Modern Critical Views

Modern Critical Views

MARGARET ATWOOD

Edited and with an introduction by
Harold Bloom
Sterling Professor of the Humanities
Yale University

CHELSEA HOUSE PUBLISHERS
Philadelphia

© 2000, 2001 by Chelsea House Publishers, a subsidiary of
Haights Cross Communications.

Published in cooperation with National Book Service
of Canada

Introduction © 2000 by Harold Bloom

Printed and bound in the United States of America

10 9 8 7 6 5 4 3 2

∞ The paper used in this publication meets the minimum
requirements of the American National Standard for
Permanence of Paper for Printed Library Materials,
Z39.48-1984

Library of Congress Cataloging-in-Publication Data

Margaret Atwood/edited and with an introduction by
Harold Bloom.
        p. cm.—(Modern critical views)
    Includes bibliographical references (p.) and index.
    ISBN 0-7910-5659-7 (alk. paper)
    1. Atwood, Margaret Eleanor, 1939—Criticism and
interpretation. 2. Women and literature—Canada—
History—20th century. I. Bloom, Harold. II. Series.
PR9199.3.A8 Z747 2000
818'.5409—dc21
                                        99-052023
                                        CIP

Contributing Editor: Tenley Williams

Contents

Editor's Note

My Introduction admires the literary skill and grim humor of *The Handmaid's Tale*.

Judith McCombs examines the strong Gothic strain in Atwood's poetic sequences, while Arnold E. Davidson concentrates upon the ironic "Historical Notes" that conclude *The Handmaid's Tale*.

The feminist critic Annette Kolodny emphasizes the political responsibility of Atwood's readership, if *The Handmaid's Tale* is not to become a prophetic novel, after which Sharon Rose Wilson takes us through the parodistic and deeply horrifying *Bodily Harm*.

J. Brooks Bouson, commenting on *The Edible Woman*, commends Atwood for (supposedly) refusing to "rescue" her heroine, while Glenn Deer returns us to *The Handmaid's Tale*, emphasizing Atwood's cunningly firm authorial control.

Emma Parker gives us "the politics of eating" in Atwood, a kind of feminist cannibalism (as Parker sees it), after which Molly Hite analyzes *Cat's Eye* as a different kind of autobiographical fiction.

Atwoodian Gothic is seen by Hilde Staels as a turning-inside-out of the genre, while Atwood's visionary metaphors in *Cat's Eye* are the concern of Coral Ann Howells.

The relation between Jonathan Swift's caustic "A Modest Proposal" and *The Handmaid's Tale* is explored by Karen Stein, after which Phyllis Sternberg Perrakis broods upon vampirism in *The Robber Bride*.

In a concluding essay, June Deery praises Atwood for bringing a woman's perspective to bear upon "scientific" notions that are masks for a supposedly male ideology.

Introduction

Literary survival, as such, was not my overt subject when I started out as a critic, nearly a half-century ago, but I have aged into an exegete who rarely moves far from a concern with the question: Will it last? I have little regard for the ideologies—feminist, Marxist, historicist, deconstructive—that now tend to dominate both literary study and literary journalism. Margaret Atwood seems to me vastly superior as a critic of Atwood to the ideologues she attracts. My brief comments upon *The Handmaid's Tale* will be indebted to Atwood's own published observations, and if I take any issue with her, it is with diffidence, as she herself is an authentic authority upon literary survival.

I first read *The Handmaid's Tale* when it was published, in 1986. Rereading it in 1999 remains a frightening experience, even if one lives in New Haven and New York City, and not in Cambridge, Massachusetts, where the Handmaid Offred suffers the humiliations and torments afflicted upon much of womankind in the Fascist Republic of Gilead, which has taken over the Northeastern United States. Atwood, in describing her novel as a dystopia, called it a cognate of *A Clockwork Orange*, *Brave New World*, and *Nineteen Eighty-Four*. All of these, in 1999, are now period pieces. Anthony Burgess's *A Clockwork Orange*, despite its Joycean wordplay, is a much weaker book than his memorable *Inside Enderby*, or his superb *Nothing Like the Sun*, persuasively spoken by Shakespeare-as-narrator. Aldous Huxley's *Brave New World* now seems genial but thin to the point of transparency, while George Orwell's *Nineteen Eighty-Four* is just a rather bad fiction. Approaching Millennium, these prophecies do not caution us. London's thugs, like New York City's, are not an enormous menace; Henry Ford does not seem to be the God of the American Religion; Big Brother is not yet watching us, in our realm of virtual reality. But theocracy is a live menace: in Iran and Afghanistan, in the influence of the Christian Coalition upon the Republican Party, and on a much smaller scale, in the tyranny over English-speaking universities of our New Puritans, the academic feminists. *The Handmaid's*

Tale, even if it did not have authentic aesthetic value (and it does), is not at all a period piece under our current circumstances. The Right-to-Life demagogues rant on, urging that the Constitution be amended, and while contemporary Mormonism maintains its repudiation of plural marriage, the Old Faith of Joseph Smith and Brigham Young is practiced by tens of thousands of polygamists in Utah and adjacent states.

Atwood says of *The Handmaid's Tale*: "It is an imagined account of what happens when not uncommon pronouncements about women are taken to their logical conclusions." Unless there is a Swiftian irony in that sentence, which I cannot quite hear, I am moved to murmur: just when and where, in the world of Atwood and her readers, are those not uncommon pronouncements being made? There are a certain number of Southern Republican senators, and there is the leadership of the Southern Baptist convention, and some other clerical Fascists, who perhaps would dare to make such pronouncements, but "pronouncements" presumably have to be public, and in 1999 you don't get very far by saying that a woman's place is in the home. Doubtless we still have millions of men (and some women) who in private endorse the Bismarckian formula for women: *Kinder, Kirche, und Kuchen*, but they do not proclaim these sentiments to the voters.

Atwood makes a less disputable point when she warns us about the history of American Puritanism, which is long and dangerous. Its tendencies are always with us, and speculative fictions from Hawthorne to Atwood legitimately play upon its darkest aspects. *The Handmaid's Tale* emerges from the strongest strain in Atwood's imaginative sensibility, which is Gothic. A Gothic dystopia is an oddly mixed genre, but Atwood makes it work. Offred's tone is consistent, cautious, and finally quite frightening. Atwood, in much, if not most, of her best poetry and prose, writes Northern Gothic in the tradition of the Brontës and of Mary Shelley. Though acclaimed by so many Post-Modernist ideologues, Atwood is a kind of late Victorian novelist, and all the better for it. Her Gilead, at bottom, is a vampiric realm, a society sick with blood. *The Handmaid's Tale* is a brilliant Gothic achievement, and a salutary warning to keep our Puritanism mostly in the past.

JUDITH McCOMBS

Atwood's Haunted Sequences: The Circle Game, The Journals of Susanna Moodie, *and* Power Politics

It was the addiction
to stories . . .
Stories that could be told
on nights like these to account for the losses,
litanies of escapes, bad novels, thrillers
deficient in villains . . .
Who knows what stories
would ever satisfy her
who knows what savageries
have been inflicted on her
and others by herself and others. . . .
—Margaret Atwood, "Gothic Letter on a Hot Night,"
You Are Happy

Return of the Gothic: Atwood's Ghosts

In Margaret Atwood's work generally, but especially in her three long poetry sequences, the neglected and long outcast stepchild of literature, the Gothic, comes to life again. An obviously Gothic terror haunts *The Circle Game* (1966), *The Journals of Susanna Moodie* (1970), and *Power Politics* (1971).

From *The Art of Margaret Atwood* by Judith McCombs. © 1981 by House of Anansi Press Limited.

Although this Gothic inheritance was spelled out in 1968, in Atwood's "Speeches for Dr. Frankenstein" and in the Gothic "Revenant" poem, which complains of the ghosts from *Wuthering Heights* that inhabit "the skull's noplace, where in me / refusing to be buried, cured, / the trite dead walk," still Atwood's Gothic voices were not widely recognized until her satiric, anti-Gothic novel, *Lady Oracle* (1976), brought the old tradition into daylight focus. Nor was this Gothic inheritance much valued by contemporary critics until Robert D. Hume, Peter Haining, Ellen Moers, and others began to reclaim the Gothic and the female Gothic tradition for serious literature.

The original Gothic inhabits that body of British literature which begins in 1765 with Horace Walpole's *The Castle of Otranto*, and flourishes in William Beckford, Ann Radcliffe, Matthew Lewis, Charles Maturin; in the nineteenth century, in *Frankenstein, Wuthering Heights, Jane Eyre, Dracula*; and, crossing the Atlantic water, in certain Poe tales, etc. The Gothic aims at terror or horror as a dominant effect; it customarily invokes the feudal past and the weird supernatural. The usual elements of the Gothic were the haunted setting—customarily a castle or forest—whose supernatural powers, be they real or deceptive, menaced and dwarfed the human characters; the hero-villain, who often goes back to the demon-lover of the ballads; the female victim or, in Radcliffe especially, the female hero-victim; and an overall reality that is either negative or, at best, deeply split between good and evil. In the twentieth century, the Gothic comes to life in (for example) certain works of William Faulkner and Flannery O'Connor, in Jean Rhys' *Wide Sargasso Sea*, Sylvia Plath's *Bell Jar* and death poems—and in much of Atwood's lyric poetry, in many of the interior monologues of her fiction, and especially in her first three poetry sequences, *The Circle Game, The Journals of Susanna Moodie*, and *Power Politics*.

These three sequences resurrect the Gothic spirit of terror in the female hero-victim, a terror emanating from the major elements of the original British Gothic literature—or from their direct descendants. Beginning with *The Circle Game*, this terror inhabits a female *I* who is, like Ann Radcliffe's heroines, "simultaneously persecuted victim and courageous heroine." As the earlier Gothic heroine (Walpole's Maddalena, Radcliffe's Emily) was trapped in chamber and cell, so Atwood's *I* is trapped in a chamber of horrors inside her skull. As the traditional female hero-victims confronted a haunted, menacing castle or a monstrous, threatening forest, so Atwood's *I*'s are menaced by an inhuman universe, grim and icy wastes, entangled and haunted wilderness. As the elder female heroes were tempted by what Atwood's recent creator of costume Gothics calls "the hero in the mask of a villain, the villain in the mask of a hero," a man who offers an exciting but threatening escape from the boredom and constraints of ordinary female life, and who might reveal himself as demon, killer, monster; so Atwood's female *I*'s are tempted by male Others whose power animates and captivates, whose guises enthrall, whose love spells death. As Mary Shelley's unique Gothic, *Frankenstein*, divides and links the creator-villain to his monster-creature, so Atwood's creating *I* is the author-victim to her love-Other. Lastly, as the elder Gothic terror fed on divided and doubled realities—the hero victim, the escape-trap, the villain-hero, the Frankensteinian monster-creature, the demonic or vampirish love-death—so Atwood's divided and redoubled images, lies in the mask of truth and truth in the mask of lies, permute and magnify the Gothic terror that her work creates.

This essay will focus first on the interior Gothic that dominates *The Circle Game*; next on the wilderness Gothic of *The Journals of Susanna Moodie*; and finally on the Frankensteinian mirrored and remirrored Other of *Power Politics*. Because, in all three books, this Gothic terror emanates from female *I*'s who are both hero and victim—and behind these *I*'s, from a female author—Atwood's work belongs to the genre Moers calls female Gothic; this essay will consider, as Moers does in *Literary Women*, how femaleness feeds or shapes this Gothic.

Interior Gothic: The Circling *I*

The Circle Game is apparently the least sequential of Atwood's first three sequences, and yet its effect is the most claustrophobically and terrifyingly Gothic. It lacks the signposts of place and time that segment Moodie's *Journals*, the epigraphs that categorize *Power Politics*. But it has a centre—the short title sequence—and framing poems at start and end; it has concurrent and encircling images, and a recurring flight from man to nature, self to Other, threat to death.

Most important, the Circle has throughout a single *I* and single setting in which the Gothic terrors gather. The female *I* is herself the setting of this Gothic; the chamber of horrors is interior to her consciousness. Though the horrors she sees are always possible—in nature, myth or man—still no other character confirms her terror; no other agent sets loose the menaces. What is visible to other characters is ordinary and harmless; only her vision opens into horror. She is simultaneously the hero and the victim of the Gothic horrors that unreel inside her skull; the author who conceives these torments and their imperiled sufferer. Like a witch or sibyl, a Faust or Dr. Frankenstein, she summons up the menaces, the villains and the shambling monster-shapes: and yet she is the corpse, the prisoner, the target in the stories that she tells.

Like a stoic hero—or a greedy adventurer—in the midst of terrors, this *I* will not cry out; like a helpless victim—or enthralled addict—she dare not voice her terror. In *The Circle Game* as in the *Journals* and *Power Politics*, only the reader and the *I* witness the terror. Literally or psychically, the *I* is isolated, a silenced scream, a paralyzed Cassandra. If an Other is present, he seems oblivious to the cause or fact of the terror; at best he ignores it; at worst, he may *be* the cause. Even in *Power Politics*, which is ostensibly addressed to an Other, there are hardly any poems in which the *I* really speaks so that the *you* really hears. For to tell an Other (where he is present) would be to test the spell, to risk his confirming and thereby aggravating the terror—or to risk his denying and thereby aggravating the isolation.

Thus, in the opening poem, only the *I* can see her body lost in nature, invisible, distorted, drowned beneath the lake. In the second poem (which reruns Ovid's Flood), only the *I* perceives, as they stroll through an apparent mist, the underlying Diluvian Flood and slowly forming brutal faces. In "A Descent through the Carpet," only this Alice adventures below the surface harbours, descending in her mind's eye to the icy, voracious, prehistoric depths that bred her mammal life, the Darwinian seas of starved dream creatures where

> to be aware is
> to know total
> fear.

In the title poem, only the *I* senses the prisoning rhythms of nature and myth, children and lover, *I* and *you*. In the following camera man poem, only the *I* sees how nature shifts and dissolves, beyond his lense's range. Only the *I* witnesses her own flight from him into nature, her dissolution into a hurricane speck. In the northern ice poems, only the *I* sees how glaciers, winter, and breakup menace self and Other. In the paired ending poems, only the *I* witnesses their future skeletons, gone back to nature, cannibalized by one of them, now fields where children play.

The natural universe, then, is in *The Circle Game* a modern version of the Gothic setting that surrounds and menaces the hero-victim *I*; here nature, in her mind's eye, drowns, obliterates, shocks, freezes, buries the self, and sometimes the Other as well. The traditional claustrophobic cells and passageways have narrowed to the smaller circle of the *I*'s skull; but have simultaneously metamorphosed into a modern, northern, and inhuman universe, where floe and flood, shifting time and expanding space, conspire against the *I*. The fictions of this universe are scientific rather then literary. The terms are modern rather than romantic or sacred. The scene is cold and vast Canadian (overlaying Frankenstein's final Arctic flight) rather than the picturesque Mediterranean landscape of much Gothic of the eighteenth and nineteenth centuries. But the effect of this universe, this nature—where to be aware is to know total fear—is the same pervasive and animating terror that galvanized the elder Gothics.

This deadly nature in a deadly universe is the coldest, vastest, and least human of the three concurrent horrors that encircle the summoning *I*. The second sort of horrors are the monster-ghosts from myth and history that come alive inside her skull; and the third sort are her menacing familiars, the joyless encircling children and the imprisoning lover of the title sequence.

These second, specific monsters are still interior Gothic, and they haunt the *I*'s vision in the midst of ordinary, harmless scenes: walking beside him, only she can see beneath apparent mist the Diluvian Flood and shambling, brutal life; outside her window, the random face of the Hanged Man (her Muse?) disintegrates,

> shouting at me
> (specific) me
> desperate messages with his
> obliterated mouth
>
> in a silent language.

As she pauses between trains, the screen-toppled lady and the razor man who travel like voodoo dolls in her suitcase come to life. Her powers summon them even as her emptiness attracts their forms, and their terror is the edge that she inhabits:

> I move
> and live on the edges
> (what edges)
> I live
> on all the edges there are.

Only the *I* sees that the billboard lady is a vampire, and the grey flannel man is food for ghouls; and that the *you* and *I* may also be those Frankensteinian "scraps glued together / waiting for a chance / to come to life."

The same interior emptiness that attracts and feeds these smaller Gothic monsters is what binds the hero to the villain-lover, the empty *you* of the central title sequence:

> You refuse to be
> (and I)

> an exact reflection, yet
> will not walk from the glass,
> be separate.

Like a clinging double, an empty Alice or a science-fiction pod, she looks to
him, and he to others, in a travesty of Victorian sex roles: he for images alone,
she for images in him:

> You look past me, listening
> to them, perhaps, or
> watching
> your own reflection somewhere.

It is he who commands the tranced and joyless children who play at
circling: "You make them / turn and turn, according to / the closed rules of
your games." The power is his, the dependency hers; it is she who is caught
in his indifferent gaze, "transfixed / by your eyes' / cold blue thumbtacks."
Lover and double, villain and fellow victim and Muse, his incarnations are
multiple, and his powers therefore inescapable. Like an evil wizard or
magician he rings her with his spells: "your observations change me / to a
spineless woman in / a cage of bones."

But does the real danger come from Gothic spell or outer world, from
him or them?

> (of course there is always
> danger but where
> would you locate it).

Sheltered by his dangerous games, caught in female dependency and female
powerlessness, she crumples in his eyes. At the end of the sequence, she is
still half-paralyzed and half-enthralled, able only to want "the circle /
broken."

After this nadir the whole book is transformed: the *I* breaks out and
flees to nature; a male Other alternately pursues or accompanies her. Though
these continuing flights, escapes, and deaths are her metaphors and her
nightmares—therefore an interior Gothic still—yet in overview these
repeated escapes and deaths, this continuing flight of the female *I* to/from
/with a male Other, to/from a nature that is both refuge and death, evoke the
fleeing Isabellas and Maddalenas of the elder Gothics. Or the Arctic ice chase
of wretched creator and wretched being that ends Shelley's *Frankenstein*: for
after the central sequence, nature becomes far vaster and far icier; deaths are

constantly foreseen; the hero-villain lover-Other is skull and skeletal; rescuer or not, he brings death. At book's end, deadly nature and deadly man have triumphed: the *you* and *I* are buried, and her bones gnawed, apparently by him.

The Circle Game, then, creates a spell of female Gothic terror, centered in a hero-victim *I* who flees from man to nature, from self to Other, from threat to death. Remove the spell, and what would be left? A plot where nothing happens: a flat enclosing circle, inside which a modern female *I* languishes, discontent and bored. Passive, she passes for normal—i.e. normal for a female. Powerless, she feels herself surrounded by powers that she cannot control or become—powers that belong to men, her sexual Others. Childless, she fears and avoids children. Menaced, she does not venture on her own; she follows or goes escorted—or else becomes a target. Dependent, she divides herself between herself and her sexual Other, and assigns to him the stronger role. Empty, circling and encircled, she is her victim and her jailor, bored with her own plight.

Return the Gothic terror, and this plot, this character, come to life. Like a vampire lover, this terror calls forth the wilder powers of the *I*, and rescues her from stagnant female "normalcy." Because this Gothic terror stays hidden, silent and interior, it is with her everywhere; it animates and inwardly subverts—but does not overtly challenge—the patriarchal status quo. Like a vampire lover, this terror carries its own punishment; for she is victim, target, paralyzed and drained.

Wilderness Gothic: The Victim and the Witch

The Journals of Susanna Moodie, Atwood's dream-conceived account of what the actual nineteenth-century Ontario pioneer and commercial writer, Susanna Moodie, witnessed but did not in her lifetime reveal, is the most Gothic of the poetry sequences to date. *The Circle Game*, as we have seen, creates the spirit of female Gothic terror, but reruns tradition in another century, another universe; *Power Politics* has a wealth of Gothic elements and exemplifies the Gothic doubleness of Atwood's thought; but in *Power Politics* the female Gothic terror is undercut by other, non-Gothic politics. Only in the *Journals* do the original Gothic spirit and elements prevail.

These three journals, which begin in the nineteenth-century backwoods of Ontario, reveal a wilderness Gothic of old patterns imported to the new continent: here the forest is menacing, invading, breeds monsters. Its inhabitants are either alien and jeering villains, or else its victims. Surrounded by its undergrowth, the hero loses her body's image and her soul's identity. The shadowy husband turns wereman; the children die and come back as brier-fingered haunts; in the last journal Moodie herself turns ghostly revenant. Like the dark woods of our foremothers' tales in Grimm and the haunted forests and castles of eighteenth- and nineteenth-century Gothic, this wilderness setting casts a spell that overpowers the humans, breaks down their civil Christian souls, and drags them deathward.

Furthermore, although this wilderness is not personified, it nonetheless tempts the hero as the Gothic Heathcliff lover tempts: for it offers Moodie an escape from the proper menfolk's rule: it provides a savage kingdom that, like a demon-lover, compels her surrender to its power. Against the forest power the menfolk dwindle, impotent as Lintons; the hero escapes from their "legitimate" order to a savagery that, as in the demon-lover ballads and Julia Anne Curtis' "Knight of the Blood-Red Plume," first excites, then takes her life. But Atwood's *Journals* does not end there: Moodie's death initiates her into a wilderness kingdom that she makes her own: at the end, like a triumphant witch or an immortal Catherine, she becomes the voice of the wilderness, the prophet of her own wild, eternal realm.

This vision of the wilderness as menace and temptor may have one other source as powerful as the Gothic, Grimm, and ballad literature: I mean the Northern forests themselves—or rather, the Northern forests as "universally" experienced by carriers of Western European culture. Moodie's terror of the wilderness, then, would not be confined to Moodie, nor to Atwood, nor to literature, nor to the literate. Fear of bodily death and spiritual disintegration may well be *the* (Western European) human response to a nature that is dark, unpeopled forest and harsh winters. Atwood was raised in such terrain, and may know. In *Survival* she argues that Canadian literature—including the historic Moodie's work—is haunted by Nature as Monster, inhuman, anti-human, freezing, and deadly. Certainly a lot of non-literary nineteenth-century settlers and trappers were panicked, threatened, crazed, and quite literally killed by the North American wilderness.

In the *Journals*, as in *The Circle Game*, the vision of nature as monster-villain stays interior to the female *I*: no other character notices or confirms the danger. Even though the horrors that Atwood's Moodie endures in the wilderness—isolation, disintegration, death—seem genderless; and even though her first-person narration, using the generic pronoun, *I*, implies a universal human voice—still it is only the female *I* who admits—and magnifies—the danger.

Like all Atwood's female Gothic heroes, Moodie is both author and character, egotist and victim:

> I take this picture of myself
> and with my sewing scissors
> cut out the face.

Now it is more accurate:

where my eyes were,
every-
thing appears.

The double portrait-frame ovals that follow this self-scissoring epigraph (and introduce each of Moodie's three journals) are empty, save for dates. Atwood's accompanying collages are scissored-out images of the hero, dead or alive, surrounded by emptiness, stuck like an encapsulated cyst into a wilderness she does not touch.

From epigraph on through the first of the three journals—the one which covers her seven years' trials in the wilderness—Moodie attacks her own vision, assumes guilt for distorting, sides with the non-human wilderness but against her species and herself. Disembarking at Quebec with book, knitting, and shawl, she seems outwardly a mirror image of Moer's Traveling Heroines of the Gothic—one of those "British ladies who in point of fact did set sail for Canada and India and Africa, with their bonnets, veils, and gloves, their teacups and tea cozies—ill-equipped for vicissitudes of travel, climate, and native mutiny, but well-equipped to preserve their identity as proper Englishwomen." But the heirloom image cracks as, disembarking, Moodie blames her "own lack / of conviction which makes / these vista of desolation, / . . . omens of winter." When the water refuses to reveal her image and the rocks ignore her, she becomes in her own eyes invisible, untranslatable.

Trapped on the backwoods farm, Moodie sees the wilderness as a large darkness: "It was our own / ignorance we entered. / I have not come out yet." A stranded Red Riding Hood, she needs wolf's eyes—not her human eyes—to see true: "Whether the wilderness is / real or not / depends on who lives there." If it depends on the men, it only seems real, for as planters they impose their own illusions of progress, force the tangled forest to become the straight Cartesian rows of their futile dream. If the wilderness depends on her, it may be real, but then she is not: her opened eyes are "surrounded, stormed, broken / in upon by branches, roots, tendrils."

With heroic courage, alone and unaided, Moodie faces the terror of her own disintegration. When she is finally able to look in a mirror, at the end of the first journal, she sees a body gone back to nature, an exhumed corpse, the proper lace and black rotted off, the skin "thickened / with bark and the white hairs of roots," the eyes bewildered, almost blind, budlike. The "heirloom face" she brought with her is a "crushed eggshell / among other debris" of shattered china, decayed shawl, pieces of letters—all those artifacts

and emblems of the English gentlewoman she once was. Helpless, invaded—
a female Gothic plight—she has been taken over by the wilderness as by an
evil spell: she is the living but unrecognizable dead:

> (you find only
> the shape you already are
> but what
> if you have forgotten that
> or discover you
> have never known).

In the tradition of female Gothic, this facing of the empty self is heroic
courage: but it is also a female lack of identity, a female dependency on the
image to *be* the self.

Throughout the journals, while men imposed their civil power on the
wilderness, Moodie lets the wilderness impose its savage, Gothic power on
her. The first journal, with Moodie as Gothic matron invaded by monstrous
lair, builds a climactic Gothic terror. But when Moodie is unexpectedly
rescued from those seven years of captive terror and is hauled back to
civilization on her husband's sleigh, then she suddenly finds herself
dispossessed of the wild eyes that had begun to glow within her; she feels
relief but also "unlived in: they had gone."

The middle journal, of Moodie's first thirty years in Belleville, shows her
recollecting in tranquillity her experiences of savagery. (You can take
the woman out of the wilderness, but you can't take the wilderness out of the
woman.) Outwardly rescued, inwardly she rejects civilization, and dwells
among danger, death, and horror. She sees her children die (literally) back into
the land and return as clutching, brier-fingered ghosts. She sees the painfully
built homesteads that were her composite self revert to forest. She sees the
land itself as icy river and unknown ocean on which the living float; only the
dead can enter its depths. Inside her head history breaks down to gibberish.
The 1837 War she witnessed unravels into "those tiny ancestral figures /
flickering dull white through the back of your skull, / confused, anxious," idiot
faces and banana-clustered hands holding flags or guns, their advances through
trees and fire no more actual than a child's crayon-scribbled fort.

Gothic victim turned celebrant of Gothic chaos and death, Moodie
shows us the universal savagery beneath our civil selves:

> (Note: Never pretend this isn't
> part of the soil too, teadrinkers, and inadvertent
> victims and murderers, when we come this way

again in other forms, take care
to look behind, within
where the skeleton face beneath

the face puts on its feather mask, the arm
within the arm lifts up the spear:

Her dreams are nightmare ghosts that claim her waking life: she is
haunted by the wet and surging horror of the long-past bush garden where
anything planted came up blood; by the suicidal and scar-throated hunter,
Brian, who killed and felt his skin grow fur, his soul run innocent as hooves.
Her dream-imagined, fear-furred night bear

is real, heavier
than real   I know
even by daylight here
in this visible kitchen

it absorbs all terror

as it moves inside her skull towards her family in the lighted cabin.

By the end of the middle journal, Moodie comes to see herself not as
the captive of exterior Gothic powers, but instead as the source of an interior
Gothic wisdom: there are two voices inside her head, dividing reality
between convention and horror. The truths she chooses are "jubilant with
maggots." Atwood's accompanying collage shows Moodie scissored out,
aged, hooded, staring witch-like from one baleful, deeply shrouded eye; a
thin emptiness divides her, not from wilderness, but from civil, steepled
Belleville.

In the last, death journal (which ranges up to the present), Moodie
transcends her Gothic horrors of decay and death by joining them as, aging,
she lets slip her human shapes and consciousness. In the "Daguerreotype
Taken in Old Age" she accepts her image as pitted, cratered, eroded, a moon-
face in the garden, a dead "being / eaten away by light." In the "Wish:
Metamorphosis" she welcomes her shrinking, furred, and feather-wrinkled
body, her puckered, burrowing mind, and exults at last in the animal eyes that
may glow within her later, underground.

Dying Moodie renounces flesh and custom, teacup and history. With a
hero's—or a witch's—spirit of adventure, she crosses over into the wilderness
and becomes its voice. Dead and underground, she prophesies against the
bulldozer's silver paradise. Atwood's collages show her buried body curving
with the strata, completely touching, blending in at last, her limbs drifting or

dancing with the earth. In a resurrection that is both Christian and pagan, she joins "those who have become the stone / voices of the land."

At the last Moodie appears as a ghostly old lady on a modern bus, unbanishable: "this is my kingdom still." Allied with snow and storm, she threatens her twentieth-century audience—us—with her wild, Gothic powers:

> I am the old woman
> sitting across from you on the bus,
> her shoulders drawn up like a shawl;
> out of her eyes come secret
> hatpins, destroying
> the walls, the ceiling
>
> Turn, look down:
> there is no city;
> this is the centre of a forest
>
> your place is empty.

Like a triumphant witch, or a science-fiction time traveller, or a medieval revenant, this hero haunts us with the Grimm and Gothic terrors of the elder, wilder realm that she has made her own.

Double or Nothing: The Victor and the Being

Power Politics is Atwood's most doubled and dividing sequence: even its Gothic structure is dual, for its victor/victim games (Atwood's critical terms, from *Survival*) reenact not only the invaded hero-victim *I* vs. the monstrous hero-villain *you* of *The Circle Game* and elsewhere; but also, concurrently, the Gothic nightmare of that early victor who dared create a monster being— Mary Shelley's Victor, surnamed Frankenstein.

These two sets of Gothic antagonists overlap, contrast, juxtapose, and superimpose upon each other, so that the victim of one set may simultaneously be the victor of the other pair: "How can I stop you / Why did I create you" asks the female *I*, shifting from imperilled victim to guilty author of her torments—and she is truly both. Each of these Gothic antagonists is paired to an external Other who is its double, shadow, outcast self—as Shelley's Victor and "being" (her term) were each other's alter images. Each of Atwood's antagonists is also self-split within, for evil or good, power or suffering: female and male compete for victory and victimhood; creator and created vie like Shelley's pair in enmity and wretchedness. The Gothic terror and the Gothic horror, so divided and redoubled, take place as in a hall of mirrors, where reality is instantly evaded and yet reflected, distorted and yet magnified.

Even the cover of *Power Politics* (conceived by Atwood and executed by William Kimber) forewarns us of reality within reality: for the warrior and his captive woman are sadomasochism in Gothic dress. But they are simultaneously the burdened male tied to dependent female, for his extended arm, tied to her dangling weight, would suffer excruciating pain. They are simultaneously a suit of rigid, empty armor (he has no flesh, no eyes) which props the female seer whose pose is the Hanged One of the Tarot, signifying "life in suspension," real bodily "life and not death."

Throughout *Power Politics* reality is thus triple: the Gothic sadomasochistic pair are true—so true that the book is usually read as sexist realism, women readers confirming it and men readers protesting, as Atwood has observed. But the pair are also true reversed, he victim and she heartless. And always they are characters within a third, Frankensteinian Gothic where as creator-seer she is Victor, he the hapless being.

Thus, in the first of the three sections, he enters as a cruel hook; then a three-headed monster, rising like Victor's being or a Canadian Indian monster from a snowbank, shivering "cunningly." Farcically stabbed, he inflates to a dirigible-sized Superman. Drunk, he plays Christ. Beautiful wooden General, he promises bronze rescues but delivers her blind, paralyzed, one of a slavish horde of female followers who casts flowers under his hooves. Strange and repellent growth, he thrives in darkness. A body with head attached, he collides and they both shatter. A dead starfish, he floats belly up on her. And when towards the end of the section he escapes, "nothing / remembers you but the bruises / on my thighs and the inside of my skull."

As the above litany makes clear, his role of monstrous Gothic villain alternates with his role as pathetic Gothic monster. The Superman gets stabbed; the beautiful wooden General fixes it so he almost wins and longs to be bandaged before he is cut; the bruiser makes *his* escape. But even his sufferings smack of romantic male egotism, a demand for female sympathy as well as female submission.

Though her role of victim alternates with, and is compounded by snarl, threat, and self-denunciation, her rebellion is all an interior female Gothic, a victim's fantasy: the restaurant stabbing is farce and wish, an act that doesn't happen, unreal as his apotheosis into Superman dirigible. The next poems show him alive and dominant, fake Christ who gets her succour, fake General who literally overrides his female followers. Her perception that he is fake is but interior female hatred, a victim's curse, silent or unheard. The double victim/villain roles of each confuse and paralyze the female *I;* her horror and her guilt confound escape, for she would escape his menace and cannot escape his suffering or her guilt.

But the above litany also reveals the *you* as a projection made monstrous by creating *I,* a Gothic Other drawn from Shelley's *Frankenstein.* As the first wretch (Shelley's term) was made outwardly hideous but inwardly humane; as he sought love from his horrified creator, fled in rain, wandered suffering and unpitied, then reappeared to his heartless creator in an Alpine sea of ice, so this monster in the opening poem "reappears" in a snowbank with needs and "cunning;" shivers, seeks love, and flees from his unloving creator, and dissolves in rain at the end of the first section. But this Victor has read *Frankenstein,* and coldly proclaims her guilt:

> I approach this love
> like a biologist
> pulling on my rubber
> gloves & white labcoat
>
> You flee from it
> like an escaped political
> prisoner, and no wonder.

As in *Frankenstein,* this creator repudiates the "body with head / attached" that is the complement to her own divided self, the "head with / body attached." The being's flight reveals the creator's monstrous and unloving egotism. As in Shelley, the two compete for power and victimhood. When one waxes, the Other wanes. But unlike Shelley's being, this Other is a sexual Other, and yet so close a mirror-double that his external reality is never sure. Throughout the first section, the creating *I* shapes him cruel, hideous, fake, evil, multiform; at the end she forgets his vanished, rain-dissolved shape, which, like the Cheshire Cat or Watchbird haunts her bed:

> My walls absorb
> you, breathe you forth
> again, you resume
> yourself, I do not recognize you.

Read as a Frankensteinian Gothic, then, the first section of *Power Politics* covers creation and flight of the wretch. The victor *I* projects an outwardly monstrous Other, and monstrously recoils from it. The second, central section corresponds roughly to the wretch's unsuccessful attempts to join humanity. In Atwood as in Shelley, humanity is revealed as murderous persecutors, and the wretch begins to imitate them. In this section the real monster is what the legend of Frankenstein has become for the whole world in the twentieth century: the atomic nightmare given life, the monster system that may destroy us all. Against the gigantic horrors of the war machine, the private Gothic costumes recede, quaint fakeries; the *I* and you struggle simply to stay alive and innocent. What does appear of private victor-victim games here is mostly defrocked; the you could be anyone generic and faceless, merely alive, ordinary, and "growing older, of course you'll / die but not yet, you'll outlive / even my distortions of you." At the end of the second section, she preaches mutual flight from power games, but there is no reply, perhaps no listener.

The third and final section turns from global horrors back to the personal Gothic duel where the *I and* you contend in sterile sadomasochism. She would go back to nature, but fears creation and refuses children; nature thereafter threatens her with death, and the literary horrors "fertilize each other / in the cold and with bulging eyes." This final section corresponds roughly to the last parts of Shelley's novel; in both books the hideous being turns from man to nature, and turns to hideous killer. The creating *I* is racked by the monster's persecutions and by guilt. Like Victor's being, Atwood's Other crosses over into nature, and flourishes there as bestial god or noble, godlike beast. The original Victor followed but died in pursuit; Atwood's creator starts to follow but, fearing death, turns back.

In Atwood's third section the Gothic sadomasochism breaks out unchecked: as in the first section, but far worse, it is she who dies, gets broken, blames herself; she who waits, dependent, for his revelation or torment; she who gets trampled in his escape; she who is the imperiled and tortured female victim; and, at the end, the human target stalked by natural monster him. The beautiful wooden General of the first section seems naive and playful compared to this monster-villain loosed from horror film, from *Frankenstein*, from sadomasochistic tales. Now he is simultaneously the evil Rochester (see Jean Rhys' female Gothic novel, *Wide Sargasso Sea*, for how Rochester changed from lover to villain, and drove his first wife mad), King Kong, and Frankensteinian monster of the film.

Now her victim's alliance *with* her tormentor is grotesque terror and masochism:

> catastrophe, I see you
> blind and one-handed, flashing
> in the dark, trees breaking
> under your feet, you demand,
> you demand

> I lie mutilated beside
> you; beneath us there are
> sirens, fires, the people run
> squealing, the city
> is crushed and gutted,
> the ends of your fingers bleed
> from 1000 murders
>
> Putting on my clothes
> again, retreating, closing doors
> I am amazed / I can continue
> to think, eat, anything
>
> How can I stop you
>
> Why did I create you.

The terror is real, the sadism is real, only the Gothic costumes are false. In the next poem, as she hesitates outside the door, telling the wrong lies, she sees him as bleeding Christ and slain God, and warns him to escape her costumes. Yet the door leads to his Bluebeard's castle stairs, his Fichter's room of bloodied, dismembered wives. But the last alternative—sans costumes, sans lies—is the worse: "In the room we will find nothing / In the room we will find each other."

Now he escapes again to nature; she briefly follows, but soon pulls back to the human side of the window. Like Victor's being in the Alpine heights and Arctic wastes he goes on, allied with earth, sea, and death, lost in water and moving shadow. In the penultimate poem the *I* repudiates all costumes; the bronze man, the fragile man, the scaling fanged Dracula she made "were all inaccurate." But were they? She is still inside a mirrored and remirrored Gothic horror chamber where the victim cannot know who is victim and cannot flee: the last poem shows him scaled again, and Frankenstein's monster again, rising from "the pits and starless / deep nights of the sea," unstoppable, bearing towards her "a new death / which is mine and no-one else's."

Power Politics, then, creates a mirrored Gothic of the Other where a male who is both wretch and victim, monster and villain, stalks a female who is both distorter and creator, adventurer and victim. Inside this doubly Gothic structure the horror and the terror redouble, divide, and multiply. Atwood's sequence thus reflects not only Gothic literature and modern, fragmented reality, but also the particular power politics of a society where men have outward power and women have inward pain: the female *I* is alienated from her body and her head, even from her terror; addict, she comes alive only in relation to a sexual Other who is a series of oppressive masculine poses. His power threatens her, his sufferings milk her; either way, she is his victim and yet guilty of her victimization. That she prefers the Gothic horrors to reality is not only her private addiction, but also the politics of how the dominated endure, and the aesthetics of how the bored escape. That the Gothic stays interior, and that the *I* creates only by seeing— not by speaking, leading, acting—is not only a Gothic addiction/vision, but is also the silence of the politically isolated and disabled.

Atwood's Frankensteinian *Politics*, then brings to static climax the Other-centered and interior Gothic of the first two sequences. Here, as in *The Circle Game*, the female *I* flees in static and recurrent terror the shifting, deadly, vulnerable, monstrous lover-Other. Here, as in *The Circle Game*, the *I* is locked into a polarized victor-victim duel with her sexual Other and/or with an inhuman, icy, post-Darwinian universe that promises her death. In *Power Politics*, the terror swings inward to the mirrored and remirrored Frankensteinian Gothic; in the nineteenth-century *Journals*, the terror swings outward to the inhuman natural universe, which becomes a monstrous, haunted lair, tempting as a demon-lover, luring the hero-victim into its deadly savage realm.

But, whether the worst danger come from sexual Other or from inhuman Other, in all three sequences the target is the same: the female *I*. And the outward power and danger, for good or evil, is the same: the Other, be it inhuman or masculine. And, in all three sequences, the Gothic stays interior to the female *I* who is its secret author, its silenced victim: no character, but only the reader can (perhaps) be trusted to share this animating and addicting terror. The politics of this terror, invisible to patriarchs yet everywhere for those who share and identify, are female-centered: for this interior terror releases, diverts, and dangerously, narrowly channels the limits and burdens and nightmares common to the ordinary, daylit female life.

This essay, having followed the Gothic terror and its elements through Atwood's first three poetic sequences, book-by-book and theme-by-theme; having pursued the more visible ghosts of Grimm and British Gothic therein; having then, like a traveller at journey's end, gathered its memories and souvenirs into a summary display (a simple one, but with a dangerous two-way metaphor of female Gothic life and literature saved for the last)— this essay could well stop here. But that summary display, which appears complete but gathers only some parts into a convenient and deceptive whole, misrepresents the protean nature and effects of Atwood's Gothic: these sequences, these Gothic elements and terrors, should not be left to fall by default into such a whole.

For Atwood's poetic work, here and elsewhere, is multifaceted as the fly's eye: to fix one aspect in one light is to turn away to darkness the other facets. These three poetic sequences reflect, refract, and like a lens distill from/to reality (whatever that appears to be) and Atwood's other work, made and not yet made; from Grimm, *Frankenstein*, the Brontës; from science fiction, comic books, horrror films; from the Bible, scientific fictions, modern politics and sexist realism, Canadian literature and North American Indian myth; from the Lord Knows What. Though Atwood's best work, in these sequences and elsewhere, is as compellingly original as Coleridge's Xanadu, in one (misleading) sense it is not original at all, but a place in which the shapes of her culture come to life, metamorphosing like Proteus, like ghosts, like caterpillars: and among these shifting forms the Gothic is one obvious yet transient shape, one kind of voice, not simple, not stable, but resonant, echoing, drifting back and forth and sideways with the other voices that it has become and will become in other readings, other sequences.

ARNOLD E. DAVIDSON

Future Tense:
Making History in The Handmaid's Tale

Margaret Atwood in *The Handmaid's Tale* conjoins two different projected futures. The first, distinctly dystopian, is Gilead, a fundamentally tyrannical order the author envisions for the Northeastern United States. The handmaid Offred's secret account (the women of Gilead are not even to have thoughts of their own, much less stories) gives us the measure of Gilead and particularly emphasizes—as even Offred's name attests—its use and abuse of women. This same account gives us, too, Gilead's genealogy, the story of its rapid rise in the last years of the twentieth century. Understandably alleviating her devastating assessment of her life in Gilead with memories of a different past, Offred records the traumatic transition from one order of things to a radically different order, all of which takes place within the limited span of her childbearing years.

Or perhaps Gilead embodies not such a radically different order after all. In fact, *The Handmaid's Tale* portrays the advent of that society as an easy slide into "final solutions" only slightly less brutal than those attempted in Nazi Germany (but solutions given a thoroughly American habitation and name) and thereby fulfills the traditional function of the dystopia. By envisioning an appalling future already implicit in the contemporary world, Atwood condemns just those present propensities that make a Gilead possible and does so on every level, even the comic. There is something

From *Margaret Atwood: Vision and Forms*, edited by Kathryn VanSpanckeren and Jan Garden Castro. © 1988 by Board of Trustees, Southern Illinois University.

humorously appropriate, for example, when the Commander's wife, formerly a spokesperson for women in the Phyllis Schlafly mode, gets exactly the life that she earlier advocated for others and does not find it good. And there is something tragically wrong when others, such as Offred, who ask for little get so much less, not even the children they are forced to bear for the state (if they are lucky enough to conceive them, since, for handmaids, the alternative to fertility is death).

Yet Offred's perturbing narration does not comprise the whole of *The Handmaid's Tale*. Appended to the fifteen titled sections that constitute her account and the bulk of the novel is a final part not numbered as another section nor even designated as a separate chapter. These "Historical Notes" give us both a second future (a future to Gilead) and the genealogy of Offred's account, which up to that point we have been reading. The resultant disjunction might well seem disconcerting. After an appalling story of tyranny, genocide, and gynocide in late twentieth-century America, we are, in effect, brought fast-forward to June 25, 2195, to the University of Denay in Nunavit and an International Historical Association's rather placid (if pompous) intellectual foray back into the Gilead Regime.

This unequal division of the text serves several narrative functions. On a most immediate level, the second part provides, as previously noted, the history of Offred's history and an account of how her private record has become a public document, the object of future historians' attention. That attention, moreover, supplements Offred's story by the very act of subjecting it to academic scrutiny. Whereas Offred describes the practices of Gilead, the Twelfth Symposium on Gileadean Studies can provide some of the theory that underlies those practices. Thus, we are given the analysis of the use of the "Aunts" as especially "cost-effective" or the observation that Gilead itself was partly the product of earlier theories such as the sociobiology of Wilfred Limpkin. A retrospective symposium attests, too, that Gilead was survived and as such constitutes a distinct note of hope for the future. But that note is countered by another consideration. The historical notes, like any scholarly afterword, also serve to validate the text that they follow, and there is something ominous in that claiming of the right to have the last word.

Retrospective analysis by a Cambridge don—male, of course—is ostensibly more authoritative than a participant woman's eyewitness account. Furthermore, the supposed "objectivity" of the scholarly enterprise of the Twelfth Symposium on Gileadean Studies is a chilling postscript to a story in which women (and others too: blacks, Jews, homosexuals, Quakers, Baptists) have been totally *objectified*, rendered into objects by the State. Is the process beginning again? And implicit in that question is a more immediate one. Do we, as scholars, contribute to the dehumanizations of society by our own critical work, especially when, as according to the distinguished professor of the novel, "our job is not to censure but to understand"? Atwood's epilogue loops back through the text that precedes it to suggest that the ways in which scholars (present as well as future) assemble the text of the past confirms the present and thereby helps to predict the future, even the horrific future endured by Offred. In short, Atwood does not let intellectuals off the hook—and the hook is a loaded metaphor in *The Handmaid's Tale*. How we *choose* to construct history partly determines the history we are likely to get.

Another version of this same problematics of history is implicit in the textual question posed by the epilogue. "The Handmaid's Tale" in its present form is not the only possible ordering of the "some thirty tapes" (we are never told exactly how many) that have been transcribed (we are never told how directly) into text. The editors, we are specifically informed, have intervened to make choices about the structure of the tale. Moreover, Professor Knotly Wade of Cambridge and Professor James Darcy Pieixoto, Director of the Twentieth and Twenty-First Century Archives at Cambridge, have ordered thirty or so tapes into an extremely intricate structure—forty-six untitled chapters arranged in fifteen labeled sections, with the heading "Night" used seven times (and the only heading repeated). Professor Pieixoto admits that "all such arrangements are based on some guesswork and are to be regarded as approximate, pending further research." But that pro forma disclaimer does not acknowledge how much the very process of assembling a text (or writing the history of any age from its surviving traces) means *creating* a fiction. Where, then, is the boundary between novel and history? This textual question becomes all the more pertinent when juxtaposed against Atwood's insistence that everything in the book is "true," has, in some form in some society, already been done (Cathy N. Davidson, "A Feminist *1984*").

In a very real sense, the future presaged by "The Handmaid's Tale" is already *our* history, just as the meeting of the Gileadean Symposium of 2195 could readily be incorporated into a contemporary literature or history convention. The relentlessness of history is partly what makes *The Handmaid's Tale* (like any successful dystopia) plausible. The plot of the novel also plays to our sense of the familiar. As Peter S. Prescott has observed, Atwood borrows the standard format of the dystopia. First, the narrator experiences hopeless despair in the face of the brutal regime, then feels some hope through discovering the possibility of resistance (the Mayday Underground and the Underground Femaleroad) and begins to perceive cracks in what seemed to be the unassailable power of Gilead (the lapses of the Commander, Fred). This political hope is strengthened by personal hope in the form of a love affair, a testament to continuing human emotion in the face of the dehumanization of the regime. Finally, there is the possibility of escape. Within the tale itself, Offred's end is uncertain, yet the very existence of the tapes suggests that, aided by Nick, she did elude the rule of Gilead.

Even the most idiosyncratic feature of this dystopia, its female narrator, is tellingly domesticated. Offred's reconstructed narration embodies the same sexual dualities that Gilead exhibits in their starkest form. She is essentially passive and in need of rescue by a man, a gender cliché underscored by Professor Pieixoto's distinction between the "quasi military" Mayday Underground as opposed to the nurturing and escapist enterprise of the Underground Femaleroad. This distinction (supported with remarkably little data, it must be emphasized) posits men aggressively striving to destroy the regime and women merely reacting to it in a compassionate capacity. This distinction is further underscored by another of the professor's little jokes, his reduction of the Underground Femaleroad to "The Underground Frailroad." And of course, the whole title of the narration is appended by Professor Wade, "partly in homage to the great Geoffrey Chaucer" but also as an intentional pun on "the archaic vulgar signification of the word *tail*." Yet it is those little jokes that give the larger game away. The grotesque transformation of women's bodies into passive receptacles for the perpetuation of the genes of the Regime's Commanders is itself grotesquely transmogrified, in the twenty-second century, into silly sexist jests. As Atwood has noted to Cathy N. Davidson in an interview, this is "what happens to history—something that's a very intense experience for the people who are living it becomes a subject of speculation, often of witticism, and rather detached analysis two hundred years later."

The countering academic text is intended to condition future readings of the Gilead regime, just as Biblical commentaries (of any era or religion) condition readings of the Bible. Nor is that analogy gratuitous. Indeed, the Biblical fundamentalism of Gilead poses crucial questions about the interpretive use of literary texts, for that society's most appalling practices all have their scriptural justification. Chapter and verse can be cited for every atrocity, but who privileges those particular chapters and verses and decides how they should be read? And more important, how does that right to textual authority itself write the larger text of the society? The novel presents us with versions of this process in the Gileadean reading of the Bible and the professional reading of Gilead:

> If I may be permitted an editorial aside, allow me to say that in my opinion we must be cautious about passing moral judgement upon the Gileadeans. Surely we have learned by now that such judgements are of necessity culture-specific.

Also, Gileadean society was under a good deal of pressure,
demographic and otherwise, and was subject to factors from
which we ourselves are happily more free. Our job is not to
censure but to understand.

Again an ostensibly marginal aside situates us right in the center of the
professor's own moral judging and his society's "hypocritical self-
congratulation." The conferees at the Twelfth Symposium on Gileadean
Studies assent to Professor Pieixoto's remarks by a round of applause.

One imagines that "The Handmaid's Tale" could provide the scholars of the
twenty-second century with a crucial text from the Gilead regime. Very little
remains of Gilead, for destroying information—obliterating marks of the
past—was part of the many purges that marked this unstable society. We are
told that, besides Offred's tapes, anthropologists have discovered "The A. B.
Memoirs" in a garage in a Seattle suburb and "The Diary of P." "excavated
by accident during the erection of a new meeting house in the vicinity of
what was once Syracuse, New York." Aside from offering us a tantalizing
glimpse of what life might be like in the United States in 2195—does the new
meeting house recapitulate the town structure of an earlier Puritan or
Quaker theocracy?—the very scantiness of the evidence underscores how
much history is the product of historians. The only other guide to the era is
a "diary kept in cipher" by sociobiologist Wilfred Limpkin, a political insider
whose theories of natural polygamy served as the "scientific justification for
some of the odder practices of the regime, just as Darwinism was used by
earlier ideologies."

If social Darwinism supports rampant laissez-faire capitalism and
sociobiology justifies the theocratic totalitarianism of Gilead, then, we must
ask, what ideologies are supported by the seemingly innocuous exercise in
literary history indulged in by those at the Twelfth Symposium on Gilead
Studies? The form of historical analysis assayed by Pieixoto is, essentially, a
pre-Foucault, pre–de Beauvoir form of historical criticism, which pretends to
"objectify," to placing texts within their historical "contexts" with little
awareness that context itself is a construct. As Mary Wilson Carpenter has
pointed out, Pieixoto continually trivializes the status of "The Handmaid's
Tale" as document precisely because he trivializes women's role in society—
in Gilead society, in his own society. In fact, much of his narration is
concerned not with the text itself but with attempting to discover the identity
of Fred, the Commander to whom the narrator of "The Handmaid's Tale" is
assigned. "What would we not give, now," Pieixoto laments, "for even

twenty pages or so of printout from [the Commander's] private computer!"

The professor's desire for what he has not and the concomitant disregard for all that he has (if he could only read it better) is finally parodic. Other comic inversions also characterize the enterprise of these future scholars. For example, Professor Gopal Chatterjee, of the Department of Western Philosophy, University of Baroda, India, is scheduled to speak on "Krishna and Kali Elements in the State Religion in the Early Gilead Period." Or the session on "The Handmaid's Tale" is chaired by Professor Maryann Crescent Moon, of the Department of Caucasian Anthropology, University of Denay, Nunavit. And even Denay, the future nation in the north that a number of native peoples in Canada currently wish to form—a nation in which the tradition ways of the natives will replace the Western ways of their oppressors—embodies obvious contradictions. With most of the United States contaminated by radioactivity and other industrial and nuclear disasters, the far north has apparently become the seat of power in North America, and with power comes a society that mimes the very Western ways it was intended to oppose. Although the existence of a Department of Caucasian Anthropology reverses the usual hierarchies—who is studied, who studies—there still *are* such hierarchies and the institutions that embody them.

Maryann Crescent Moon's role as chair of the conference session on "The Handmaid's Tale" does not prove an egalitarian future. On the contrary, as soon as the keynote speaker ascends to the podium, we are shown the real distribution of textual and sexual power. The eminent Professor Pieixoto of Cambridge (another enduring hegemony despite his non-Anglo name) begins his talk with the standard speaker's ploy of breaking the ice with a joke. Yet his opening comment, ostensibly marginal to the topic at hand, effectively centers the professor's discourse, and from the very first he sounds his key note. A most dubious note it is. His joke turns upon a bad pun conjoining the "charming Arctic Char" that "we all enjoyed" last night at dinner and the current "Arctic Chair" that "we are [now] enjoying." Lest the full racist and sexist implications of that equation go unappreciated, he also spells out the different senses of "enjoy" and thereby elicits his audience's laughter. The chairwoman/charwoman thus assumes her marginal place as mere handmaiden to Pieixoto's central text.

Pieixoto's discourse mirrors, then, the structure of the novel of which it is a part, and by that mirroring it also claims the part it would play. "The Handmaid's Tale" as text serves as handmaiden to the career-enhancing epilogue provided by the academics. Is this what history is for? To round out the vitae of historians? Or does the asserted marginalization of one text set forth itself still another text and a context in which to read it? We know—

from both Offred's narration and Pieixoto's speech—that the Caucasian birthrate declined disastrously in Gilead, thanks to such factors as radioactive fallout, chemical pollution, and a backfired plan for gene warfare against the Russians. Women who could bear children were therefore vital (literally) to the survival of the regime. But prospective mothers were nevertheless the most controlled, powerless, and demeaned members of that society. In short, there is no necessary relationship between one's importance to the perpetuation of society and one's privilege within that society. Significance and status are both constructs manipulated by those in power. Just as the conference chair in 2195 is peripheral to the proceedings themselves, so is Offred merely a marginal (and ultimately disposable) tool of the patriarchy that cannot exist without her. What Atwood has written is not just a history of patriarchy but a metahistory, an analysis of how patriarchal imperatives are encoded within the various intellectual methods we bring to bear on history.

The historical notes with which *The Handmaid's Tale* ends provide comic relief from the grotesque text of Gilead. Yet in crucial ways the epilogue is the most pessimistic part of the book. Even with the lesson ⟨of⟩ Gilead readily at hand, the intellectuals of 2195 seem to be preparing the way for Gilead again. In this projection of past, present, and future, the academic community is shown to have a role, not simply an "academic" role (passive, accommodating) but an active one in recreating the values of the past—which is, Atwood suggests, the way to create the values of the future. Professor Pieixoto's title is "Problems of Authentication in Reference to *The Handmaid's Tale*," and his very mode of speaking authenticates her tale by retrospectively duplicating the suppression her society inflicted upon her, by claiming the right to determine the meaning of her experience. But because his reading of her experience verges back towards Gilead again, our reading of his reading can authenticate Offred's account in a different sense than the professor intended and can also show how insidious are the horrors at the heart of his dark narrative.

The professor, too, concludes with mixed metaphors of light and dark: "As all historians know, the past is a great darkness, and filled with echoes. Voices may reach us from it; but what they say to us is imbued with the obscurity of the matrix out of which they come; and, try as we may, we cannot always decipher them precisely in the clearer light of our own day." It is a brief peroration that elicits his audience's applause and prepares the way for any discussion that might follow. Indeed, when he ends, with again a standard ploy—"Are there any questions?"—that question itself well may be rhetorical. And even if it is not, the speaker has already indicated what he thinks the questions are. His questions, however, need not be our questions, especially when we consider the matrix out of which his asking comes. His persistent assertion of gender prerogatives darkens his claimed "clearer light of [his] own day" and conjoins his world with Gilead's and ours.

ANNETTE KOLODNY

Margaret Atwood and the Politics of Narrative

More than twenty years before its publication, Margaret Atwood's novel *Life before Man* (1979) had been anticipated by Kenneth Burke. The prologue to the 1954 edition of Burke's *Permanence and Change* outlined "a kind of melodrama" played out on a stage clearly demarcated as foreground and background:

> In the foreground . . . there was to be a series of realistic incidents, dealing with typical human situations, such as family quarrels, scenes at a business office, [or] lovers during courtship. . . . In the background, like a set of comments on this action, there was to be a primeval forest filled with mythically prehistoric monsters, marauding and fighting in silent pantomime.
>
> These two realms were to have no overt connection with each other. The monsters in the "prehistoric" background would pay no attention to the everyday persons of the foreground; and these everyday persons would have no awareness of the background. But the pantomime of the background would be in effect a "mythic" or "symbolic" way of commenting upon the realistic action of the foreground.

From *Studies on Canadian Literature: Introductory and Critical Essays*, edited by Arnold E. Davidson. © 1990 by The Modern Language Association of America.

If the exhibits of the Royal Ontario Museum have replaced Burke's primeval forest in Atwood's novel, the relationship between background and foreground is otherwise in place. Against a backdrop in which reconstructions of long-extinct creatures "rear their gigantic heads and cavernous eye-sockets," Atwood's human characters play out analogous scenarios of territoriality and survival.

For Burke, the conceit attained full meaning only when background and foreground collided. "Gradually, . . . with increasing frequency," wrote Burke, "there were to be fleeting moments when the two realms seemed in more direct communication. And the play was to end with a sudden breaking of the frame, whereat the monsters of the background would swarm forward, to take over the entire stage." For Atwood, by contrast, narrative integrity depended on the two realms remaining separate. Lesje, a museum paleontologist, might on occasion daydream her way into Jurassic swamps and try to imagine *what it would be like if suddenly the dinosaurs came to life,"* but in the end she finds "she can't do it. . . . In the foreground, pushing in whether she wants it to or not, is what [a co-worker] would call her life." By collapsing the background into the foreground, Burke moved his "modernized morality play" from allegory to romance. In *Life before Man*, Atwood purposefully rejected the narrative strategies of romance—strategies she had employed successfully in the past—and composed her first true novel.

The distinction derives from Nathaniel Hawthorne, with whose work Atwood became familiar in the early 1960s at Harvard, while attending Perry Miller's lectures on American Romanticism. Articulating the distinction for the first time in his preface to *The House of the Seven Gables* (1851), Hawthorne declared that the novel aims "at a very minute fidelity, not merely to the possible, but to the probable and ordinary," while the romance may swerve from the probable in order to give the writer's imagination freer play. Taking up the argument a year later, in his preface to *The Blithedale Romance* (1852), Hawthorne again declared that, unlike the novelist, the romancer "is allowed a license with regard to every-day Probability." What the romancer wanted to create, he explained, was "a theatre, a little removed from the highway of ordinary travel, where the creatures of his brain may play their phantasmagorical antics." In effect, Hawthorne was describing Burke's final "breaking of the frame": the imagined theater stage on which the allegorical and symbolic intermingle with, even swarm forward to take over, the ordinary.

Measured by Hawthorne's narrative categories, Atwood was essentially a romancer until *Life before Man*. In *The Edible Woman*, *Surfacing*, and *Lady Oracle*, she allowed her characters their "phantasmagorical antics," inventing worlds in which the marvelous and the mundane easily intermingle. In the comic romance *The Edible Woman*, for example, the monsters have already taken over the stage. Images from prepackaged consumer goods so invade daily perception that the grittiness of reality all but disappears and people's expectations become delusory. Advertisements for girdles promise purchasers that "they were getting their own youth and slenderness back in the package," while beer commercials depict hunting and fishing scenes in which the fish have "no slime, no teeth, no smell," and "the hunter who had killed a deer stood poised and urbane, no twigs in his hair, his hands bloodless." When the central character, Marian McAlpin, momentarily breaks through the packaging to the reality it would mask, she is unprepared. Cellophaned and neatly labeled supermarket meat is intended to conceal the fact that what is being sold is "part of a real cow that once moved and ate and was killed." When Marian realizes that this, in fact, is what is on the plate before her, she becomes increasingly unable to eat. In true romance fashion, however, she shows no signs of wasting away, no evidence of malnutrition. After all, Marian continues to consume in the one way her society most approves: she goes to a beauty parlor for a new hairdo and buys a red dress for her fiancé's party.

If *The Edible Woman* amusingly examines the impossibility of living authentically amid the self-induced delusions of consumer society, *Surfacing* is a serious romance about escaping inauthenticity. The monsters who invade the stage here, though, are sources of healing and refuge. For, in *Surfacing*, it is the magical and the numinous that swarm forward to initiate the narrator's transformation, and, in this narrative, the breaking of the frame results in the woman's assumption of "the power for what I must do now." What she must do is give up the false myth of personal powerlessness that she has so carefully constructed for herself over the years. "This above all," she asserts at the end, "to refuse to be a victim. Unless I can do that I can do nothing. I have to recant, give up the old belief that I am powerless and because of it nothing I can do will ever hurt anyone."

Encountering the dry spare prose in which the narrator tells her story, the reader does not expect a romance. But as in a gothic romance (to which Atwood would turn next, in *Lady Oracle*), the reader of *Surfacing* must work at untangling the real from the unreal. What proves unreal is the narrator's account of her wedding, her failed marriage, and a child given over to the husband she had divorced. It is this version of events, she claims, that has left her "inoculated, exempt" from further emotional entanglements. When she enters a numinous wilderness, however, the fabricated past unravels to reveals only a collage of random memories pieced together so as to camouflage what she cannot accept: "the mutilation, ruin I'd made, I needed a different version." There had been no wedding, we learn, only a tawdry affair with an older man, her college art professor. And there had never been any child, only a back-alley abortion, urged on her by her married lover. For this unwilling complicity in the taking of a life, she believes herself a destroyer, "a killer." And so she has ever after clung to a belief in her own powerlessness and fabricated "a different version" to live with. "If it hurts invent a different pain."

Having taken to heart Hawthorne's advice to "make a very moderate use of the privileges" of romance (*Seven Gables*), Atwood grounds the transition from mundane to numinous in physiological plausibility. The narrator's first visionary experience in the lake—when she sees something "drifting towards me from the furthest level where there was no life"— follows upon a third dive. She is dizzy, weak, and suffering from the symptoms of oxygen deprivation, which, among other things, can cause hallucinations. Days later, after she has abandoned her parents' cabin in order to live like an animal in the woods, the narrator feels herself merging with the natural world: "I lean against a tree, I am a tree leaning." She is hungry—in itself an explanation for hallucinatory experience—but she has also just eaten wild mushrooms. "They taste musty," she admits, "I'm not sure of them."

In the narrator's view, she has entered one of "the sacred places" and been granted "true vision." The text itself never determines whether oxygen deprivation, exhaustion, hunger, mushrooms, or the powers of ancient Indian gods account for her altered perceptions. What is certain is that, whatever the plausible physiological explanation, this woman slips the confines of everyday rationality to momentarily immerse herself in the ground of being: "I am not an animal or a tree, I am the thing in which the trees and animals move and grow, I am a place." That the narrator now experiences herself as a source of life—rather than death—signifies the process as healing, whatever its origin. When she feels "separate again," moreover, the narrator for the first time sees the human symbol of the generativity that she seeks both to know and to become. There, "standing in front of the cabin, . . . her hair . . . long, down to her shoulders in the style of thirty years ago, before I was born," she sees her mother.

Another renewal marks the end of *Lady Oracle*—but in this case, the monsters that invade the stage are the conventions of romance's most highly stylized form, the gothic. The heroine, Joan Foster, composes popular "costume gothics" aimed at female readers and, as well, lives out the genre's fantasies of escape and transformation. As a slim, attractive adult, Joan conceals a former life: her unhappy childhood, when she was chronically overweight. She also conceals her secret identity as Louisa K. Delacourt—the name under which she publishes books like *Love, My Ransom*. In a brief excursion into the occult, she experiments with automatic writing and ends up composing a best-selling volume of poetry, entitled *Lady Oracle*. When the success of *Lady Oracle* causes her to become prey to a blackmailer who threatens to expose her alternate identity as Louisa Delacourt, Joan fakes an accidental drowning and escapes to Italy—under yet another assumed name. In each of her successive incarnations, Joan Foster eagerly identifies with "the pure quintessential need of my readers for escape, a thing I myself understood only too well."

Plainly, Joan Foster's life is a catalog of the gothic conventions she employs in her writing. The transition from fat child to stunning young woman represents the magical transformation. She flirts briefly with the supernatural in her experiment with automatic writing. And, like every gothic heroine, she is fatally attracted to a lover who "liked creating images of virtue violated." If this interpenetration of one world by another proved a source of knowledge and healing for the narrator of *Surfacing*, for Joan Foster it is otherwise. "Why did every one of my fantasies turn into a trap?" she cries. The answer is that this is a romance about the dangers of romance.

As the chapters progress, Joan's different lives become indistinguishable from those of the characters she is inventing for *Stalked by Love*, the working title of the costume gothic she is currently composing. In Italy—stalked by a strange man whom she cannot identify and isn't even certain exists—Joan (like the Surfacer) momentarily slips the bonds of everyday rationality and enters the garden of her gothic imaginings. The punning statement *"Suddenly she found herself in the central plot"* refers both to Redmond's garden and to the story line. Here, then, in the penultimate chapter, the merging of the frames is complete.

The problem is that, like all Joan's fantasies, the fabled garden maze of *Stalked by Love* is a trap. Offering rescue is the menacingly handsome Redmond, the ambiguous male protagonist of *Stalked by Love*, who in turn takes on the appearance of all the men in Joan Foster's life, from her father to her husband. "'*Let me rescue you*,'" appeals Redmond, and then—sounding like one of Joan's former lovers—"'*we will dance together forever, always.*' . . . *Once she had wanted these words, she had waited all her life for someone to say them.*" But this time the appeal fails. The familiar plot has unraveled, and Joan realizes that her belief in miraculous rescues and timely escapes is the real danger. Breaking the pattern, she opens her eyes, accepts the potential threat of the present moment, and prepares for a man who may actually be following her.

The man at the door turns out to be a reporter who has tracked her from Canada. Uncharacteristically for her, Joan tells him the truth about herself, and "the odd thing is that I didn't tell any lies." "I suppose I could still have gotten out of it. I could have said I had amnesia or something. . . . Or I could have escaped." That she does neither signals the cessation of gothic fantasies in both her life and her work. She will not give up writing, she affirms, but "I won't write any more Costume Gothics. . . . I think they were bad for me."

In Joan's statement, Atwood was announcing her own intention to take up a different narrative design. Having explored the major conventions of romance—from the comic in *The Edible Woman* to the serious in *Surfacing*— she ended up parodying the form in *Lady Oracle*. The ruthlessness of the parody (for all its comedic effect) suggests a certain impatience on Atwood's part with the romance's propensity for fantasies of escape, rescue, and transformation. In fact, in the fictions to follow, Atwood resolutely rejected these as narrative strategies, replacing romance's interpenetrating frames with a Sartrean "no exit." If she had not altogether exhausted the possibilities of romance, Atwood was nonetheless embarked on a new project for which romance would not serve. The practice piece for that project was *Life before Man*, "a novel novel," Atwood told an interviewer. "It stays very firmly within the boundaries of realism."

The foreground action of *Life before Man* takes place before two different background frames, each imaged in the buildings between which Nate jogs on a Sunday afternoon in 1976. "Behind him are the Parliament Buildings," squat pinkish reminders "that he once thought he would go into politics." "Ahead of him" are the gray buildings of the Royal Ontario Museum, where Nate's wife, Elizabeth, and his mistress, Lesje, are members of the professional staff and where Elizabeth's lover, Chris, had worked until his suicide. Against the novel's images of political statecraft, Nate, Elizabeth, and Lesje negotiate their own terms for power and territory. Against museum exhibits in which prehistoric form and movement are simulated out of bone fragments and fossil remains, these three middle-class Torontonians piece together lives from the fragments of childhood traumas and out of the shards of broken marriages and failed affairs. What secures *Life before Man* its status as a novel is that neither politics nor prehistory threatens to invade reality—as in *The Edible Woman*; nor do they provide alternate realities for healing or escape—as in *Surfacing* or *Lady Oracle*. The frames remain firmly fixed *as frames*. In that capacity, they provide a variety of commentaries— ironic, symbolic, sometimes even prophetic.

Nonetheless, *Life before Man* is very much a transitional text, replete with reminders of the romance narratives that preceded it. Elizabeth's former lover, Chris, for example, appears cut from the same mold as Redmond, the dangerous seducer of Joan Foster's *Stalked by Love*. As Elizabeth remembers him, "Chris had been a dangerous country, swarming with ambushes and guerillas, the centre of a whirlpool, a demon lover." For Nate, Lesje is another romance icon: the unattainable, otherworldy exotic. "Holding Lesje," Nate muses, "would be like holding some strange plant, smooth, thin, with sudden orange flowers. *Exotics*, the florists called them." And Lesje, a paleontologist by both vocation and avocation, is first introduced as "wandering in prehistory. Under a sun more orange than her own has ever been, in the middle of a swampy plain lush with thick-stalked plants and oversized ferns," Lesje likes to imagine herself "watching through binoculars, blissful, uninvolved," as "a group of bony-plated stegosaurs" graze and "a flock of medium-sized pterosaurs glides from one giant tree-fern to another."

The purpose of flirting with—but never employing—the romance possibilities is to expose them for what they are. The demon lover turns banal in his dependency and ultimately pathetic in his desperate suicidal vengeance. Nate's initial response to Lesje as an otherworldly exotic is a throwback to adolescence, and Nate quickly identifies the "image, place[s] it in time: a Saturday matinée of *She*, seen when he was an impressionable twelve and masturbating nightly." Nor can Lesje's Jurassic swamps offer solace or escape. In the end, although she still hungers to imagine *"what it would be like if suddenly the dinosaurs came to life,"* she finds "she can't do it. . . . In the foreground, pushing in whether she wants it to or not, is what Marianne would call her life." *Life before Man* thus goes beyond *Lady Oracle* in rejecting the generic conventions of romance, aiming instead at Hawthorne's "minute fidelity, not merely to the possible, but to the probable."

The probable, it turns out, proves wholly adequate to the transformations these characters seek. For, no less than the romances, *Life before Man* also recounts change and transformation. Elizabeth survives both her lover's death and Nate's leaving, realizing that, despite all, she has managed to build "a dwelling over the abyss." Nate emerges from the passivity of his marriage to Elizabeth and makes a commitment to Lesje. Lesje, in her turn, gives up her daydreams of prehistoric Jurassic swamps and makes a commitment to the future by throwing away her contraceptive pills. If none of these entail the mystery of the Surfacer's metamorphosis into wilderness creature or the eerie psychodrama of Joan Foster's entry into the garden of her gothic imaginings, that is precisely the narrative point. In the novel, as in life, people must learn to negotiate within the confines of being "worn, ordinary, mortal." Atwood the romancer had turned realist.

Her audience, by habit, remained loyal to the romancer. A number of critics had difficulty with *Life before Man*, and, as Atwood herself acknowledged in an interview, "they didn't know quite what to do with that

one because it didn't have the things in it that they were looking for." To
ensure against further misunderstandings, Atwood anchored even the most
bizarre elements in her subsequent novels to demonstrable realities. The
police station's pornography collection in *Bodily Harm* replicated sequences
in the Canadian Film Board documentary *This Is Not a Love Story* (a film in
which Atwood reads a poem). In interviews and public readings, Atwood left
no doubt that the novel's St. Antoine had both a geographic and a political
counterpart in a West Indies island she had been fond of frequenting. And
review copies of *The Handmaid's Tale* arrived from the publisher with
selections from a CBC interview in which Atwood declared that every event
in the novel was now happening or had already happened somewhere in the
world. "I clipped articles out of newspapers," she told the interviewer. "I now
have a large clipping file of stories supporting the contentions of the book."

This new emphasis on a realistic base underpinning the fiction was
crucial because the shift in narrative strategy was intended to enable a shift
in thematic focus. After *Life before Man*, Atwood turned away from her
previous concentration on the power politics of intimate relations and
looked, instead, at the abuse of power in the public arena. It was not an
entirely new focus for her, to be sure. In a series of poems that would be
published in *True Stories*, she had written, "power / like this is not abstract."
But the examination of this kind of power was new to her fiction. The moral
dimension of that change, she knew, would be lost if readers believed they
were taking in only fictive inventions, the phantasmagoria of a romancer's
perfervid imagination. Ironically, therefore, even as contemporaries like
Ariel Dorfman and J. M. Coetzee turn to romance fantasies to cope with
political horrors that defy rational understanding, Atwood reverted to what
Hawthorne called the "minute fidelity" of the novel in order to render the
dread palpable.

II

The narrative structure of *Bodily Harm* follows a pattern familiar in Atwood's
fiction. As the action of the plot unfolds, memory and association trigger
flashback sequences. Thus, revelations from earlier years help the reader
understand the central character's actions and responses in the present. In
this case, what we learn through flashback is that Rennie Wilford spent her
childhood in the narrow and repressive town of Griswold, Ontario, finally
escaping to Toronto as a university student. After college she supported
herself as a freelance journalist specializing in "lifestyles." In college she had
taken on controversial issues, writing a piece "on blockbusting as practiced
by city developers and another on the lack of good day-care centers for single

mothers." When she graduated, "it was no longer 1970," editors were not interested in social issues, and Rennie put away the "ambitions, she now thinks of as illusions."

What intrudes upon Rennie's carefully constructed complacency is the appearance of a cancer requiring a partial mastectomy. The operation so traumatizes her that she withdraws sexually from her live-in lover, Jake, and he moves out. At the same time, Rennie develops a crush on her surgeon, Dr. Daniel Luoma, but that too ends badly. Then one afternoon she returns to her apartment to discover that an intruder has entered and left a coiled rope on her bed. Unable to cope with what seems an increasingly threatened existence in Toronto, Rennie attempts an escape. She persuades the editor of *Visor* magazine to let her do a travel piece and ends up with an assignment "off the beaten track": a Caribbean island she "had never heard of."

Rennie's experiences on St. Antoine and its neighbor, Ste. Agathe, are the novel's present and constitute the unfolding of the plot. Essentially, the plot is about recovery. Rennie recovers her capacity for sexual pleasure in a brief affair with a small-time local drug runner named Paul. She recovers her capacity for compassion in her relationship with Lora (whose life story also winds its way through the narrative). And through Dr. Minnow—a local politician who is assassinated—Rennie recovers the outrage at injustice that had once fueled her journalism. The irony is that Rennie comes back to life when she is, in fact, most vulnerable: jailed in wretched conditions, uncertain that she will ever be let out, hearing the cries of the tortured all around her, and thinking about "her own lack of power . . . what could be done to her." Under these circumstances, her cancer scar "seems of minor interest, even to her. . . . She may be dying, true, but if so, she's doing it slowly, relatively speaking. Other people are doing it faster: At night there are screams."

The catalyst for these transformations is Rennie's belief in the possibility of being "away . . . invisible . . . safe." But because St. Antoine is so far off the regular tourist path and because she arrives on the eve of the first election since the British gave up colonial rule, her very presence arouses suspicion. Rather than becoming invisible, she is watched wherever she goes. Finally, when the corrupt local government attempts to thwart the election results, Rennie is suspected of being a foreign agent. In a place where corruption and unbridled power mean that "nothing is inconceivable," Rennie learns that there is no such thing as safety. Once and for all, she abandons the notion that "she's a tourist. She's exempt."

Rennie first attracts curiosity when she tours the island in the company of Dr. Minnow, a man she met on the plane from Barbados. Rennie expects to be shown the local attractions, but Minnow has a different itinerary. He takes her to a squalid encampment where the victims of a previous year's hurricane huddle, without adequate food or shelter—even though the "sweet Canadians" have given the government ample funds with which "'to rebuild their houses. . . . Only it has not yet happened, you understand.'" Minnow's tour highlights the island's poverty and the corruption of the present regime. What Minnow also reveals in the course of the afternoon is that he is the major opposition candidate in the upcoming election, and he wants Rennie to cover that event. "'Look with your eyes open and you will see the truth of the matter,'" Minnow pleads. "'Since you are a reporter, it is your duty to report.'" But "Rennie reacts badly to the word *duty*. Duty was big in Griswold."

Politics is "not my thing," protests Rennie, "I do lifestyles." Minnow takes the word literally and agrees that this, too, is what *he* is after. "'It is our duty to be concerned with lifestyles,'" he says. "'What the people eat, what they wear, this is what I want you to write about.'" Only later, when Minnow appears to have won the election and is shot by the new CIA agent on the island, does Rennie understand the urgency behind his pleading. "Now she knows why he wanted her to write about this place: so there would be less chance of this happening, to him."

In the aftermath of Minnow's assassination, some of his followers attempt to overthrow the present government. The tiny insurrection is brutally put down, and Rennie, having been seen in Minnow's company, is jailed as a subversive. Rennie's cellmate is Lora, another white woman who had drifted to the island and become involved with "Prince," the second opposition candidate.

The two are unlikely companions. In contrast to Rennie's stolidly middle-class upbringing, Lora is the child of poverty and abuse. Where Rennie is university-educated, Lora has had to become streetwise. In fact, as Rennie is slow to realize, some of the privileges they enjoy in jail—Lora's supply of cigarettes, a comb, a package of chewing gum—result from Lora's sexual favors to their guards during the daily latrine run. For Rennie, silently repeating the wisdom of Griswold, "it isn't decent." To the hardened Lora, it is simply a survival tactic. It's "'not any different from having some guy stick his finger in your ear.'"

Not that Lora is doing it for cigarettes or chewing gum. The guards have promised to arrange for her to see Prince, whom they claim is also incarcerated. As the days go by, Lora becomes increasingly impatient: the guards keep promising, but they never deliver. When Lora cries over her dilemma, Rennie finds herself "embarrassed. She looks down at her hands, which ought to contain comfort. Compassion. She ought to go over to Lora and put her arms around her and pat her on the back, but she can't." Finally, a new guard blurts out that Prince was never imprisoned, having earlier been "caught in the crossfire." Lora realizes that he, too, has been assassinated and that she has been used. Her rage and grief explode, provoking the two guards, and Rennie watches, helpless, as Lora's body endures their relentless beating. At last, against her will, Rennie is doing what Minnow had asked: "'Look with your eyes open.'" "She doesn't want to see, she has to see, why isn't someone covering her eyes?"

Unlike *Life before Man*, *Bodily Harm* is tenaciously novelistic, refusing even a flirtation with romance elements. Rennie may have once found it "soothing to think of Daniel," her kindly but deeply conventional surgeon, but she knew all along that this was only "a fantasy." The intended escape to "somewhere warm and very far away" has embroiled her in Third World political upheavals. And her lover, Paul, never rescues her from jail. When she is released, she knows, it is sheer luck—it might easily have been otherwise. Indeed, what Rennie learns on St. Antoine is that "she will never be rescued." There is no rescue from the realities on which this novel insists.

Moreover, where *Life before Man* still utilized framing backgrounds as symbolic commentary, in *Bodily Harm* the symbolic commentary is itself a product of the foreground. Rennie's cancer, which precipitates her journey to the Caribbean, is not only a plot device. It is also a metaphor for a malignant world. The disease really to be feared, Rennie comes to realize, is the capacity to take pleasure from another's pain. When the police arrest her at her hotel, she recognizes on the hotel manager's face "a look of pure enjoyment. *Malignant*." In prison she watches a guard with a bayonet menacing a group of bound prisoners. The guard "walks slowly around to the back of the line with it, strolling, hips rolling, taking his time, luxuriating. He's not doing this just because he's been ordered to," thinks Rennie. "He's doing it because he enjoys it. *Malignant*." In the end, what will save her sanity is what she had once most feared: massive involvement. Only now the term has a different meaning.

If there are neither romance elements nor background frames in *Bodily Harm*, there is what the novel calls "a subground, something that can't be seen but is nevertheless there." That subground is Griswold, where Rennie "learned three things well: how to be quiet, what not to say, and how to look at things without touching them." As such, Griswold does not offer commentary but is does help to define the absences, or lacunae, in Rennie's personality. First and foremost, as Rennie remembers it, Griswold was a place without compassion. "In Griswold everyone gets what they deserve. In Griswold everyone deserves the worst." Second, the old Victorian house of Rennie's childhood is a place of emotional withholdings, remarkably without touching or intimacy.

One of Rennie's most vivid memories is of her aging grandmother complaining that she has lost her hands: the hands "I had before, the ones I touch things with." Repeatedly during such episodes, Rennie had been unable to respond to her grandmother's anxiety. She "cannot bear to be touched by those groping hands," and so "she puts her own hands behind her and backs away."

By the time she first arrives on St. Antoine, Rennie's emotional withdrawal has become so complete that her grandmother's delusion is now her own nightmare. On her second night on the island, Rennie dreams she's "rummaging through her slips, scarves, sweaters. . . . It's her hands she's looking for, she knows she left them somewhere, folded neatly in a drawer, like gloves." But as she stays on St. Antoine, Rennie's hands again become capable of touch—first with Paul and then, more important, with Lora.

Rennie had never responded well to the living Lora, but after witnessing the beating, she is unable to ignore Lora's dying body. Bruised beyond recognition, Lora's face makes Rennie want to throw up and turn away, as though from a stranger. But "she can't do it . . . it's the face of Lora after all, there's no such thing as a faceless stranger." Rennie reaches out, finds the use of her hands, and takes hold of Lora's cold hand with both of her own. By the sheer act of will, Rennie attempts "to pull her through." It "is the hardest thing she's ever done": "She holds the hand, perfectly still, with all her strength. Surely, if she can only try hard enough, something will move and live again, something will get born." What gets born is a new Rennie. Upon her release, Rennie is aware that she has been changed irrevocably. For the first time, "she's paying attention, that's all." "What she sees has not altered; only the way she sees it." On the flight back to Canada, Rennie feels "the shape of a hand in hers, both of hers, there but not there, like the afterglow of a match that's gone out."

Ironically, the time on St. Antoine has made her what before she's been in name only: "A reporter. She will pick her time; then she will report." The Canadian official who passes on a request from the local government that she not write about what happened to her, we know, has no influence. Rennie has become what they accused her of: "a subversive. She was not once but she is now." The feel of Lora's hand in hers— "it will always be there now"—is the pledge that Rennie will eventually bear witness to what she has seen.

As has been characteristic of all of Atwood's longer fictions, then, the central character of *Bodily Harm* also undergoes a major transformation. As with *Life before Man*, however, the transformation takes place without the alternate realities, interpenetrating worlds, or colliding frames of romance. What distinguishes *Bodily Harm* from *Life before Man* is that the unsparing brutality of the later novel makes the reader long for precisely such illusions— even as it renders them at once immoral and inaccessible. Rennie's craving for exemption, her impulse toward escape and invisibility, are inherently romantic. But it is these very conventions that must be denied if *Bodily Harm* is to have its intended narrative force. For the message of *Bodily Harm* is the message of a novel: "She will never be rescued. . . . She is not exempt."

III

In contrast to Rennie, who learns to "'look with [her] eyes open,'" the narrator of *The Handmaid's Tale* pays the price of living "as usual, by ignoring. Ignoring isn't the same as ignorance, you have to work at it." Atwood's 1985 long fiction is thus a cautionary tale, illustrating the consequences of refusing the lessons of *Bodily Harm*. At the same time, *The Handmaid's Tale* represents the agony of telling that Rennie only contemplates. Where *Bodily Harm* asserts the moral imperative for bearing witness, *The Handmaid's Tale* elaborates the pain of that process. "I don't want to be telling this story," Offred repeats. "It hurts me to tell it over, over again."

The time frame of the narrative is the not-too-distant future when everything that we would recognize as familiar has been relegated to "the other time, the time before." The United States has undergone a coup d'état. The president has been shot, Congress "machine-gunned," and the Constitution "suspended." Taking control is a well-armed, highly organized right-wing fundamentalist faction whose politics combine sociobiological justifications for literal interpretations of the Bible with an appeal to a return to "traditional values." The new regime declares a state of emergency and establishes a police state named the Republic of Gilead.

The driving motive behind all this is racist anxiety at the declining Caucasian birthrate. Rather than direct its animus at the environmental causes of sterility—"nuclear plant accidents, . . . leakages from chemical and biological-warfare stockpiles and toxic-waste disposal sites, . . . the uncontrolled use of chemical insecticides, herbicides, and other sprays"— Gilead points its finger at the erosion of family values and the liberation of women from the home. Gilead's solution is a white supremacist ideology and a skewed reinstitution of the patriarchal family. Blacks are deported to "homelands"; Jews are given the choice of conversion or immigration to Israel; and homosexuals are executed as "gender traitors."

The white women remaining in Gilead are prohibited gainful employment and the right to hold property or money in their own name; they are no longer permitted to read or write. The only exception to this last stricture are the Aunts, a small group of relatively privileged older women who police the rest. Those resisting the new order are declared Unwomen and are banished to the Colonies—forced labor camps or toxic cleanup sites, where the life expectancy is two to three years.

Males in Gilead are organized by a rigid hierarchy of class and power, each man's status announced by the female services to which he has access. Low-status males are presumably celibate until they gain sufficient status to be assigned Econowives, women who must both reproduce and take care of all household chores. Econowives wear dresses striped in blue, green, and red, indicating their multiple functions. Upper-echelon males enjoy Wives, always dressed in blue; household servants, called Marthas, dressed in dull green; and Handmaids, attired in red.

The sole function of the Handmaids is breeding. Assigned to the childless households of high-status males and their wives, the Handmaids engage in a formal copulation Ceremony—once monthly, when they are ovulating. The Ceremony replicates the scene of Rachel and Bilhah in Genesis 30 and thus claims biblical precedent. The Ceremony notwithstanding, the odds are against successful reproduction because most of Gilead's adult males are sterile. And even when impregnation does take place, "the chances are one in four" that the fetus will miscarry or the infant prove deformed. When a Handmaid produces a healthy infant, she nurses it for a brief period but then turns it over to its legal parents and moves on to her next posting. Unless terminated by a successful pregnancy, each posting lasts two years. The reward for successful reproduction is the promise that the Handmaid will never be sent off to the Colonies. Should she fail to produce a healthy child after three postings, her fate is sealed. Because Gilead does not recognize male sterility but only female infertility, the Handmaid who does not conceive is declared an Unwoman and is banished.

For almost a year, watching with her as the seasons change, we live inside the head of one such Handmaid, known to us only as Offred. Like all Handmaids, her name denotes her possession by the high-status male in whose home she is currently posted (that is, she is the property *of Fred*). Because women are not persons so much as functions in Gilead, her given name, like her individual identity in the time before, is what the regime is bent on obliterating. Struggling to retain some vestige of her former personality, Offred hoards her memories. "The night," she says, "is my time out. Where should I go?" Alone in a sparsely furnished room at the top of the stairs, the "somewhere good" she chooses on one occasion is a college reminiscence. At other times, she remembers scenes from her childhood or from her marriage.

Offred's willed excursions into the "distant past"—along with her nightmares—flesh out the narrative. In these sequences, we learn something of her personal history—her prickly relationship with her ardently feminist mother, her marriage to Luke, the birth of their daughter, and her tendency to take "too much for granted; I trusted fate, back then." We also get her fragments of knowledge about the coup and the changes gradually instituted in the months following. Women were let go from their jobs, denied employment, and—with the regime in command of all the computer data banks—their money and property were transferred to the control of husbands or male relatives. "There were marches, of course," Offred recalls, "a lot of women and some men." But "when it was known that the police, or the army, or whoever they were, would open fire almost as soon as any of the marches even started, the marches stopped." For her part, the narrator attempted withdrawal into domesticity, "doing more housework, more baking." Too often, though, she found herself crying "without warning." When Luke remained insistently assuring, she realized—to her horror—that "he doesn't mind this. . . . He doesn't mind it at all. Maybe he even likes it. We are not each other's any more. Instead, I am his."

Only when their marriage is decreed invalid—because of Luke's prior marriage and divorce—does Luke attempt escape. But their forged documents are detected at the Canadian border, and a desperate run into the woods is quickly thwarted. Luke is shot, the narrator captured, and their five-year-old daughter taken away. In the worst of her nightmares, Offred can still "see her, . . . holding out her arms to me, being carried away." Except for a small Polaroid photograph purloined by Serena Joy, Offred never sees her daughter again; nor does she know what became of Luke, whether he is alive or dead.

Following the capture at the border, her memory lapses. "There must have been needles, pills, something like that. I couldn't have lost that much time without help." When the narrator regains full consciousness, she is at the Leah and Rachel Centre, formerly a high school, now converted for the training of Handmaids. Here—in a flashback sequence—the novel opens. The present time of the plot, however, covers the period from Offred's arrival at the home of the Commander and his wife, Serena Joy, through her final escape from Gilead in a black van. Thus, in what is by now a familiar pattern in Atwood's longer fiction, the events of the present are set against an interweaving of the past, with the past requiring the reader's active reconstruction.

If the narrative structure is familiar, the narrative voice is not. Offred's is the most anguished voice in Atwood's fictions to date, and the most self-conscious. She struggles with the process of telling, trying out different versions, inventing—then recanting—scenarios that might show her in a better light, and agonizing over missed opportunities in a past she can never recover. "I wish this story were different" is her repeated refrain. The anguish is heightened by Offred's uncertainty that she has an audience. Everything she has suffered and her attempt to bear witness to that suffering, after all, are rendered meaningless without a recipient who will honor her survival by learning its lessons. Offred therefore has no choice but to take a leap of faith and will her audience into being. "By telling you anything at all I'm at least believing in you, I believe you're there, I believe you into being. . . . I tell, therefore you are." But willing the audience's existence is not enough. She must also ensure that her audience will interpret her story as she intends.

Her narrative is not to be taken in the spirit of George Orwell's *Nineteen Eighty-Four*—that is, as a fable about totalitarian control. Offred thinks she has another lesson to teach. "Maybe none of this is about control," she muses. "Maybe it isn't really about who can own whom, who can do what to whom and get away with it, even as far as death. Maybe it isn't about who can sit and who has to kneel or stand or lie down, legs spread open." Instead, she speculates, her story is "about who can do what to whom and be forgiven for it." The speculation arrests attention. First and foremost, it suggests that Offred might consider forgiving the Commander, an architect of the regime that now enslaves her. Second, it underscores the travesty of Christianity that this repressive monotheocracy represents, by reminding us of the absence of anything like charity or forgiveness in Gilead. And, finally, in the face of a totalitarian police state that has seemingly appropriated all power to itself, Offred proposes that power takes many forms. "Remember," she enjoins, "forgiveness too is a power. To beg for it is a power, and to withhold or bestow it is a power, perhaps the greatest."

In the narrative as we have it, we never hear the Commander beg for forgiveness. Even so, we know that he has at least dimly understood that the Handmaids suffer and, because of this, he has embarked on an awkward effort to make Offred's situation endurable: he begins a clandestine friendship of sorts with her. Late at night in his study, he invites her to play Scrabble with him, provides forbidden reading material, and supplies a bottle of contraband hand lotion. On one occasion, he even sneaks her into Jezebel's, Gilead's underground version of a Playboy Club and whorehouse for the male elite. For all that, Offred never tells us that she bestows the single power she can still claim as her own. Having seen this sympathetic side of her Commander, she admits that "he was no longer a thing to me." But it is, at best, a "realization" that "complicates," not one that leads ineluctably to forgiveness.

Offred worries the point because she wants her audience to understand what it would mean if this *were* "about who can do what to whom and be forgiven for it." For all his attempts at amelioration, her Commander wields power on behalf of a regime that outlaws love, charity, intimacy, and forgiveness, ruling by terror and intimidation. To forgive such brutality would imply unthinkable power—not to the bestower but to the recipient—because it confers ultimate impunity. Rennie's nightmare on St. Antoine, where "nothing is inconceivable," pales in comparison to Offred's hint at a moral constellation in which nothing is unforgivable. "If you happen to be a man, sometime in the future, and you've made it this far," Offred appeals, "please remember: you will never be subjected to the temptation of feeling you must forgive, a man, as a woman. It's difficult to resist, believe me." But resist she does.

The "man, sometime in the future" who takes charge of Offred's narrative turns out to be the exegete Offred had tried to guard against. In "Historical Notes," which follows as an appendix, Professor James Darcy Pieixoto, Director of the Twentieth and Twenty-First Century Archives at Cambridge University, England, addresses an academic conference in the nation of Nunavit (a nation carved out of what was once northern Canada by the native peoples). The date is 25 June 2195. Gilead no longer exists, but in its wake the map of North America has been radically redrawn. Pieixoto's subject is the provenance of the *Tale* and the problems he has had, as a historian, in authenticating it. The narrative we have just read, it turns out, is Pieixoto's (and his collaborator, Professor Knotly Wade's) arrangement and transcription of some thirty tape cassettes "unearthed on the site of what was once the city of Bangor," Maine. The cassettes are "of the type that became obsolete sometime in the eighties or nineties with the advent of the compact disc." Offred is presumed to have made the tapes while hiding out at a "way-station" en route to Canada on "The Underground Femaleroad" that operated secretly in Gilead.

Pieixoto opens his remarks with a series of sexist puns. He then details the discovery and transcription of the tapes, briefly digressing to what he terms "an editorial aside" before launching into his main subject. The editorial aside is a caution against "passing moral judgement upon the Gileadeans." His main subject is the attempt to "establish an identity for the narrator" or for any of the personages mentioned by Offred. Bringing his remarks to a close, Pieixoto registers disappointment at the "gaps" in information within the narrative and reiterates his contention that voices from the past are "imbued with the obscurity of the matrix out of which they come."

The reader who has been moved by Offred's rendering of the dailiness of suffering in Gilead is unprepared for this kind of discourse. Because of the subject matter of the Handmaid's testament, what jolt us in Pieixoto's remarks are both his delight in salacious puns—especially those "having to do with the archaic vulgar signification of the word *tail* "—and his "editorial aside" against "passing moral judgement." Pieixoto subscribes to the relativist argument that all "such judgements are of necessity culture-specific." As a congress of historians, he states, "our job is not to censure but to understand."

The implied objectivity of this stance has the effect of repressing moral valuation because it flattens the uniqueness of Offred and her telling into a domesticating matrix. She has been consigned safely to history. Her document is merely additional evidence for fleshing out a context that no longer exists. As Pieixoto puts it, "Our author . . . was one of many, and must be seen within the broad outlines of the moment in history of which she was a part." As a result, what Pieixoto means by *understanding* comes dangerously close to what Offred would have named forgiveness. By telling his audience that "Gileadean society was under a good deal of pressure, demographic and otherwise," Pieixoto has not so much explained as *explained away* racist and sexist policies that led to a virtual reign of terror. This refusal to judge or censure thus makes of historical discourse—at least as Pieixoto practices it—a discourse of exoneration.

The "Historical Notes" was an inspired device. Pieixoto's analysis of the history and ideological underpinnings of Gilead, along with his pursuit of the identity of Offred's Commander, provides Atwood a mechanism for offering information to which her first-person narrator could not have had access. At best, Offred had managed "to see the world in gasps." At the same time, the "Notes" section provides Atwood with a mechanism for posing profound questions about what should constitute the narrative of history. The progress from the romantic to the increasingly realistic had brought Atwood to the view that "life can never be truthfully represented as having the kind of formal coherency met with in the conventional, well-made fabulistic story." She therefore put forward two opposed narrative possibilities: Offred's halting reconstruction of her own "limping and mutilated story" followed by Pieixoto's orderly excavation of identifiable personages, relationships, and motivations that might be derived from it. The two stand opposed not because of content—both are incomplete attempts at accurate reconstruction—but because the single response demanded by the primary document is the same response that its interpreter categorically refuses.

Offred bears witness that lessons may be learned, judgments made, future atrocities avoided. Her recollections are an admonition. "There were stories in the newspapers, of course," that gave clues too a right-wing takeover in the offing, Offred remembers, but most people "lived, as usual, by ignoring." Pieixoto records past social and cultural practices *for their own sake*. Among "his extensive publications" is an article entitled "Sumptuary Laws through the Ages." Pieixoto does not read the Handmaid's tale as *we* have been reading it: that is, as a call to critical awareness of the praxis current in one's own society. Thus Pieixoto is able to congratulate his era for being "happily more free" of the adverse demographic and environmental factors to which Gilead reacted, but he is oblivious to the Gileadean echoes in his own sexist jokes. As Pieixoto would construct it, in other words, history is not a narrative that asserts moral awareness or hones a critical perception of the present.

The point in all this goes beyond George Santayana's observation that "those who neglect the study of the past are condemned to repeat it." As Hayden White has commented, "It is not so much the study of the past itself that assures against its repetition as it is how one studies it, to what aim, interest, or purpose. Nothing is better suited to lead to a repetition of the past than a study of it that is either reverential or convincingly objective in the way that conventional historical studies tend to be." By engaging the reader first in an empathetic identification with Offred, Atwood has ensured that Pieixoto's putative objectivity will not be ours. In so doing, Atwood places us in the peculiar position of rejecting one kind of formal historical narrative—Pieixoto's—about a past—Offred's—that has not yet occurred but might be our future. The result is that we, as readers, are doubly inscribed in this text as the *writers* of history. On the other hand, jolted by Offred's narrative to reexamine current praxis, we realize that our action—or inaction—in the present is already writing the future that is Offred's past.

Because *The Handmaid's Tale* is a dystopia set in an invented future, there is some temptation to regard it is a romance fantasy. Atwood herself, however, insisted that she had projected only "a slight twist on the society we now have." In the widely publicized CBC interview, she explained: "There isn't anything in the book that isn't based on something that hasn't already happened in history or in another country or for which the materials are not already available." Futuristic though it is, then, in its "fidelity, not merely to the possible, but to the probable," *The Handmaid's Tale* adheres to Hawthorne's definition of a novel.

Unlike a romance, moreover, *The Handmaid's Tale* functions without interpenetrating alternate realities that could invite fantasies of rescue or escape. The best that Offred can manage is "time out" through memory. But even this is never a sure refuge. If she lingers too long in the past, she calls forth scenes painful to endure. And, finally, the past is not even surely there. "I ought to have . . . paid more attention, to the details," she agonizes. She didn't, though, so now Luke, too, is "fading. Day by day, night by night he recedes."

That said, there is a way in which *The Handmaid's Tale* might be read as romance. Offred's "time out" is the time we live. Ours is the world she attempts to conserve in memory. When we find fault with Pieixoto's commentary, we become the appropriately responsive audience whom Offred has willed into existence. In effect, *we* are the alternate possibility brooding over Gilead, ours the realm of potential interpenetration. *We* are the romance element that this novel everywhere invokes. Atwood has come full circle. She has offered her readers a return to romance—*if*, that is, we are willing to take on the obligations of history. We can both *re*write Pieixoto's narrative and *un*write Offred's if only we attend to the warnings in her tale and guard against the Gileadean impulses in the contemporary United States. To recognize these obligations is to recognize that we are Offred's ultimate fantasy of escape. To do otherwise is to measure Offred's future suffering in the magnitude of our present complacency. The generic choice is ours. Whether *The Handmaid's Tale* proves prophetic novel or cautionary romance depends on how seriously we take our political responsibility as readers who inevitably write history.

SHARON ROSE WILSON

The Artist's Marriage to Death in Bodily Harm

Written within a few years of *Bodily Harm* (1981), Margaret Atwood's *Murder in the Dark, Bluebeard's Egg,* and *Interlunar* (including the previously published *Snake Poems,* 1983) share intertexts, motifs, themes, and techniques similar to those in *Bodily Harm.* In varying degrees these works use fairy-tale intertexts alongside mythic, biblical, native, and/or literary ones (Dante, T. S. Eliot) to portray "hollow" wasteland artists who are figuratively, sometimes literally, married to death. Like the narrator-illustrator in *Surfacing,* these *"solde"* females and males, sometimes contrasted to heroic artists, are divided from others and from parts of themselves but are seeking transformation. Connected themes include sacrilege or debasement of art and of the sacred, natural, and human; humanity's simultaneous attraction to destruction (poison, murder) as well as to creation; and the artist's heroic/ironic/parodic journey out of the underworld (wasteland/prison/hell). Other themes these works share are sexual/textual/cultural politics; the colonization of the alien "other"; and transformation toward individual and global wholeness, healing, and wisdom (sometimes through special eating). Among shared motifs in these texts are magic, dismemberment, vision, cannibalism and ritual eating, silence versus speech or singing (poetry), hands, and the folk motif, also used in *Double Persephone* and *Procedures for Underground,* of descent to the underworld of the dead.

From *Margaret Atwood's Fairy-Tale Sexual Politics,* by Sharon Rose Wilson. © 1993 by the University Press of Mississippi.

In *Bodily Harm*, the Grimms' "The Robber Bridegroom," "Fitcher's Bird," "The Girl Without Hands," and a deconstructed combination of the Grimms', Perrault's, and Disney's "Cinderella" are major intertexts. In addition, *Oedipus Rex* and Oedipus folklore, goddess (especially Demeter, Pandora, Hecate) myth and related fisher king legend, the biblical story of humankind's fall, current critical theories, popular detective stories and games, spy stories, and other popular culture texts, playfully reflect and refract one another in *Bodily Harm*. Canadian riddles of the Robber Bridegroom type, Sir Walter Scott's *Ivanhoe*, and John Berger's *Ways of Seeing* are also important. Fairy-tale and other intertexts in *Interlunar, Bluebeard's Egg*, and *Murder in the Dark* are discussed (in Chapter 9).

To varying degrees, most of Atwood's work is, on some level, about the artist's marriage to death. Atwood's comic and serious artists include the poetry personae, Marian, *Surfacing*'s narrator, Joan, Nate, Offred, Elaine, and such short fiction protagonists as Julia ("Lives of the Poets"), Joel ("Ugly Puss"), Loulou and the poets ("Loulou; or, The Domestic Life of the Language"), and Joanne ("True Trash"). In *Lady Oracle* (1976), dancing in the red shoes all women wear means at least amputation of talent, goals, or desires: a psychic death. In *Bodily Harm* and *True Stories*, the marriage to death can be literal; and even in *Interlunar, Murder in the Dark*, and *Bluebeard's Egg*, the political and cultural implications of this theme have moved from subground to foreground. Because potential artists in these works are married to death, the "robber" is not simply a male or even patriarchy *per se* but the kind of dead or death-worshipping culture Riane Eisler associates with "the Blade" rather than "the Chalice," societies in which art and the artist serve commercial, military, and colonial ends. By being part of this increasingly global culture, Atwood's artists thus become not just victims but "robbers" of life colluding in their own and their world's "cannibalism" and "dismemberment." Ironically already in the kind of personal, urban, or societal hell Lessing portrays in *Briefing for a Descent into Hell* (1971), in *Bodily Harm, Murder in the Dark*, and *Interlunar* Atwood's artists descend into an inner and sometimes external healing or purifying landscape. Their initial self-deception sometimes makes them more parodic than heroic; and when they return to "ordinary life," they may again face speechlessness. Although such protagonists' life quests follow a deconstructive pattern, they still resemble those of medieval romance, where journeys (and thus texts) never end.

Originally entitled "The Robber Bridegroom," *Bodily Harm* resembles *The Edible Woman* and the short fiction, "A Travel Piece," in again using the Grimms' "The Robber Bridegroom" intertext. This fairy tale about a suitor who chops up and eats prospective brides and the woman who witnesses and tells about his crime dramatizes personal, interpersonal, aesthetic, national, political, and "earth" survival problems in a cannibalistic world.

Much more than source material for understanding Atwood's intentions or the changed vision many critics see, "The Robber Bridegroom" intertext is, with "The Juniper Tree," the basis for the cannibalism motif throughout Atwood's work and for distinctive features Irvine and others find in *Bodily Harm*. Along with "The Girl Without Hands" and the "Fitcher's Bird" fairy tales with which Atwood associates it, "The Robber Bridegroom" intertext illuminates the book's splitting of subject and object; disembodied, italicized language fragments; apparent narrative dismemberment; multileveled themes of cannibalism and dismemberment; surrealistic tone; patterned doubling; unreliable narration; and metafictional frame. Significantly, it structures the breastless and symbolically handless Rennie's transformation toward wholeness.

An "artist" married to death, as are protagonists in virtually all of Atwood's work, Rennata Wilford is the bride of the Robber Bridegroom, Fitcher and the father/devil ("The Girl Without Hands") in the novel's deadly sexual and global politics. Like all of us—male and female—however, she is married to the human condition, including her own relentlessly approaching death. As she discovers, because there is no longer an inside and outside, a here and there, there is no separation between the robber and his band or culture, the robber and his land, the robber and his bride, or the bride and other women. Thus, little separation exists between the man who breaks into Rennie's Toronto apartment (the man with the rope) and other men, the man with the rope and Rennie, Rennie and other women, Rennie and world imperialism, or Rennie and an invaded mother nature. Although she is a "sweet Canadian," Rennie is no more exempt than *Surfacing*'s narrator: she resembles "The Americans" who keep dictators in power either through foreign aid or CIA manipulations. A food specialist like *The Edible Woman*'s Marian, Rennie is literally and metaphorically eating and being eaten: Rennie's eyes "twin and reflect" those of the Robber and the closely related Fitcher and Devil father ("The Girl Without Hands"). Thus, Atwood's postcolonial themes and postmodern techniques are perhaps more evident in *Bodily Harm* than in any of her other work.

Not only is another evolving female "artist," Rennata Wilford, married to death, but Western and third-world culture and values are similarly consumed, internally and externally. As Patton suggests, the Caribbean country Rennie visits is also a "girl" in danger of being consumed by "robber bridegrooms'" cannibalistic imperialism. Massively involved, not only by literal and metaphorical cancers but also by consciousness, Rennie becomes a cell in the global body: she must "turn inside out" to connect the personal and political in order to create and to speak rather than to colonize and consume.

As in *Surfacing*, where disease is symbolically spreading up from the south, the main narrator of *Bodily Harm* exists in a diseased landscape that is her body, her "art," her nation and world, and the earth, all characterized with the "out of control" motif. Not only her own cancerous cells but also her relationship with Jake; her trendy articles; pornography; crime; Ste. Agathe and St. Antoine's government, revolution, and prison; Toronto's urban sprawl; Western imperialism; and, by extension, the narrative itself seem out of control.

Rennie is a parodic fisher king whose knights are more interested in killing dragons than in rescuing her or attaining the holy grail, a female symbol of regeneration. She lives in a world, not just one country, where "Ellis [not Christ] is King." The "Prince of Peace" and the fish symbol are reduced to campaign poster decoration, and Christ (parodically Prince and Minnow), no longer a savior, is either ineffectual or dead. In Atwood's feminized "Wasteland," neither Rennata Wilford, the island probably named after a saint (Agatha) whose breasts were cut off, nor Rennie's world can be healed by patriarchy's "bionic cock." In *Bodily Harm* we can no longer fail to see that the cancer is already within the narrator and that she is the wasteland she seeks to escape, first by living on its surface and then taking a more literal "vacation." As the narrator's aborted fetus and sliced-apart body in *Surfacing* symbolize personal, national, and societal dismemberment, Rennie's cancer and mastectomy, evidence of a "break-in" on multiple levels, suggest similar, more explicitly global themes: the cell image symbolizes cancer of the female and world body and represents "all women, all victims and oppressors, all human beings, all." Thus, the invaded cells of the body also suggest cancer of the earth. Because of the goddess's stature as the mother of all, the womb of the earth, these diseased cells also suggest a colonized Mother Nature, prefiguring the demonic, fallen world of *The Handmaid's Tale*.

Again Atwood simultaneously develops these artist, sexual-political, and global themes through re-visioned fairy-tale, mythic, and related intertexts about marriage to death and the need for the female artist to recover the godmother or goddess in herself. In this case Rennie is a simultaneous parody of Fitcher, the Robber, and the devil-father of "The Girl Without Hands" and their victims, Cinderella, and both patriarchal and matriarchal versions of Pandora, Mother Earth, and Eve in the Garden of Eden. Rennie is Barthes's "zero" or absent author, Rennie's and Atwood's readers, a parodic fisher king, and Berger's seen and acted upon woman. She is also Oedipus, the smart/dumb detective who discovers that he is the murderer in his life text; and Tiresias, the blind oracle. Simultaneously, she is also some of these texts' re-visioned hero.

Initially, Rennie is both cannibal (imperialist) artist and reader/consumer at the same time as she is the consumed "bride" in *Bodily Harm*'s at least six interlaced levels of "Robber Bridegroom" story: the personal body (disease, mortality), personal relationships (sexual politics, competition, friendship), the world of literature and culture, the national/political/global arena, the human condition, and the earth body. In the Grimms' "The Robber Bridegroom," disruptive female speech depends upon paternal and patriarchal absence or permission. Symbolically, like the caged bird, the old woman in the cellar becomes the voice of the girl's subconscious: the old woman is able to offer warnings and help only insofar as the robbers do not know about them. After the Robber Bride and the old woman escape from the Robber's den, the Bride tells her father about the Robber's crimes; the marriage feast goes on as scheduled. After each of the wedding guests and presumably the Robber has told a story, the Robber Bridegroom's condescension ironically releases silenced—internally and externally repressed—female rage: "'Come, my darling, do you know nothing? Relate something to us like the rest.' She replied: 'Then I will relate a dream'" (alternatively, "'Well, my dear, can't you think of anything? Tell us a good story.' 'All right,' she said. 'I'll tell you a dream'"). "This is how I got here, says Rennie," as she begins the story that the Robber Bridegroom requests and we read; some drafts of the novel even use an epigraph from the fairy tale.

Both the fairy tale and *Bodily Harm* present dreamlike stories that challenge readers' realities. In "The Robber Bridegroom," recounting the Robber's murder and cannibalism of another prospective bride, the Robber Bride undercuts her narrative with the increasingly sarcastic statement, "My dear, it was only a dream." *Bodily Harm*'s recurring question, "What do you dream about?" (is now Rennie's "last wish, it's all she really wants to know." Asked by a Rennie seeing literal or symbolic death not only in her dreams but everywhere she goes, in everything she eats, and in everyone or everything she touches, the question is, like its "Robber Bridegroom" corollary, still directly or indirectly answered with death (Paul's dreams of a hole in the ground, Minnow's actual death). Even Lora's answer, that she dreams of bearing "a son for Prince," fosters the destructive system underlying the book's action. Like the Robber, however, we are surprised at the form, content, and real effect of the "dream."

As in the Grimms' "The Robber Bridegroom" and Atwood's *Surfacing* and *True Stories*, *Bodily Harm* breaks the fictional frame supposedly separating dream or fiction from reality, suggesting the "truth" of fiction and the fiction or multiple stories of "truth." In the case of the fairy tale, when the Bride produces the severed finger of a formerly dismembered and cannibalized bride at the end of her "dream" tale, the Robber and his band are "actually" tried and executed. One of the voices in "True Romances" warns us that one day we will discover such a severed finger in the bottom of our own breakfast coffee or tea cup. *Bodily Harm* again subverts our desire to know the "true story," lying among all the other stories, "multiple and untrue / after all" and yet all the more believable for the disclaimers. As Paul says and Rubenstein discusses, there are at least three versions of everything in this novel. Resembling some of Angela Carter's fiction, Rennie's dreams blend into her and our realities.

Also reminding us of Iris Murdoch's texts, Rennie's self-conscious narrative, including Lora's parallel self-conscious narration "snaking" through hers, punctures the story illusion. The comments parodying popular genres and the book we are reading make *Bodily Harm* not only metafiction (metaromance) but anti-romance. Discussing publication of the story Minnow wants her to write, Rennie tells him, "I can't think of anyone who would touch it. It isn't even a story yet, nothing's happened. It's hardly of general interest." Later, when her Sunset Inn room is broken into, "This, thinks Rennie, is an exceptionally tacky movie. . . . It's not even a good lunchtime story." She recognizes that her relationship with Paul "is the biggest cliché in the book, a no-hooks, no-strings vacation romance with a mysterious stranger." As Atwood points out, by using the point of view of one of the females outside the central action of a conventional spy story and never totally uncovering the mysteries it poses, the book undercuts even its thriller story. Parodying the narrative form of "The Robber Bridegroom," Atwood first breaks the "frame" separating the Robber's known but unauthored text (his unacknowledged cannibalism) from the Bride's narrative, and then, more radically, the frame between the Bride and Rennie's narratives.

A parodic fusion—of metaphysical detective story, spy thriller, the ghost story, the Gothic romance, and the doctor/vacation romance—that Atwood calls an anti-thriller, *Bodily Harm* is, on one level, also an anti-comedy like *The Edible Woman*. Rather than resolving the action through marriage of the wrong people, however, *Bodily Harm* begins with marriage, in this case a profoundly ironic marriage to death. Despite its deconstructed romance form, *Bodily Harm* is sometimes mistaken for novelistic realism. Like *The Handmaid's Tale*, it is paradoxically grounded in "demonstrable realities" and recounts actual events: in this case pornography depicted in the Canadian Film Board documentary *This Is Not a Love Story* and a failed revolution on a Caribbean island Atwood visited but prefers not to identify. After reading *Bodily Harm*, readers may be afraid to face what is in their own cellars, closets, and bedrooms.

Prior to her Caribbean experience, Rennie is a camp, poststructuralist author: if not yet appropriately "dead," she is the impersonal blank, "replaceable by something else," that contemporary critical theory seems to approve. Atwood admits Rennie could be the writer of the novel, *Bodily Harm*. If, as Kristeva suggests, "the creator" "is not an individual . . . , not an identity," but "the one who produces a text by placing himself or herself at the intersection of this plurality of texts" on their semantic, syntactic, or phonic levels, creative subjectivity is a "kaleidoscope." "On the basis of this anonymity, this zero where the author is situated, the *he/she* of the character is born."

If we apply Kristeva's theory more literally than she might to Rennie's narrative, we could call Rennie's uncommitted life-style journalism the art of the faceless stranger. For Rennie's similarly escapist readers, such "faceless" writing falls into an existential void not only of Platonic substance but also of authorial and reader presence. The Toronto art world of *Bodily Harm*, also represented by *nouveau wavé* Jocasta, is as comic as Atwood's other parodies of current "trends" both in the arts (the Royal Porcupine's "con-create" freezer art) and in criticism of them (Charna's catalogue comments in *C⟨at's⟩ E⟨ye⟩*.) With the possible exception of *The Handmaid's Tale*, however, *Bodily Harm*'s authorial, reader/critic, and literary parody has a darker side than in any other novel. Rennie's colonialist discussion of what she eats in the Sunset Inn and what people wear on St. Antoine's streets could, for hundred or thousands of people, constitute "the Caribbean." Similarly, writing flip articles on such topics as boredom for the ironically named *Visor, Crusoe,* and *Pandora* magazines, Rennie assumes the passive females and active males of Berger's warning *Bodily Harm* epigraph and thereby perpetuates rather than challenges a view supported in some versions of fairy tales and myths: "A man's presence suggests what he is capable of doing to you and for you. By contrast, a woman's presence . . . defines what can and cannot be done to her" (*Ways of Seeing*). *Bodily Harm* self-consciously foregrounds the irresponsibility of Rennie's authorship and innocuous "pieces" in its own internal parodies: "What To Do If the Thief Visits You" and Madame Marvelous's "Problem Corner" in *The Queenstown Times*.

In *Bodily Harm*'s satiric pluralism of texts and intertexts, pictures of a calendar sunset, a rat in a vagina, a judge in *Pandora*'s "Woman of Achievement Series," the gallows of the prison (ironically named Fort Industry) where Rennie and Lora are incarcerated, a winking sun in *Leisure* magazine, an "exposed" brown-skinned woman on a Heather Cooper poster, and a tourist brochure's woman in a modesty-paneled bathing suit exist side by side with "Rex Morgan" comic strips, Dell mysteries, the game of Clue, and Rennie's "mental films" or superficial "camera vision." Refracted by the

Grimms' fairy tales and, as we shall see, by myth and *Oedipus Rex*, these interacting postmodern texts structure the larger postcolonial text that Rennie writes and we read.

Of course, we, like the novel's characters, are "under no obligation to see" or to reflect on a pluralistic void. Despite a common "marriage to death," "few can read" what matters on St. Antoine or anywhere else in Atwood's world: until the Robber Bride speaks, few can read the Robber Bridegroom's hidden text. Prior to the "massive involvement" that eventually turns Rennie into the subversive writer of the book we read, Rennie's life, her unvalidating notebook, and the eyes of the sun-glassed men (Paul, Masden, Ellis's minister of justice and his body guards) responsible for deaths in Ste. Agathe's short-lived revolution resemble the *nouveau wavé* book, *Death by Washing Machine*, after page 63. Despite subground conditioning and motives reeking of "authorial" intention, they all look "blank." Like the never seen but omnipresent dictator Ellis and the absent Paul, who simply disappears from the book after performing as "the connection," Rennie thinks of herself as invisible.

Although Daniel suggests after Rennie's mastectomy that she should think of her life as a clean page and write whatever she like, Rennie and her life are, of course, already partly inscribed, despite her admission of emptiness ("empty" is not the same as "clean"), her frequent wearing of Diana white, and her repudiation of her small town Ontario background. She even complains to Jake about his doodling inscription of her. Despite the narcissistic absence of self implied in Rennie's looking at herself from the outside—through the male gaze—at her body under glass during the mastectomy, and at others through reflecting sunglasses, *she* is reflected in what she sees or reads, including others' efforts at nonimpingement: their reflecting sunglasses. In addition to mocking the absent author of both formalism and poststructuralism, Robbe-Grillet's zero narrator, and the "faceless stranger" of the news and of Rennie's, Atwood's, Berger's, and our own fictions, *Bodily Harm* deconstructs the absent reader: "he" and "they" are also "I." As in the art gallery cheese and grapes of *Cat's Eye*, the taste of death—a major "Robber Bridegroom" motif—is omnipresent. *Bodily Harm* may thus (unintentionally?) deconstruct borders between author, narrator, reader, text, and intertext.

Atwood ridicules the concept of the dead or missing author: "I think I am a writer, not a sort of *tabula rasa* for the Zeitgeist or a non-existent generator of 'texts.'" Nevertheless, she is uncomfortable with simplistic autobiographical readings of her works and prefers to "cover" both author and authorial "intent" (signified with a paper bag in Michael Rubbo's autobiographical film, *Margaret Atwood: Once in August*). While she stops short of Beckett's "Crritic!" as the final insult, she jokes about kicking deconstructionists and seems to repudiate poststructural readings of literary criticism as texts among other texts, that is, as a variety of, or of the same status of, literature. Ironically, it is her own literary criticism that not only establishes a Canadian literary tradition (*Survival*) but also speaks movingly about the writer's moral responsibility and the opportunity books give us "to review, to re-view what's being presented": "I've implied that the writer functions in his or her society as a kind of soothsayer, a truth teller; that writing is not mere self-expression but a view of society and the world at large, and that the novel is a moral instrument. *Moral* implies political. . . . By "political" I mean having to do with power: who's got it, who wants it, how it operates."

We may be more aware of Atwood's soothsaying voice in her recent work, such as *The Handmaid's Tale* (1985) and "Three Chronicles" (1990). Although a number of critics have stated that 1981, the year both *Bodily Harm* and *True Stories* were published, marks a turning point, however, Atwood's moral commitment does not begin with *Bodily Harm*. Like *Are You Happy*'s Circe and many of Atwood's other poetry or fiction artists, Rennie does not remain faceless. By "spying" as the Robber Bride does and telling her multileveled story (the one Minnow, the Deaf and Dumb Man, and Lora want her to tell and the one we read), Rennie, too, becomes a soothsayer speaking for the voiceless.

However, Rennie also resembles the Grimms' Robber Bride, first in disregarding her instincts against following "the path" and later, after seeing and hearing the Robber Bridegroom's text, in initially "remain[ing] still and . . . not utter[ing] a word." For much of the book Rennie is the kind of escapist reader targeted in *Lady Oracle*, this time of several sub-species of the romance genre including "the ultimate male writing": the voyeuristically dismembering and devouring genre of detective fiction parodied in *Bodily Harm*'s deliberately complicated and unsolved or unresolved mysteries. Ironically, as Patton suggests, if Rennie had not been "bookless" on the plane (she finishes the thriller purchased in the Toronto airport before she reaches her "destination") and so undefended against conversation with Dr. Minnow, she might never have become involved in Caribbean politics and might have avoided jail. Rennie reads murder mysteries on the night of Ste. Agathe's first election since the end of British colonial rule. Even in prison she wishes for a book and tries to shield herself from reality, paradoxically in this case the *story* of Lora's rape, by recasting it as media entertainment. As a voracious reader of stories littered with female bodies, Rennie is again both Robber and Robber Bride.

In order to subvert both the thriller and travel romance form as well as Rennie's method of reading (predicting the murdered victim, guessing the killer, and skipping to the end to discover "the truth"), Atwood obfuscates narration, genre, settings, characterization, structure, and plot. She denies possible expected endings or even a resolved ending (Rennie's rape, murder, or marriage) while offering two alternate future-tense conclusions. Engaging the reader in a narrative game of Clue while Rennie reads clues to her own involvement as murderer, victim, and detective, Rennie's retrospective, unreliable narration has caused more than one reader to misread details of plot or structure as Rennie initially misreads her life.

The name of Rennie's friend Jocasta helps us recognize the comic *Oedipus Rex* intertext that not only carries tragic "Robber Bridegroom" themes but also foregrounds Rennie's insufficient "reading" ability. In addition to providing the basis of Freud's Oedipus complex, *Oedipus Rex* is based on myth explaining the Triple Goddess's suppression. In the play, Jocasta is symbolically married to death from the moment she gives birth to the son she will marry. In *Bodily Harm* Jocasta is an incestuous mother only of lame *nouveau wavé* trends. Like Lora always on the move, she embraces trends when, in changed form, they return to her. Thus, as "oracle" of the future and Rennie's braver alter ego, she is also a likeable Tiresias, the physically blind prophet of Sophocles' play. She even recommends the gender-shifting experience Tiresias embodies: based on the seven years Tiresias is supposed to have spent as a harlot, he judged that women experience more sexual pleasure than men.

Rennie plays Oedipus, Creon, and Tiresias roles. As a blind detective, naively obtuse but convinced of her own cleverness in solving riddles, Rennie is a parodic Oedipus in danger of being devoured, and not by the Sphinx. She is even an "oracle" in her job. Although editors think she sees into the future, she tells them, "I see into the present, that's all. Surfaces." In order to become a genuine Tiresias figure, the soothsayer who speaks against "bodily harm" rather than either the raped and murdered victim or the evil murderer her reading seems to predict, Rennie reads clues and tries to detect the "author" of the crime: her cancer, the book's many robberies, the rape and selling of females and the third world, Minnow's death, Lora and the Deaf and Dumb Man's beatings, world imperialism and corruption, and all the book's other "bodily harm" and betrayals. Before the "break in," the break into her consciousness, Rennie, like Oedipus, symbolically blinds herself so that she will not see what she begins to know about herself and her "Toronto-chic" life.

Also like Oedipus, Rennie was symbolically maimed in childhood. Her grandmother, who eventually "loses" her own hands, never lost her temper but locked Rennie in the cellar with unclean, crawling things. Accustomed to being silenced and controlled, Rennie, too, hides her misgivings (shuts them in the "cellar")—in her case about such matters as Jake's sexual bondage games, the pornography exhibit, her frivolity compared to the happy, successful judge she interviews, the possibility of being responsible for her own cancer—behind a precarious pride so that she will be able to continue her life. Rejected as well as abandoned by her father and remembering her grandfather mostly for cutting holes in women's stomachs and amputating men's legs, Rennie even becomes, in a sense, "incestuous," particularly with Daniel and the older Paul. She wants a strong male to "father" or passively protect and take care of her.

Like Creon, Rennie even "banishes" the person her Griswold subground identifies as the culprit: herself, first from Griswold and then from the scene of the first break-in. If the exact location, weapon, victim, and crime seem unclear because of the book's surrealistic spaces and times and doubled imagery, events, and characters, the novel's clues still lead to everyone's complicity in a continuing crime. Paradoxically, Rennie's Griswold training has its uses. She knows how to read events in terms of the narrow Griswold version of the biblical fall: one gets what he or she deserves. Everyone is, therefore, guilty (a murderer) and is punished (murdered). Unlike the English woman at the Sunset Inn, however, both Rennie and the reader are denied the Griswold gossip detective's malicious joy of discovering and reporting.

The biblical story of the fall is, like the fisher king and *Oedipus Rex* interstories, intertwined with several levels of "The Robber Bridegroom," "The Girl Without Hands," and Pandora intertexts. Reversing the pattern of fisher king legend and fairy tales, Adam and Eve "fall" from innocence in paradise to knowledge and death. Although with the completion of the pattern they may return to paradise in the form of heaven, their transformation—from immortal to mortal beings in a similarly transformed setting—is, at least at this point, negative. As in so many fairy tales ("The White Snake"), myths (Demeter/Persephone), and children's books (*Alice in Wonderland*), the transformation is linked to eating, in this case the forbidden apple. In *Bodily Harm* a nameless, hidden or "underground" evil invades Rennie, the cells of her body, her consciousness, and her relationships—including those with Minnow, Jocasta, and Lora. In addition, evil invades other female and male bodies, Ste. Agathe's political coalition, and the novel's real and remembered settings: Rennie's apartment, the Toronto art world, Paul's garden, an abandoned coconut plantation, Lora's childhood (cellar) apartment, the twin Caribbean islands of Ste. Agathe and St. Antoine, Ste. Agathe's dock where Rennie and Lora hide, the prison where they are jailed, Rennie's room at the Sunset Inn, the cellar of her grandmother's Griswold house.

This cancer or cannibalism is symbolically suggested by rats (in vaginas, in Lora's apartment, in the prison), maggots, fleas and other insects, crabs and snails, and by the motifs of nibbled flesh (Lora's fingers, Rennie's mastectomy), massive involvement, and something or someone "out of control" (cell division, the revolution, the government, the prison). Since Atwood's motifs characteristically begin to reverse as her narrators regain amputated senses, in *Bodily Harm* self-birth, growth, and flying overtake disease, death, and the fall as, at least mentally, Rennie moves "out of control" to report what is under the surface.

In terms of the biblical intertext, *Bodily Harm* tantalizes readers with thriller forewarnings and premonitions of evil and death in "paradise," giving ordinary details of setting a partly parodic charge. Images of hell, the underworld, mortality, death, and the Garden of Eden's snake quickly replace stereotypical images of humdrum Toronto and the Caribbean as paradise. Descending and crossing over, as her name suggests, Rennata (Rennie) enters an underworld where dead people elect the government, the head of the government is invisible, and the Minister of Justice dresses like an undertaker. In *Snake Poems*, snake imagery connotes goddess power and shamanistic vision rather than biblical sin or evil, and Oedipus myth links Tiresias' oracular powers to snakes. The snake in *Bodily Harm*, however, is a phallic coiled-snaked-rope. The first clue the police, Rennie, and reader-detectives discover, the rope on Rennie's bed warns of bondage, invasion, possible dismemberment and cannibalism, and, ironically, of the massive involvement that readers as well as Rennie encounter in tying seemingly separate events and narrative strings together.

"Rope Quartet" was an early title for the book that became *Bodily Harm*. Although Atwood cut at least one passage dealing with rope, there are still fifteen or so references to ropes and people, objects, or activities associated with rope, including the man with the rope and his doubles, the rope, the coil, tying, binding, strangling, and hanging.

Playing against the biblical fall and the disease and mortality it brings, "ropes" in *Bodily Harm* usually suggest the evil of "bodily harm." After Rennie's plane "falls" and lands, "the heat slips over her face like thick brown velvet." Although she thinks she is escaping not only the man who left a coiled rope on the bed of her Toronto apartment but also the breast cancer that ties her to a dying body, her Sunset Inn room contains another coiled signifier. Close to a picture of a cut-open melon and a lamp featuring a mermaid with exposed breasts and next to the Bible by her bed, Rennie finds a mosquito "coil" from the Blood Protection Company. Since she ironically overcompensates for learned Griswold prudery by metaphorically sleeping with the Robber or death throughout the book—sometimes confusing symbolic rape with love—her descriptions of the coiled rope, coil, and other ropes are ominous and surrealistic.

If the island country of St. Antoine and Ste. Agathe is a parodic Eden, "bush garden," and Gethsemane, then Rennie is its parodic Eve / Pandora and Robber Bride / Girl Without Hands. Jake, Daniel, and Paul share roles as ironic Adam, Robber, and Devil-father, and Paul and Marsden, especially, as coiled snake and Judas. Right before Marsden stops Rennie and Lora from leaving Ste. Agathe, Paul (possibly covering his own tracks before heading south) accuses Marsden of being the new CIA agent. Lora even approximates a "hiss." Although we never know for sure who the agent is and who kills Minnow, evil and betrayal permeate all the book's settings, including hypocritical Griswold with its punishing cellars.

Usually Rennie associates both rope and coil, like the mosquito netting that guards against being bitten in bed on the islands, with the bed and sex. After seeing Keith's bound women pieces and film clips of strangled and abused women in the police pornography collection, Rennie has trouble with Jake's holding her so she can't move during sex. Several times after the Toronto "break-in," including once in Paul's bed (Lora, too, finds this experience "like being with someone who wasn't there"), Rennie dreams that the man with the rope is in bed with her. After the Sunset Inn break-in she wants "A warm body, she doesn't much care whose." Ironically, Rennie parodies the policeman's presentation of pornography, including the kind of strangled women Rennie reads about on Paul's bed, as entertainment for "normal" (heterosexual) people. She does so by indirectly contrasting the book we read with her earlier stories. Once, Rennie would have served the man with the rope as an entertaining lunch story: "She would have told it at lunch, with the strawberry flan. . . . [but] the story had no end, it was open-ended. . . . And when you pulled on the rope, which after all reached down into the darkness, what could come up? What was the end, *the end*? A hand, then an arm, a shoulder, and finally a face. At the end of the rope there was someone. Everyone had a face, there was no such thing as a faceless stranger." The rope reaches down into darkness, suggesting the folk motif of the rope to the lower world.

At the end of this rope, however, is a hand. In addition to suggesting the presence of evil, ropes in *Bodily Harm*, like the character Paul, symbolize connection and signification. Although for most of the book this connection is "someone's twisted idea of love" rather than genuine love, touch, and communication, the motif suggests how all of Rennie's experiences, all of the settings and the separate pieces of narrative, eventually braid into the "rope" of narrative Rennie throws to us. Since ropes in *Bodily Harm* are not intrinsically evil, hands used either like binding or saving rope focus the book's opposition between Robbers and Lovers. If any one strand is followed to its terminus, we find hands, either of the Robber/Devil-father—the many-faced person with the rope who does evil (imperialistically controls, beats, rapes, tortures, amputates, or "eats") because it is possible—or the lover: the one who gives, who pulls the other to safety, through instead of down. Ironically characteristic of Atwood's postcolonialist vision, the lover can be a wiser ex-Robber.

In keeping with *Bodily Harm*'s "Robber Bridegroom," "Fitcher's Bird," and "The Girl Without Hands" intertexts is another implicit "murder" of the Grimms', Perrault's, and especially Walt Disney's "Cinderella" story. As we have begun to see, on the sexual-political level of the six-dimensioned Robber Bridegroom narrative, most of the men Rennie and her alter egos Lora and Jocasta encounter are in some sense robbers or betraying devil-fathers rather than princes. To *Bodily Harm*'s unreliable but developing narrator—a Rennie who has just become aware of her mortality—the male strangers in her life, with and without known faces, are comically and parodically if not seriously the ultimate Robber Bridegroom with whom she has a brief affair: Death, or in other guise, time, who will eventually "get" her. Understandably, after the first "bite" is taken out of her, she is frequently nauseous and uncomfortable when she recognizes that others have been "nibbled." In *Bodily Harm*'s nonchronological narration, Rennie's first bedroom encounter is not with a lover but with the rope the Ovaltine-drinking intruder leaves on her bed. In the "romantic" Caribbean, the fast-growing love vine strangles everything in the garden, and the island country considers chopping up women (an activity Rennie associates with cookbooks) less offensive then stealing. Despite Lora's story of love at first sight, Prince, of course, is neither the Prince of Peace nor a fairy-tale prince. Certainly not (except comically and parodically) the Prince of Darkness Rigney suggests, Prince fails to be either Lora, Rennie, or his country's rescuer in this book's enactment of the Rapunzel syndrome. Like Minnow—a potential rescuer whose icons (minnow, whale) suggest Atwood's food chain watercolor—Prince is eaten by the "sharks."

In addition to the men Rennie has sex with and the actual robber or man with the rope who breaks into the false security of her existence, robbers include many doubles: the older policeman who investigates, the robber in a bathing suit, Marsden, Ellis, Prince, Lora's stepfather Bob, Lora's rapist, the prison guard Morton, and even Dr. Minnow. Although it is Rennie who is "hungry enough to eat an arm" when Minnow, "his bottom teeth clasped over the top ones like folded hands," takes her to lunch, his tour of St. Antoine and its prison parodically foreshadows and even helps determine her entrapment in the Robber's "cellar."

Again parodically, however, instead of the Robber and Fitcher's successive chopped-up and eaten brides, Rennie has successive "grooms" whose amputating abilities, like her own, threaten their societies. Each of the men Rennie has sexual relationships with and several other characters (male and female) still use touch (hands) to control, like a rope that ties one in place. Sometimes comically, each also "amputates" or "eats" her. But Atwood repudiates the male bashing both fans and foes gratuitously assume in her work: *Bodily Harm*'s Robber Bridegroom intertext is not a simplistic equation of men with the bodily harm of the novel's title. Still, if no one, female or male, is exempt from the cancer with which humanity is invaded, it is already apparent that one level of symbolism deals with the evils of what "he" and the patriarchy or andocracy do with what Eisler calls "the blade": rape, war, guns. Although not linked either to "The Robber Bridegroom" or "The Girl Without Hands" intertext, other discussion of *Bodily Harm*'s sexual politics and hand imagery also make brief treatment of the Robber/father's amputating hands possible here.

If there is a parodic Prince Charming in *Bodily Harm*, he is obviously Jake, all surface and style without any depth. Few readers would argue his already apparent Robber/"Devil" qualities. Resembling *Interlunar*'s artful Robber, Jake has long canine teeth and is expert at designing attractive packages and "layouts" for consuming Rennie. From his point of view, women exist as objects, such as warm wet washcloths, to be arranged for his convenience and pleasure; if Rennie's body is not available, he is entitled to a substitute. In Rennie's mind, Jake's "love-making" blurs with scenes and implements of paradigmatic female bondage: footage of bound or strangled women in the pornography collection, whips, Keith's sculpture of chained women, Lora's story about a man who wants to tie her to a bedpost, and pornographic "snuff films."

Since Jake uses his hands as a binding rope, symbolically removing Rennie's hands, his actions, along with the poster he picks for Rennie's Toronto apartment, epitomize the sexual-political crimes of the Grimms' "The Girl Without Hands": "Jake liked to pin her hands down . . . to hold her so that she couldn't move." In Rennie's bedroom Jake hung "a Heather Cooper poster, a brown-skinned woman wound up in a piece of material that held her arms to her sides but left her breasts and thighs and buttocks exposed. She had no expression on her face." Like the Girl Without Hands, the bound woman is upright, physically able to move but in her case unaware that she might walk away from her conditioned bondage.

The poster's ironic title, "Enigma," even reminds us of the "enigma" some critics find in the Grimms' "The Girl Without Hands." Like Rennie, *Lady Oracle*'s Joan, and the woman on *Power Politics*' cover, this "triply" bound woman still wears the "red shoes." Even before Rennie is able to make connections, she recognizes one facet: "Being in love was like running barefoot along a street covered with broken bottles." Rennie associates this poster with Keith's pornographic tables and chairs featuring bound women locked into degrading positions: "The women were dressed in half cup bras and G-string panties, set on their hands and knees for the tables, locked into a sitting position for the chairs. One of the chairs was a woman on her knees, her back arched, her wrists tied to her thighs. The ropes and arms were the arms of the chair, her bum was the seat."

In "The Girl Without Hands," after the incestuous father sells his daughter to the devil, he cuts off her hands and sometimes her breasts. Far from being simply an altruistic healer or a source of compassion in the book, Daniel resembles Jake in amputating and using Rennie. As Rennie's surgeon, Daniel is, in a sense, an abusive "father": he consciously abuses the trust of a privileged relationship in which Rennie feels like a "child" hoping to earn "a gold star." Even though he knows patients in Rennie's circumstances are prone to low self-esteem, he violates his oath by having sex with her. Although Daniel uses his "healing hands" to save Rennie's life and to comfort her after her partial mastectomy, the same hands literally amputate part of her breast and the person under it, just as Prince's grandmother Elva uses her "magic hands" to carry the box with the machine gun. Parodically, Daniel is even a cannibalizing Robber who frequently takes her to lunch, but he doesn't want "to be stuck with the whole package. She might be the icing on his cake but she sure as hell [isn't] the cake." Rennie imagines a "lineup," "a harem" of Daniel's patients, "each with a bite taken out of them, one breast or the other." However, Daniel is not really a "devil." Like *Lady Oracle*'s Joan Foster, Rennie learns that people don't fit neatly into the Gothic romance categories she and Jocasta enjoy nailing them into; she resents Paul's playing a similar game with her, pronouncing her "nice" after he realizes her genuine need for companionship.

Paul supposedly "deals" with the devil. If he is not "a buffet casserole or a spare room" Lora has the right to give away, he is, like Lora and ironically Rennie, still "for sale," apparently providing guns, including the gun that kills Minnow, to anyone who asks. However, unlike amputating Jake, whom Rennie thinks is afraid of her because she has "the kiss of death on her, you c[an] see the marks," Paul ironically helps Rennie recover touch. He does not look away from her mastectomy, "the missing piece, the place where death kissed her lightly, a preliminary kiss." Although death seems to be as real to Paul as life and he cannot stay in the present, paradoxically, momentarily, he still achieves, and gives, the gift of loving rather than robbing touch. Like the protagonists of all the novels, Rennie realizes that

"This much will have to do, this much is enough. . . . she's solid after all, she's still here on the earth, she's grateful, he's touching her, she can still be touched."

In terms of *Bodily Harm*'s sexual politics, Rennie is "afraid of men and it's simple, it's rational, she's afraid of men because men are frightening." Significantly, however, she says this when she sees a man victimized and recognizes her own culpability for the system. Not just females are victimized by men, and the patriarchy is partly supported by women. "There's no longer a *here* and a *there*": as *The Handmaid's Tale* literalizes in the "particicution," she, too, holds the rope.

The evil of the coiled rope and Robber or devil-father's amputating or colonizing hand is not confined to sexual politics. Without noting "The Girl Without Hands" intertext, a number of critics have commented on Rennie's "symbolic handlessness" and "the emblematic episode of the severing of hand contact": her grandmother's "prying [her] hands away finger by finger." Having learned silence and the ability to look without touching, Rennie resembles *Life Before Man*'s Elizabeth in going through life with folded hands, culminating in Rennie's initial inability to find her hands with Lora. Some scenes in *Bodily Harm* remind us of the Amnesty International reports so familiar to Atwood. Black and brown people, men as well as women, political suspects and prisoners are all tied with ropes. In one instance, while pairs of women suspects have their hands tied behind their backs, men are tied together in bundles of three or four and stacked like cargo in the hold of a ship.

The backgrounds of Atwood's scenes can be overlooked only at the reader's peril. Referring also to a man's "ropy arm" helping Rennie into the boat and a boat with "looped ropes thick as a wrist," Lucking notes another historical use of ropes: the gallows Rennie looks at but does not see, first as a tourist and then outside her and Lora's cell window. Readers, too, sometimes overlook the ironic language of this scene: "Rennie opens her eyes. She fails to see the point, but it's something to do. . . . 'There's nothing to see,' she says when she's back down." Later, after dreaming that the man with the rope's eyes "twin and reflect her own," she sees the victimizer's face in her own. Rennie breaks through into a different dimension of consciousness as, from the same window, she sees the archetypal face of the victim. She witnesses apparently breastless figures endure a hair-cutting "ceremony" more physically brutal than the traditional one for Jewish brides: the deaf and dumb man, tied to other prisoners with rope, is sliced with a bayonet, kicked, and tortured with a cattle prod. "The deaf and dumb man, who has a voice but no words . . . wants her to do something, pleading, *Oh please*."

Like the coiled rope and other means of death, bondage, and torture, the gallows and marriage to death are at the other end of the motif *Oh please* and in the background of everything Rennie reports throughout the book. Rennie recognizes that she, like most of the book's other characters, is not only Robber Bride but also Robber. Even if she doesn't directly kill, she, too, has exploited others' rights to their own lives, values, or taste; silence about "raw material" supports colonization.

In the much-discussed prison scene after Lora has been beaten, Rennie regains her hands. Like Fitcher's third bride who puts the dismembered pieces of her sisters back together and magically revivifies them, Rennie pulls Lora, and her own reborn self, "through" with a saving "rope." Despite her and all human beings' marriage to death, she symbolically gives birth: "she's gritting her teeth with the effort, she can hear herself, a moaning, it must be her own voice, this is a gift, this is the hardest thing she's ever done. She holds the hand, perfectly still, with all her strength. Surely, if she can only try hard enough, something will move and live again, something will get born." Rennie passes on the gift of loving or healing touch to Lora, and "magically," by extension, to the "handless" grandmother she could never before touch. By acting to help another, as her mother and Elva had, she also symbolically "clasps hands" with the duty-bound, red-knuckled mother she, like her father, once escaped. In addition, she links hands with the breastless women in Daniel's "lineup" and with all women, with the deaf and dumb man who once blessed her with his touch, and with all "lovers" and saviors rather than Robbers or killers. As Atwood's "Five Poems for Grandmothers" and both title and content of Irvine's *Two-Headed Poems* discussion indicate, "one woman leads to another" and, I might add, to the other.

By extending her own "good-fairy" hand, Rennie symbolically collapses time to transform her grandmother from the once-menacing and then impotent witch in her mind into the no longer frightening godmother or goddess of her earlier dream. Sequentially following Lora's "Hansel and Gretel" newspaper story and parallel childhood memories, Rennie's dream "told" her that her mastectomy was not her only amputation. "Bound" in the bedsheet when she partly awoke, wearing a white gown tied in the back, Rennie searched for her hands in bureau drawers. As the narrators of *Surfacing*, *Lady Oracle*, *Life Before Man*, and *Cat's Eye* must do with their "framed" images of gods or monsters, she lets the past go so that she will not be "stranded" without hands either there or in "the future." Both past and future are now present: in a scene recalling the narrator's vision of her mother in *Surfacing*, "[Rennie's] grandmother smiles at her, the hummingbirds are around her head, lighting on her hands. Life everlasting, she says."

Finally, in addition to being Robber Bride, Robber, and Girl Without Hands, Rennie is also both patriarchal and original matriarchal versions of Pandora. Sometimes usefully discussed, the Pandora myth has unrecognized significance as an intertext in *Bodily Harm*, particularly when Pandora's "first woman" connection to Eve and other goddess figures is explored. Like Eve, Pandora is sometimes seen as a temptress and has been traditionally blamed for all human ills, including disease. In best-known patriarchal versions of the story, Pandora was given a box or jar containing all the evils that can trouble humanity. Although she was told not to open it, she was curious and did so and the evils spread over the earth. The box contained one good, however: hope. The box Rennie carries, stored under her bed and later in Paul's bedroom closet, is paradoxically not only a metaphor for the vagina and womb and all the book's literally and symbolically invaded inner spaces but also the kind of phallic rather than matriarchal "snake" closely linked to the man with a rope and his break-ins. Rennie is afraid to touch the box and worries that it might hatch. In a sense, it does, breaking the thin shell separating "life-tourist" Rennie from real experience so that she can be "reborn."

If we supply motives in the nightmare, the literal and symbolic box is the reason the robber breaks into Rennie's bedroom, both in Toronto and at the Sunset Inn, and a major reason that she is arrested on the fairy-tale seventh day of her stay. By extension, Atwood implies, all women, innately possessors of "the box," ironically resemble Kafka's Joseph K. in being under "suspicion," "on trial" in their and other's eyes—in Rennie's case, the dissecting gaze of Marsden and other men—and therefore guilty without knowing why (*The Trial*). Traditional interpretation of archetypal feminine symbolism, including the mouth, the breasts, and the womb, suggests why, revealing an unconscious basis in male sexual frustrations, fear, and envy: "as container, [the Feminine] also holds fast and takes back." As Dworkin suggests, "that slit which means entry into her—intercourse—[and/or human beings' associations with it] appears to be the key to women's lower human status. . . . She is defined by how she is made."

Literally, Pandora is the all endowed, with one quality from each of the gods, or all-giver, like the earth-goddess Rhea, made out of earth in the underworld. Like Persephone, in matriarchal myth Pandora is an underworld goddess associated with Hecate and Ge, the earth mother, sometimes called Pandora. Pandora's box was originally a honey vase or jar symbolizing the womb and used as a vessel of death and rebirth. Thus, contrary to what many believe, the womb-box traditionally contains the blessings and benefits of humankind. A number of folk motifs associate a box with the moon, magic, underground kingdoms, love, and even money.

In Hesiod's misogynistic version of the story, however, Pandora, in herself part of the gift from the gods, has become "a deathly vessel of the Feminine" designed to enact revenge upon "mankind." Thus, from this point of view, Pandora's box suggests another myth and folktale motif apparently rooted in male fear or envy: the castrating toothed vagina found in North American native, Chaco, and Guiana tales, in male dreams, and in Jung's archetype of the Great Mother. "The hero is the man who overcomes the Terrible Mother, breaks the teeth out of her vagina, and so makes her into a woman."

Ironically, although vagina dentata tales may suggest a reversed-gendered "Robber Bridegroom," still with cannibalism and sexual-political themes but with female victimizer and male victim, they also remind us of the rat no woman would put into her own vagina and of the tendency to view goddess iconography "through the lens of 20th century bias" ignorant of its religious and social context.

As in patriarchal versions of the Pandora myth, the womb in *Bodily Harm* anticipates the womb in *The Handmaid's Tale*: it is "packaged." Pandora's box no longer belongs to Pandora: it is the property of a faceless stranger who, in this case, uses more than one woman to deliver it. Ironically, the box returns to "poison" both owner and carriers. Thus, as in Hesiod's "anti-feminist" version, it contains a curse. Again ironically, in *Bodily Harm* even the healing hands of the grandmothers (the matriarchy) now carry the means of destruction and betrayal (the machine gun). Guns supplied by the American "connection," Paul, presumably for a coup d'état, not only keep the current dictator in power: they kill his opposition (Minnow, Prince). Dr. Minnow jokes that one can't eat culture; but disguised as food, the box facilitates Robber-Baron cannibalism of the island. In terms of the Pandora version most people know, Rennie brings on her own and others' undoing not only by touching but by looking into the forbidden box, apparently especially damaging actions when a woman performs them.

Again, however, Atwood remythifies and heals amputations, not only those of Rennie and the book's other characters but also those of the novel's male and female readers, of myth, of fairy tales, and of all women. Ironically, Rennie's error really is in not opening the box and her eyes sooner, in remaining passive under a colonizing gaze and touch and depending upon "the phallic opening power of the male" to disclose even her own inner spaces, her own "forbidden room." For example, she is fascinated with Daniel's secret knowledge of what is under her surface, but even she is annoyed with her "fluffiness" and irritated to be "seen through" as she quietly listens to Paul tell who she is. As other motifs are reversed, however, Rennie shifts from being "opened" to actively opening. Like Fitcher's brides and Pandora, who do the forbidden, Rennie does open the box and finally does open the forbidden door: into Paul's extra bedroom, where the box is hidden, and into her own "underworld," "earth-womb" or "goddess" power associated with both door and regeneration. In discovering the Robber's identity and choosing to be a lover rather than a robber, Rennie is reborn, not as a goddess but as a human being. As in some versions of the myth, hope, the possibility for her world's rebirth, remains.

Throughout the book Rennie literally is missing part of a breast: not only her ability to "feed" (sustain, nourish, comfort) another but also the regenerative power once associated with the sometimes multibreasted source of nourishment—milk/rain—or Giver of Life in general, and, in human rather than superhuman terms, necessary for Rennie and other characters' psychic health. Like other goddess attributes, including the womb, breast symbolism is too frequently subjected to the same kind of disparagement as are women and parts of their bodies: as objects of both external and internalized gaze, breasts are, thereby, stripped of natural, historical, religious, and personal meanings. Viewed as a burden or trap, part of a heavy "feminine" package one might need to lose in order to be taken seriously or, paradoxically, to be a full human being (a man), such externally defined breasts are part of the antiquated dualism entrapping not only Atwood's characters but all human beings. Structuralists caught by our inability to see and account for our own standpoints, most of us (including feminist theorists) can talk about patriarchal conditioning without recognizing how much what we see is still distorted by it. Not just worn like clothing to be displayed or, as Jake advises, flaunted, breasts are part of the body Atwood's artists sometimes have difficulty accepting. Much as Atwood's *Cave Series* deals with both physical and mythological womb, to the extent that Rennie's body *is* metonymically *Bodily Harm*'s landscape, the twin islands she initially visits as a tourist may even be seen as her breasts, and those of a personified, no longer sacred Mother Earth.

Symbolically, Rennie also lacks other body parts closely related to senses (touch, vision, speech, hearing, even smell and taste) amputated or cannibalized by "the system": family, gender, national, patriarchal, and Western colonialist conditioning. If she can't literally become whole, like St. Agatha, Rennie can symbolically regain her breast and *Bodily Harm*'s four other most important parts of the body: her mouth, hands, heart, and womb. She can learn to love and respect first herself and then the other, communicating this through touch and speech. Since Rennie's invaded cells, organs, and senses also represent cancer of the earth and a colonized Mother Nature, her healing prefigures the possibility of the earth's healing.

Some readers deny Rennie's transformation, insisting she is still in jail telling the story we read to Lora and that she only dreams her release. As I have already suggested here and elsewhere, Atwood deliberately denies closure, especially the cliché endings of "happily ever after" and marriage as solution, in *Bodily Harm* as in other novels and many stories and poems. As in *Dancing Girls'* "Lives of the Poets," she often does so by shifting to the future tense. The manuscript drafts of *Bodily Harm* are particularly revealing, demonstrating that, in addition to the two alternate future-tense conclusions Atwood compares to nineteenth-century double endings in the published version, Atwood actually experimented with and rejected two more resolved endings. One conclusion is similar to the published version with two very significant differences: Rennie does not connect Lora's hand to her grandmother's, so that when she is on the plane and feels a shape of a hand, she has "forgotten whose hand it is." However, the other variant reads: "You can fly, she says . . . she's back, flat-land criss-crossed by roads, buildings foreshortened by the height, there's snow on the ground already, her shadow's on it, blue-grey, beneath her feet the scarred earth rises up to meet her."

Rather than landing or almost landing the plane, in the book Atwood uses the flying image that is associated with art, imagination, and the transcendence of growth and that will also "close" *Cat's Eye*. Like *Bodily Harm*, Rennie "ends" in "the air," flying in a plane with faith in its and her ability to fly. The magical scene of holding Lora's hand and the lyrical tone of Rennie's resolve to be a subversive writer leave little doubt about her transformation or about the "magic" that can empower human beings: "She will never be rescued. She has already been rescued. She is not exempt. Instead she is lucky, suddenly, finally, she's overflowing with luck, it's this luck holding her up." In order to read ourselves as well as Atwood, we must like Rennie read the subtexts—including intertexts of sometimes amputated myths and fairy tales—and make connections.

J. BROOKS BOUSON

The Edible Woman's *Refusal to Consent to Femininity*

Atwood wrote her first novel in 1963 when she was twenty-three. The novel—which she handwrote at night in her room in a Toronto rooming house and typed during the day at her job with a market research company—was set near a swamp. "It was very existential," as she describes it. "There was a lot of marsh gas in it. People committed suicide and also drowned. It ended with the female protagonist wondering whether or not to push one of the male characters off a roof, which would be perfectly acceptable now but was, then, considerably in advance of its age." Although "downcast" when she was unable to find a publisher for her novel, before long she began writing another novel about a market-research employee living in a Toronto rooming house.

"I wrote *The Edible Woman* in the spring and summer of 1965, on empty examination booklets filched from the University of British Columbia, where I had been teaching freshman English for the previous eight months," Atwood remarks in her "Introduction" to the novel. "The title scene dates from a year earlier; I'd thought it up while gazing, as I recall, at a confectioner's display window full of marzipan pigs. It may have been a Woolworth's window full of Mickey Mouse cakes, but in any case I'd been speculating for some time about symbolic cannibalism. Wedding cakes with sugar brides and grooms were at that time of particular interest to me." Like

From *Brutal Choreographies: Oppositional Strategies and Narrative Design in the Novels of Margaret Atwood*, by J. Brooks Bouson. © 1993 by The University of Massachusetts Press.

71

the story Atwood tells about her first, unpublished novel, which ends with the female protagonist thinking about pushing a male character off a roof, the story she tells about her first published novel—with its focus on the "symbolic cannibalism" of marriage in patriarchal society—registers protest as it reveals the cultural and literary expectations she openly challenged at the outset of her novel-writing career.

"*Edible Woman* was written in 1965, before the Women's Liberation Movement had begun," Atwood recalls. At the time, it was "still very much the model pattern, in Canada anyway, to take a crummy job and then marry to get away from it." When her manuscript, which had been misplaced by the publisher, was finally published in 1969, "just in time to coincide with the rise of feminism in North America," some commentators wrongly assumed that her novel was "a product of the movement." It was, in fact, "protofeminist rather then feminist" inasmuch as there was "no women's movement in sight" when she composed the book. While some lauded Atwood's novel for its feminism, others, invoking traditional gender expectations, viewed *The Edible Woman*'s critique of marriage and motherhood "as essentially 'young' or 'neurotic.' I would mature, they felt, and things (i.e., marriage and kids) would fall into place." Caught in an inadvertent act of repetition, such commentators, in effect, reenacted the central drama—and trauma—of the text by pronouncing Atwood's oppositional art as a sign of her rejection of her own femininity. These conflicting early readings of Atwood's novel, reflective of the changing cultural climate of the late 1960s, reveal how different interpretative communities can produce different constructions of the text, each having its own political aim: the culturally conservative reading of *The Edible Woman* concerned with maintaining the status quo, and the feminist intent on challenging traditional cultural and literary practices.

If the woman writer chooses to write a female-centered story "based in specifically female experience," comments Joanne Frye, "she is choosing a story that requires passivity and self-denial, a story with a prewritten ending: self existing *only* in relationship, with marriage and/or motherhood as the appropriate denouement, or the demise of the self." Described by Atwood as a novel that makes "a negative statement about society," *The Edible Woman* does have a definite political and literary agenda. Focusing her narrative on traditional female rites of passage—courtship and marriage—Atwood is aware of the limitations imposed on theme and novelistic format by the masculine plot of desire, and she self-consciously resists the romantic love-plot formula. Atwood's oppositional intent is apparent in her description of *The Edible Woman* as an "anti-comedy." If in the "standard 18th-century comedy" the young couple must "trick or overcome" the "difficulty" of an individual "who embodies the restrictive forces of society" so they can get married, in *The Edible Woman*, in contrast, Peter—Marian MacAlpin's fiancé—embodies society's repressive forces. Because Peter "and the restrictive society are blended into one," Atwood remarks, the marriage resolution of the standard comedy would be "a tragic solution" for Marian.

Unlike the traditional courtship novel in which the couple must overcome a series of frustrating obstacles to achieve the endpoint of marriage, *The Edible Woman* is patterned around, not a frustrated progression toward, but a frustrated movement away from romantic affiliation. *The Edible Woman* contradicts the traditional story of female maturation in which the "growth" of the heroine is viewed "as synonymous with the action of courtship," and marriage is regarded as the "climactic event" that "confers on the heroine her entire personal identity." Enforcing the reader's discomfort with the romance scenario, Atwood's narrative elaborates on Marian's persecutory fears and disintegration anxiety as Peter assumes dominance over her. The novel contests the traditional story of female experience with its prescribed ending that insists on marriage and/or motherhood as the expected outcome for the female heroine. Instead, *The Edible Woman* shows how female passivity and submersion in the traditional wife and mother roles can lead not to self-fulfillment but to an intensifying sense of self-diminishment. Narrative with a vengeance, *The Edible Woman* focuses attention on the sexual objectification and potential victimization of Marian MacAlpin as she consents to femininity. But although Atwood presents her character as a potential victim, she also expresses her oppositional intent by disrupting the romance plot line, by interrupting romantic discourse, and by staging female revenge fantasies in *The Edible Woman*.

"Because all language is 'inherited' and because it is all socially and ideologically charged, the conflict of voices in a novel can reveal power structures and potential resistances to those structures," remarks Dale Bauer in her study of feminist dialogics. Through the dialogized female voices in the novel, Atwood both presents and undercuts the conservative messages given to Marian by the mid-1960s culture. Unlike Clara whose attitude toward her husband is "sentimental, like the love stories in the back numbers of women's magazines," Ainsley asserts that the "thing that ruins families . . . is the husbands." "[I]f I were you I'd get married in the States, it'll be so much easier to get a divorce when you need one," Ainsley tells Marian. But although Ainsley shuns marriage, she insists that every woman ought to have "at least one baby," sounding, when she makes this pronouncement, "like a voice on the radio saying that every woman should have at least one electric hair dryer." Ironically, while Ainsley accepts the inherited cultural belief that motherhood "fulfills" a woman's "deepest femininity," Clara urges Marian not to "believe what they tell you about maternal instinct"; moreover, Clara de-idealizes the mother-infant bond by comparing her baby to a leech or an octopus covered with suckers.

Enacting a pregiven feminine script as she begins to acquiesce to Peter, Marian finds herself speaking in a "soft flannelly" feminine voice that she barely recognizes as her own. "I'd rather leave the big decisions up to you," she says to him. Although Marian also speaks in an oppositional voice— "I've chopped Peter up into little bits. I'm camouflaging him as laundry and taking him down to bury him in the ravine," she tells Ainsley—she learns to silence this voice when she is with Peter and subject to his social control. "I was about to make a sharp comment, but repressed it," Marian remarks. "Well you needn't bite my head off," she says to Peter, thinking to herself that she would have to "watch how she spoke" to him. "[L]ife isn't run by principles but by adjustments," Marian tells herself, as she becomes increasingly dominated by Peter and thus assumes the preestablished feminine role assigned to her by romantic ideology: that of the passive sexual object.

Insistently exposing the female fears encoded in the traditional romance plot, *The Edible Woman* depicts Marian's intensifying paranoia as she becomes romantically involved with Peter. Explaining that one of the functions of the popular romance novel is to "deal with women's fears of and confusion about masculine behavior," Tania Modleski observes how such literature reflects the need of women to "read" men, to "engage in a continual deciphering of the motives" for their often frightening behavior. That Marian's "reading" of Peter's behavior becomes increasingly infected with Gothic fears as he assumes dominance over her is telling. When Marian first attempts to "read" Peter, he appears ordinary enough. Fulfilling the culture's prescribed—and commodified—image of masculinity, he is "nicely packaged": he resembles the young, well-groomed men in the cigarette ads and the plaid-jacketed sportsman in the Moose beer ad. And she imagines that Peter's attempts to have spontaneous sex with her—on a blanket in a field and on the sheepskin rug on his bedroom floor—are enactments of mass-culture fantasies found in men's magazines. "The field was, I guessed, a hunting story from one of the outdoorsy male magazines; I remembered he had worn a plaid jacket. The sheepskin I placed in one of the men's glossies, the kind with lust in pent-houses." But when Marian tries to "read" Peter's motive for wanting to have sex in the bathtub, her hidden fears surface. She imagines that he may have borrowed the idea for bathtub sex from "one of the murder mysteries he read as what he called 'escape literature'; but wouldn't that rather be someone drowned in the bathtub? A woman."

Although Marian initially takes Peter at face value, she soon becomes preoccupied with discovering "what lay hidden under the surface, under the other surfaces" of Peter, "that secret identity which in spite of her many guesses and attempts and half-successes she was aware she had still not uncovered." It is suggestive that Marian fantasizes that Peter might secretly be the Underwear Man, an obscene phone caller who poses as a representative of Seymour Surveys doing a study on underwear. An otherwise normal man, the Underwear Man is "crazed" by the girdle advertisements found on buses, Marian imagines. "Society flaunted these slender laughing rubberized women before his eyes, urging, practically forcing upon him their flexible blandishments, and then refused to supply him with any. He had found when he had tried to buy the garment in question . . . that it came empty of the promised contents." Pointing to one of the central premises—and anxieties—of *The Edible Woman*, Marian's comic-paranoid fantasy of the Underwear Man focuses attention on the cultural commodification of women, showing how men treat women as packaged goods, as objects of exchange and consumption.

The fact that Peter's grisly hunting story about killing a rabbit prefaces his pursuit of and proposal to Marian underlines the narrative's view of the sexual hunt as a form of predation. Describing how he gutted the animal after killing it with one shot, Peter tells how he slit the rabbit's stomach, grabbed "her" by the hind legs and then "gave her one hell of a crack, like a whip you see, and the next thing you know there was blood and guts all over the place. All over me, what a mess, rabbit guts dangling from the trees, god the trees were red for yards. . . ." Adumbrating *Surfacing*'s description of the "Americans," the "happy killers" who slaughter the heron and string it up like a lynch victim to "prove they could do it, they had the power to kill," Marian envisions Peter and his hunting friends as callous killers, their "mouths wrenched with laughter." Unconsciously identifying with the rabbit in his story—"surprised" to find her feet moving, "wondering how they had begun"—Marian flees only to be pursued and caught by Peter. In her "game of tag" Marian unwittingly enacts the courtship ritual in which female flight attracts male pursuit and capture.

A precursor of the split good/bad male, who repeatedly appears in Atwood's fiction, Peter is "ordinariness raised to perfection," but he also harbors a secret, dangerous identity. Adept at masculine role-playing, Peter, when he becomes engaged to Marian, readily exchanges his "free-bachelor images for the mature-fiancé one," and he adjusts "his responses and acquaintances accordingly." But Marian also begins to perceive Peter as a menacing presence. When she becomes the object of his sexual conquest as he is about to propose, she sees him as a sinister Gothic figure: his face is "strangely shadowed, his eyes gleaming like an animals," his stare "intent, faintly ominous." And when Peter proposes to her, she sees herself as "small and oval, mirrored in his eyes," for as the object of male desire, Marian is subjected to the male gaze which seeks to assimilate, and thus erase, the female self. Trying to "read" Peter's dehumanizing gaze—he concentrates on her face "as though if he looked hard enough he would be able to see through her flesh and her skull and into the workings of her brain"—Marian imagines that he is "sizing her up as he would a new camera, trying to find the central complex of wheels and tiny mechanisms, the possible weak points, the kind of future performance to be expected: the springs of the machine. He wanted to know what made her tick." If Peter sounds "as though he's just bought a shiny new car" when he becomes engaged, Marian, treated like a female commodity, gives him a "chrome-plated smile," her mouth feeling "stiff and bright and somehow expensive."

When Peter, just before he asks Marian to marry him, acts as if she were a "stage-prop; silent but solid, a two-dimensional outline," she feels that he is not "ignoring" but instead "depending on" her. As a "stage-prop" and later as a "silent and smiling" object that Peter takes "pride in displaying" to his friends, Marian is caught up in a masculine script which will slowly lead her to a frightening sense of self-alienation. For as Rita Felski observes in her remarks on the feminist narrative of self-discovery, the "internalization" of the notion of "female identity as supplementary to and supportive of a male figure" is indicative of "the deep-seated influence of patriarchal ideology." Moreover, the "sense of female identity as a lack, a problematic absence, offers no basis from which to challenge existing ideologies of gender as they are manifested at the level of commonsense assumptions and everyday practices." Providing a psychological assessment of the inherent pathology of the traditional male/female relationship, *The Edible Woman* actively undercuts the popular romance formula which, as Tania Modleski observes, "insists upon and rewards feminine selflessness" by showing that the heroine achieves happiness "only by undergoing a complex process of self-subversion." In *The Edible Woman*, Atwood reveals the dangerous gender politics inherent in the traditional marriage economy and in romantic discourse, which encodes and naturalizes the essentialist constructions of feminine selflessness and masculine self-assertion and conquest. The fact that the narrative shifts from first-person to third-person narration serves not only to emphasize Marian's self-alienation and threatened loss of self as she is objectified by the culture, but also to indicate that Marian's "sense of herself as sexual object makes her the object of someone else's discourse."

In an essaylike passage that both describes women's entrapment in masculine expectations and points to the central narcissistic anxiety dramatized in the text, Joe Bates chronicles the sad fate of women like his wife, Clara. When such a woman gets married, her "core"—the "centre of her personality, the thing she's built up; her image of herself"—gets "invaded." "Her feminine role and her core," as he explains, "are really in opposition, her feminine role demands passivity from her. . . . So she allows her core to get taken over by the husband. And when the kids come, she wakes up one morning and discovers she doesn't have anything left inside, she's hollow, she doesn't know who she is any more; her core has been destroyed." To be "invaded" is to be rendered void within as the self is "taken over" and assimilated. While this passage clearly contains a political message—through Joe Bates, Atwood is telling her women readers to avoid such a fate—it also gives voice to the key anxiety found in the text. And by informing readers of the thematic significance of the nightmarish experiences Marian is undergoing, this passage is further designed to assuage potential reader anxiety about being enmeshed in the increasingly pathological world of the text.

Speaking a kind of body language, *The Edible Woman* reflects both the cultural identification of women with body and the pervasive fear of the uncontained, uncontrollable female body as it puts the "mature" female body on display and scrutinizes its isolated parts. At the office Christmas party, Marian examines the bodies of older women "with interest, critically, as though she had never seen them before." To Marian, the "mature" figure is a grotesque spectacle. "[N]ow she could see the roll of fat pushed up across Mrs. Gundridge's back by the top of her corset, the ham-like bulge of thigh, the creases around the neck, the large porous cheeks; the blotch of varicose veins glimpsed at the back of one plump crossed leg, the way her jowls jellied when she chewed. . . ." Observing the other women as they eat and talk, Marian is struck by their "dune-like contours of breast and waist and hip; their fluidity sustained somewhere within by bones," and she is fascinated with and repulsed by "the continual flux between the outside and the inside, taking things in, giving them out, chewing, words . . . babies, milk, excrement."

Insistently the narrative thematizes Marian's anxiety—her "bridal nerves"—as symptomatic of her repudiation of her femininity. But what subtends her rejection of the female body and bodily functions is a much deeper fear: what Adrienne Rich calls "matrophobia"—the fear "of *becoming one's mother*." When Marian's distanced observation of women with "mature" figures gives way to transient identification, the "matrophobia" underlying her reaction becomes apparent. Fantasizing that she is "one of them, her body the same, identical, merged with that other flesh," Marian feels "suffocated by this thick sargasso-sea of femininity" and fears she will be "sucked down" into "that liquid amorphous other." Anxious to reestablish the fixed boundaries of the self to avoid this dreaded merger with the archaic mother, Marian wants "something solid, clear: a man . . . a fixed barrier." In Nancy Chodorow's view, women have more fluid self-other boundaries because in girlhood they tend "to remain part of the dyadic primary mother-child relationship." But as Jean Wyatt remarks, females can also undergo the process Chodorow defines as unique to the male developmental track: "the process of negative identity formation," the "definition of the self as 'not-mother.'" Indeed, as Wyatt comments, women's fiction "is full of daughters who, like Chodorow's male children, define themselves through denial of the mother in them."

Although *The Edible Woman* omits the story of Marian's relationship with her mother and indeed depicts Marian as free from family strictures—for her family "no longer" seems "to belong to her"—it nevertheless dramatizes the dangers of an extended symbiotic mother-daughter bond. It does this in the displaced, peripheral drama of the tyrannical landlady and her "cretinous," infantalized daughter, a "hulking creature of fifteen or so" who is called "the child" by her mother and who wears a hair-ribbon "perched up on top of her gigantic body." Marianne Hirsh, in her analysis of nineteenth-century novels in which the mother is "silenced, denigrated, simply eliminated, or written out," remarks that such "[m]aternal absence and silence is too much the condition of the heroine's development, too much the basis of the fiction itself; the form it takes is too akin to repression." If in *The Edible Woman* the mother's absence is the condition of the daughter's development, the narrative also expresses repressed fears of the overbearing mother through the character of the landlady, who fits the "malevolent yet inconsequential" brand of maternal representation described by Hirsch. For although the landlady is the precursor of the hostile mother figure that occurs repeatedly in Atwood's fiction, she is easily mastered in the text. Operating by the "law of nuance," the landlady speaks for the official culture, making Marian feel as if she is "forbidden to do everything." But the landlady is ultimately silenced by Ainsley, who asserts her right to speak in dialogic opposition to the repressive maternal voice. When the pregnant Ainsley accuses the landlady of being a "hypocrite" and a "bourgeois fraud" and claims she does not want her "exerting any negative pre-natal influences," Marian is surprised at how "easily" the landlady is "deflated" and wonders why she has been "slightly afraid of her."

It is ironic that Marian perceives Peter as a "fixed barrier" against the amorphous world of femininity which she dreads. Because romantic love assigns her the male-defined feminine roles she wishes to escape and insists that she consent to femininity, her romantic affiliation with Peter leads not to heightened self-definition but to a frightening sense of self-diminishment.

Fearing assimilation by the archaic mother, she finds herself, instead, being slowly assimilated—taken over—by Peter. As Peter increasingly dominates her and invades her "core" self, Marian becomes plagued by narcissistic fears of body-self disintegration. In a dream that occurs early in the text, she imagines that her body is dissolving: "I had looked down and seen my feet beginning to dissolve, like melting jelly, and had put on a pair of rubber boots just in time only to find that the ends of my fingers were turning transparent." When she wakes up the morning after she has accepted Peter's proposal of marriage, she feels that her "mind" is "as empty as though someone had scooped out the inside" of her skull. Later, when she has dinner with Peter and experiences her first significant loss of appetite, she looks at her distorted image reflected in the bowl of a spoon, observing how her "huge torso" narrows "to a pinhead" at the spoon's handle end. This, in turn, recalls Marian's fantasy of the pregnant Clara as body, not mind-identified: as "a swollen mass of flesh with a tiny pinhead." Disintegration fears also emerge in Marian's response to Clara's pregnancy: she imagines that Clara is being "dragged slowly down into the gigantic pumpkin-like growth" that envelops her body or that she is "being absorbed in, or absorbed by, her tuberous abdomen." Having babies is psychically equivalent to a threat to the self, in Marian's view. For the pregnant Clara's body seems "somehow beyond her, going its own way without reference to any directions of hers," and during the "later, more vegetable stage" of her pregnancy, Marian tends to forget that Clara has "a mind at all or any perceptive faculties above the merely sentient and sponge-like."

That Marian, after she becomes engaged to Peter, feels trapped in a temporal sequence reveals how difficult it is to escape the inexorable logic of the romance plot. Marian imagines "time eddying and curling almost visibly around her feet, rising around her, lifting her body . . . and bearing her, slowly and circuitously but with the inevitability of water moving downhill, towards the distant, not-too-distant-anymore day they had agreed on . . . that would end this phase and begin another." Plotting to forestall this closural moment, Atwood ushers Duncan into the text. But while Duncan functions structurally in the novel as the rival lover, he is no victim of romantic illusion. Mocking the myth of romantic attraction, Duncan claims that Fish picked up his notion that he will experience an "electric shock" when he meets the "right person" from "Some Enchanted Evening or D. H. Lawrence or something." And for Duncan, lovemaking is "too literary," the "scenes have been done already." When he is with a "limp and sinuous and passionate" woman, he thinks, "oh god it's yet another bad imitation of whoever it happens to be a bad imitation of" and he loses interest or starts to laugh. In *The Edible Woman* Atwood not only presents a rival lover whose dialogic speech disrupts romantic discourse, but she also deliberately subverts the "double suitor convention" in which the heroine "must be weaned from an initially mistaken male object of desire by a second, more responsible wooer, who, as her mentor figure, provides a model of the correct behavior to which she herself needs to aspire in order to become an autonomous adult." Whereas in the traditional courtship plot the heroine's developing maturity is gauged by her relationship to the rival lovers—one being regarded as socially responsible and the other as irresponsible—*The Edible Woman* makes the asocial, self-absorbed Duncan into Peter's rival and Marian's mentor.

An interpretation actively promoted by the text—and embraced by numerous critics—is that Duncan represents a hidden aspect of Marian's self. Occurring in a gap in the novel's realistic surface, Duncan suddenly materializes as if in response to Marian's unacknowledged needs. Suggestively, he tells her that he is "not human at all," that he comes "from the underground." When Marian puts on Duncan's dressing gown, he says to her, "you look sort of like me in that." To explain why he broke his bathroom mirror, he tells her, "I got tired of being afraid I'd walk in there some morning and wouldn't be able to see my own reflection in it. . . . [I]t was a perfectly understandable symbolic narcissistic gesture. . . ." Responding to Duncan's confusing speech, Marian fears that "if she said the wrong thing, took the wrong turning, she would suddenly find herself face to face with something she could not cope with."

As if intent on rescuing Marian from her anorexia, the text does not depict her as becoming dangerously thin. Instead, this threat to Marian's body-self becomes figured in Duncan's "long famished body." Duncan is "cadaverously thin," his ribs "stuck out like those of an emaciated figure in a medieval woodcut." When Marian kisses him, she has the "impression of thinness and dryness" as though his body and face "were really made of tissue paper or parchment stretched on a frame of wire coathangers." Later she imagines that if she were to reach out and touch him, "he would begin to crumble." Similarly, in Duncan's "womb-symbol"—the skeleton found in the museum's ancient Egyptian exhibit room—the text provides yet another monitory image of Marian's endangered self. Marian finds the "stunted figure pathetic: with its jutting ribs and frail legs and starved shoulder-blades it looked like the photographs of people from underprivileged countries or concentration camps." Partially displacing Marian's fears onto the enigmatic Duncan—a character readers are forced to decode—the narrative temporarily deflects attention away from the anxiety subtending the description of Marian's self-starvation.

Unlike Duncan, who declares that he wants to be "an amoeba" to avoid the complications of personhood, Marian is afraid of "losing her shape, spreading out, not being able to contain herself." Presented with Marian's anorexic disorder, the reader is prompted to offer a diagnosis. If Marian's self-starvation concretizes her growing sense of self-fragility and diminishment, it also reflects her resistance to the cultural constructions of femininity. For in the text's code, the anorexic body can be read not only as a dissent from the body-identified, sargasso-sea femininity found in the amorphous, uncontainable "mature" figure or the pregnant female form, but also as a protest against the "slender laughing" women depicted in advertisements or the image of womanly fragility found in the "translucent perfume-advertisement" brand of femininity. Remarking on the "continuum between female disorder and 'normal' feminine practice" observable in "a close reading of those disorders to which women have been particularly vulnerable," Susan Bordo comments that the "bodies of disordered women . . . offer themselves as an aggressively graphic text for the interpreter—a text that insists, actually demands, it be read as a cultural statement, a statement about gender." In a disorder like anorexia, "the woman's body" can be viewed "as a surface on which conventional constructions of femininity are exposed starkly to view." Describing the "painfully literal inscription, on the anorexic's body, of the rules governing the construction of contemporary femininity," Bordo posits that the "control of female appetite for food" provides a "concrete expression" of the general rule which governs the construction of femininity in our culture: "that female hunger—for public power, for independence, for sexual gratification—be contained, and the public space that women be allowed to take up be circumscribed, limited." Required to develop "a totally other-oriented emotional economy," women "learn to feed others, not the self, and to construe any desires for self-nurturance and self-feeding as greedy and excessive." As Duncan tells Marian, "[H]unger is more basic than love. Florence Nightengale was a cannibal, you know." What subtends the "other-oriented" ideal of femininity—embodied in the cultural representation of the self-sacrificing nurse—is a deep and all-consuming female hunger. Through the anorexic's "long famished body," then, *The Edible Woman* protests the contained, other-oriented femininity embodied in the slender female form.

Warning against the dangers inherent in women's acquiescence to masculine expectations, *The Edible Woman* depicts Marian's transformation into the consumable female object that Peter desires. During her preparations for Peter's engagement party, Marian goes to the hairdresser's where she is operated on "like a slab of flesh, an object," while her hair is "carefully iced and ornamented" like a cake. Her body "curiously paralyzed," she passively gazes at her "draped figure prisoned in the filigreed gold oval of the mirror." Surveying the "totally inert" women sitting under mushroom-shaped hairdryers, their heads "metal domes," she wonders if she, too, is being pushed toward this semimechanical existence, "this compound of the simply vegetable and the simply mechanical." In the hairdresser's scene, *The Edible Woman* dramatizes what Catherine MacKinnon describes as the "thingification of women who have been pampered and pacified into nonpersonhood." Later, when Marian sees her reflection in the silver globes of the bathtub taps, she perceives herself as a "curiously-sprawling pink thing," for her "waterlogged body" appears "bulging and distorted." And when she looks down at her body, it seems "somehow no longer quite her own. All at once she was afraid that she was dissolving, coming apart layer by layer like a piece of cardboard in a gutter puddle."

Metamorphosed into the object of Peter's desire—an artificial doll in a red dress—Marian surveys herself in the mirror after make-up is applied to her face and finds herself staring "into the egyptian-lidded and outlined and thickly-fringed eyes of a person she had never seen before." Later, when she inspects herself in Peter's mirror, she perceives herself as fragmented, not whole. Unable to grasp the "total effect" created by the assortment of details of her new appearance, she wonders what "lay beneath the surface these pieces were floating on, holding them all together?" When she gazes at her arms in the mirror, the only part of her without some artificial covering, they appear doll-like and "fake" to her, "like soft pinkish-white rubber or plastic, boneless, flexible." In her "finely-adjusted veneers" and with her "huge billboard smile, peeling away in flaps and patches," Marian feels unreal. Anticipating *Surfacing*'s paranoid vision of people turning into machines, Marian, who earlier imagined that she had a "chrome-plated smile," fantasizes that as her billboard smile peels away, the "metal surface beneath" shows through. But, predictably, Peter admires her new appearance, which fulfills the male ideal of a glamorized and sexualized femininity. When he tells her that she looks "absolutely marvelous," the "implication" is "that it would be most pleasant if she could arrange to look like that all the time." Duncan, in contrast, is appalled when he sees her. "You didn't tell me it was a masquerade. . . . Who the hell are you supposed to be?" he asks Marian.

Femininity, as Atwood dramatizes in *The Edible Woman*, is a male-assigned role, an act and an acting out of feminine scripts, a masquerade. Indeed, femininity has been compared to transvestism, since, for a woman as for a transvestite, femininity is a role requiring "make-up, costumes, and well-rehearsed lines . . . in order to be properly performed." According to Luce Irigaray, when women perform the masquerade, they "participate in man's desire, but at the price of renouncing their own," and "they submit to the dominant economy of desire in an attempt to remain 'on the market' in spite of everything." But even as Atwood shows Marian submitting to the masquerade, she constructs a feminist reading position by focusing attention on femininity-as-masquerade. As Mary Ann Doane observes in her analysis of female spectatorship and film, the foregrounding of the masquerade "constitutes an acknowledgment that it is femininity itself which is constructed as mask." Thus masquerade has the potential "to manufacture a distance from the image, to generate a problematic within which the image is manipulable, producible, and readable by the woman."

Attracting Peter's gaze as she performs the feminine masquerade at his party, Marian becomes increasingly aware of her object status. Thus she panics when Peter asks to take her photograph, for to be photographed, she imagines, is to be "stopped, fixed indissolubly in that gesture, that single stance, unable to move or change." As her sense of self-unreality grows, she envisions herself as a "two-dimensional small figure in a red dress, posed like a paper woman in a mail-order catalogue, turning and smiling, fluttering in the white empty space." Anticipating *Surfacing*'s critique of women like Anna, who become imitations of imitations as they try to conform to the commercialized images of women presented in glossy magazines, Marian assumes a billboard smile and the pose of a woman in a mail-order catalogue. All but overwhelmed by her persecutory fears, she imagines that Peter, with his camera/gun aimed at her, is a dangerous predator. "That dark intent marksman with his aiming eye had been there all the time, hidden by other layers, waiting for her at the dead centre: a homicidal maniac with a lethal weapon in his hands." If, in the text's code, the camera/gun is a signifier of the voyeuristic male gaze which fixates woman as sexual object, to be "shot" by the camera/gun is to undergo a terrifying loss of self.

Marian's persecutory fears also erupt in her fantasies about her future life with Peter. At first she imagines that the "real Peter, the one underneath," is a "bungalow-and-double-bed man," a "charcoal-cooking-in-the-backyard man," a "home-movie man." But when she searches through time's corridors and rooms and finds the middle-aged, balding Peter standing beside a barbecue, she discovers that he is holding a large cleaver in one of his hands. That Marian has no real subjective presence in the masculine plot of desire is signaled in her chilling recognition that Peter is alone, that she isn't "there." Caught up in a sinister Gothic plot, Marian fantasizes that her husband-to-be is a potential murderer, a Gothic fear that will continue to preoccupy Atwood's novels.

"[M]aybe you want me to rescue you? What from?" Duncan asks Marian after she escapes from Peter before he can photograph her. In the complex scene that follows, in which Marian and Duncan have sex in a cheap hotel room, Atwood uses the conventional love triangle plot both as a weapon and as a device to rescue Marian from her relationship with Peter.

Invoking and parodying the male fantasy of the split good/bad woman, the text casts Marian, who has shunned the culturally scripted roles of wife and mother, as a prostitute. In her red party dress, which Peter admired and which she felt made her "a perfect target" for his camera/gun, she is the "Scarlet Woman." "[I]f I'm dressed like one and acting like one, why on earth shouldn't he think I really am one?" Marian says to herself when the night clerk at the hotel leers at her. Assigning Marian yet another role—that of the rescuing noble nurse who is intent on curing Duncan's sexual problem—the narrative enacts a fantasy of female sexual empowerment. Marian recognizes the lure of the mass-culture nurse fantasy, for she is aware of the "embryonic noble nurse that is supposed to be curled, efficient and self-sacrificing, in the heart of every true woman." Using and subverting the culturally sanctioned nurse fantasy—which is associated with the traditional feminine virtues of pleasing and serving others—the text reveals what is latent in this collective fantasy of womanly self-sacrifice: the wish to take control.

"I can tell you're admiring my febrility. I know it's appealing, I practice at it; every woman loves an invalid. I bring out the Florence Nightingale in them," Duncan had earlier told Marian. In a deliberate reversal of roles, Marian is the sexual aggressor as she assumes the "starched nurse-like" role in the lovemaking scene and Duncan is the passive (and temporarily impotent) recipient. When Marian orders Duncan to remove his clothes and get into bed, he hangs his head "like a rebuked child." Unlike Peter who threatens Marian with his destructive male gaze, Duncan goggles at her in "a frog-like manner." As she walks "doggedly" toward the bed, she thinks that what she is undertaking will demand "perseverance" on her part. "If she had had any sleeves on she would have rolled them up." And indeed she does find it difficult to evoke any response from the "seemingly-passive surface, the blank white formless thing lying insubstantial in the darkness before her." Duncan echoes Marian's revulsion at the "mature" female body when he tells her that he feels "like some kind of little stunted creature crawling over the surface of a huge mass of flesh. . . . There's just altogether too much flesh around here. It's suffocating." Reversing the gender hierarchy by assigning Duncan the role of the passive sex object, *The Edible Woman* acts out a fantasy of female sexual domination and male subordination.

Even more telling, the predatory, sexually aggressive Len Slank, who is "a seducer of young girls," is openly punished by the narrative. Using parody to provide a feminist-dialogic commentary on the traditional seduction plot, the narrative depicts Len Slank's unwitting seduction by Marian's roommate, Ainsley, who, despite her "young and inexperienced" demeanor, is "in reality a scheming superfemale carrying out a foul plot against him, using him in effect as an inexpensive substitute for artificial insemination with a devastating lack of concern for his individuality." That women are defined by their culture as passive objects for male consumption is one of the central premises of *The Edible Woman*. But Atwood's narrative also expresses a subversive female anger through its elaboration on a male myth voiced by Peter: that women are "predatory and malicious."

Forced to assume a "pink-gingham purity" to attract Len Slank, Ainsley resembles "one of the large plump dolls in the stores . . . with washable rubber-smooth skin and glassy eyes and gleaming artificial hair." But despite her doll-like appearance as she performs the feminine masquerade, she is a female predator. "[I]t doesn't seem ethical," Marian says of Ainsley's campaign to get impregnated by Len Slank. "It's like bird-liming, or spearing fish by lantern or something." As Ainsley plays the little girl role designed to appeal to Len Slank's desire for sexual conquest, her "inert patience" resembles that of a "pitcher-plant in a swamp . . . waiting for some insect to be attracted, drowned, and digested."

When he later learns that Ainsley is pregnant, Len is "crushed." Marian compares his behavior to that of "a white grub suddenly unearthed from its burrow and exposed to the light of day. A repulsive blinded writhing. It amazed her though that it had taken so little, really, to reduce him to that state." In a reversal of the narrative's dominant plot—in which Peter preys on Marian—in this peripheral drama the woman preys upon and sexually uses the man. "All along you've only been *using* me. . . . Oh, they're all the same. You weren't interested in me at all. The only thing you wanted from me was my body!" Len complains to Ainsley. When Len expresses his anxieties about being "mentally tangled up in Birth. Fecundity. Gestation," which he finds physically disgusting, Ainsley angrily accuses him of "uterus envy." As in the description of Marian's seduction of Duncan, the Ainsley/Len seduction plot reverses the gender hierarchy and acts out female desires for power and revenge. Indeed, Len Slank is not only emasculated by the text, he is also infantilized, reduced to sharing a room with Clara's infant son, Arthur.

In a strategic subversion of the traditional closure of the romance plot, *The Edible Woman* resolves Ainsley's plot through her marriage to Fish. Ainsley, who initially makes pronouncements against marriage, determines to find a husband when she learns that psychological studies "scientifically" prove that a child needs "a strong Father Image in the home." When Len Slank refuses to marry her, she marries Fish, who views her not as a person but instead as an embodiment of the womb symbolism which so fascinates him. "I think I already know who you are," Fish says to Ainsley when he first meets her, "patting her belly tenderly . . . his voice heavy with symbolic meaning." "In traditional comedy, boy meets girl, there are complications, the complications are resolved and the couple is united," Atwood remarks.

"In my book the couple is not united and the wrong couple gets married. The complications are resolved, but not in a way that reaffirms the social order."

Determined, in *The Edible Woman*, to tell the "other side of the story," Atwood also provides a postromantic critique of the conventional resolutions of the love story. In the view of Rachel DuPlessis, "One of the great moments of ideological negotiation in any work occurs in the choice of a resolution. . . ." Describing the romance plot as a "trope for the sex-gender system as a whole," DuPlessis explains how traditional romance plot resolutions—the happy ending which rewards the heroine with marriage and the unhappy ending which punishes her with death—are part of the "cultural practice of romance." Whereas marriage "celebrates the ability to negotiate with sexuality and kinship," death results from "inabilities or improprieties in this negotiation." Joseph Boone, in his discussion of the "privileged role played by modes of closure in the traditional love-plot," observes that "the impetus toward concluding stasis" works to "cut short any serious or prolonged inquiry into the ideological framework informing the fictional construct. For by leaving the reader in a state of unquestioning repose and acceptance, the self-contained or 'classic' text inculcates a vision of a coherence or stability underlying social reality and cultural convention alike. . . ." In contrast, *The Edible Woman* refuses to reaffirm the social order or provide the traditional "closed" ending of the marriage resolution. Instead, it incorporates elements of female protest and revenge in the novel's final—and controversial—cake-woman scene.

Interestingly, before reaching this final "resolution" to Marian's problems, the narrative invokes the inherited closure in which the price for the heroine's failure to successfully negotiate the romance plot is death. When Marian finds herself totally unable to eat—"Her body had cut itself off. The food circle had dwindled to a point, a black dot, closing everything outside"—she faces the prospect of "starving to death." In the displaced drama of Duncan, who is the very image of suicidal depression as he sits "crouched on the edge" of the snow-covered ravine cliff "gazing into the empty pit," the text enacts the traditional tragic closure. The state Duncan is attracted to is "absolute zero." "[I]n the snow," he tells Marian, "you're as near as possible to nothing." Refusing to offer Marian advice when she tells him she does not want to go back to Peter, Duncan remarks, "[I]t's your own personal cul-de-sac, you invented it, you'll have to think of your own way out." Invoking but then discrediting the tragic ending of the failed love plot, the narrative finds a "way out" for Marian in the cake-woman scene, which is designed to puzzle readers and force them to interpret. Both using and refusing the master narrative of the traditional romance plot in *The Edible*

Woman, Atwood is aware of what Joanne Frye describes as the "power of a male-dominant sexual ideology" to entrap "woman characters and women novelists within outworn plots," but also of the ability of fictional narrative to resist "fixity" and to respond to its "social context through interaction rather than simple ideological miming."

When Marian creates the cake-lady as "a test, simple and direct as litmus-paper," she wants to avoid words and entanglement in a discussion. Although she has a "sudden desire" to tell Peter "the whole story," she also asks "what good" that would do. Marian, who recognizes the power of masculine discourse to silence the female voice, finds another way to communicate meaning. Through the cake-woman "text," she signifies her own transformation into a consumable object. Asserting active mastery over passive suffering, Marian does to the cake-woman what was done to her. She begins "to operate" on the cake-woman, just as she was operated on at the hairdresser's; she scoops out part of the cake and makes a head with it, repeating her feeling that the contents of her head had been "scooped out" after she became engaged to Peter; and she uses icing to draw "masses of intricate baroque scrolls and swirls" of hair on her creation, reenacting what was done to her when her hair was decorated like a cake.

After Marian completes the cake-woman, she offers it to Peter. "You've been trying to destroy me, haven't you," she says to him. "You've been trying to assimilate me. But I've made you a substitute. . . ." Refusing to devour the cake, Peter flees, and then Marian, finding herself suddenly hungry, begins to eat the cake herself. When Marian subsequently tells Duncan that Peter was trying to destroy her, he replies that in actuality she was "trying to destroy" Peter. "What does it matter," he tells her. "[Y]ou're back to so-called reality, you're a consumer." What the culture's official story of women as passive objects of male consumption leaves out, the text suggests, is the consuming female hunger for power and revenge. The fact that Peter's eyes widen "in alarm" and he leaves "quite rapidly" when Marian presents him with the cake-woman and accuses him of trying to destroy her is also suggestive. For as Dale Bauer remarks, "When women step out of their traditional function as sign; when they refuse the imposition of the gaze; when they exchange their sign-status for that of manipulator of signs, they do so through dialogic polemics. And, at that moment of refusal, they become threatening to the disciplinary culture which appears naturalized."

A novel that makes a negative statement about society as it focuses on Marian's initial consent to and ultimate dissent from femininity, *The Edible Woman* is also potentially anxiety-provoking as it involves readers in the troubling plight of Atwood's character. Finding *The Edible Woman* a "perplexing book" that has an "uneasy appeal," T. D. MacLulich describes the narrative as "a series of haunting images, a sequence of dreamlike hallucinations which flicker through the mind" of Atwood's heroine. "Where, in this stream of subjective images," asks MacLulich, "can the reader find a firm point of reference? Is there any way of seeing past the obviously distorted perceptions of the central character?" Sherrill Grace similarly comments that the reader becomes "enmeshed" in the novel's "increasing improbability" and is "locked within" Marian's perceptions. If, as these comments suggest, reader proximity to Atwood's character can be unsettling, Atwood also uses novelistic form and design to provide a "firm point of reference" for her reader and to defensively aestheticize the persecutory fears and disintegration anxiety that impel the narrative.

In an oft-discussed passage that, at once, parodies academic discourse, thematizes the text, and indirectly focuses attention on the artistic design of *The Edible Woman*, Fish—a graduate student in English prone to long-winded discourses on literary symbolism—discusses *Alice in Wonderland*. "Of course everybody knows *Alice* is a sexual-identity-crisis book that's old stuff, it's been around for a long time . . . ," insists Fish, who indulges in grandiose displays of his intellectual mastery of the text. In Fish's analysis, Alice is "trying to find her role" as a woman. "Yes, well that's clear enough. These patterns emerge. Patterns emerge. One sexual role after another is presented to her but she seems unable to accept any of them, I mean she's really blocked." This embedded passage provides an interpretive key to *The Edible Woman*, indicating that what happens to Marian can be understood as a "sexual-identity crisis." Pointing to a pattern of signification within *The Edible Woman*, the Alice passage specifies the kinds of details and descriptions that can be isolated and connected together. The *Alice* passage also anticipates a common critical interest in the emerging patterns of signification within *The Edible Woman*. Critics, for example, have traced the novel's *Alice in Wonderland* parallels (see, e.g., Harkness, Nodelman, Rigney, Stow) or have found analogues to Atwood's narrative in Conrad or in the fairy tale (see Carrington, "'I'm Stuck'"; MacLulich; Wilson, "Fairy-Tale Cannibalism"). In a similar vein, Linda Hutcheon, who sees the novel as "highly structured," claims that *The Edible Woman* "is as tightly knit as a lyric poem" and that the narrative's "thematic configurations . . . can actually be mapped out."

A carefully designed narrative, *The Edible Woman* promotes, at least in part, a defensive reading strategy as it draws attention away from the female anxieties dramatized in the text and onto the controlling authorial presence behind the text. It is, nonetheless, a book that has an "uneasy appeal," and the novel's ending seems designed to add to the reader's sense of uneasiness.

"One of us has to be the sympathetic listener and the other one gets to be tortured and confused," Duncan tells Marian in the final section of the novel, just as Atwood both invites her readers to sympathize with Marian and confuses them about the meaning of the closure. The cake-woman scene, with its enactment of female revenge, does serve to rescue Marian from her immediate problems. For after making the cake-woman and offering it to Peter, Marian is cured of her eating disorder, her engagement to Peter is broken, and she is able to think of herself "in the first person singular again." Yet the ending remains puzzling. In a maneuver meant to entice and frustrate literary interpreters, the closure indicates that the cake is a "symbol" and insists that it is "only a cake." Because the closure both tells and refuses to tell what it knows, readers are left with the uneasy sense that they have not mastered the text but rather that the text has mastered them. "Duncan sheds more darkness than light on the symbolic significance of the cake, and on the meaning of the novel as a whole," writes one critic who seems frustrated with the novel's closure. "Perhaps there are as many interpretations of Marian's symbolic cake and of the ending of *The Edible Woman* as there are readers," writes another. Ironically, Marian's nonverbal communication—her desire to avoid words and escape becoming "tangled up in a discussion"—has provoked a seemingly endless critical conversation as critic/readers have felt compelled to insert themselves into and to supplement the text as they attempt to make sense of the novel's conclusion.

As a reader of her own novel, Atwood, too, has felt compelled to join the debate about *The Edible Woman*'s closure. In a positive reading of the cake-woman scene, Atwood comments that Marian is "acting, she's doing an action. Up until that point she has been evading, avoiding, running away, retreating, withdrawing." And yet, in another, more pessimistic reading, Atwood—describing the narrative as a "circle"—comments that Marian ends where she began. Moreover, Fish's comment on the conclusion of *Alice*—"you can't say that by the end of the book she has reached anything that can be definitely called maturity"—seems designed as an authorial gloss on the closure of *The Edible Woman*. Mirroring Atwood's conflicting readings of the closing scene, critics are divided in their interpretations of the ending.

Responding to Duncan's assertion that Marian has returned to "so-called reality" by becoming "a consumer," Robert Lecker feels that "Duncan's words suggest that Marian's plight is not resolved, and that the plot of *The Edible Woman* is metaphorically circular." According to Lecker, in offering Duncan and Peter the cake and in consuming it herself, Marian "re-enacts her female as food role." For Gayle Greene, Duncan's words are similarly troubling, suggesting that Marian "resumes her place in a system that threatens her life." And while Marian's cake-woman "is a gesture of defiance, a way of saying 'no' to a system that defines women as commodities and devours them," Greene still finds it "difficult to see what Marian *will* be when she grows up, what she will do—what, in the terms of the novel, she will 'turn into.'" Describing the "politics" of Marian's act of eating the cake-woman, Pamela Bromberg argues that in consuming the cake-woman, Marian "is quite literally joining her subject and object selves. . . . She has become active again, an agent, a subject, a consumer, rather than a consumable object of exchange traded on the marriage market." But Bromberg is also bothered by the novel's closing description of Duncan finishing the cake. "[S]ince Marian has not been able to put her understanding into words, the reader is left to wonder whether he will then devour her." Marian "is more self-assertive and healthy, but for how long?" Bromberg asks. Also bothered by the ending, Jerome Rosenberg feels that while the experiences undergone by Marian "suggest the possibility of a positive transformation in her life," she, nevertheless, appears to have "changed very little" by the novel's conclusion.

Other critics are more positive in their reading of the closure. Responding to Atwood's comment that Marian's "choices remain much the same at the end of the book as they are at the beginning: a career going nowhere, or marriage as an exit from it," Barbara Rigney is "tempted to argue with Atwood about the ending" of the novel. "[S]urely Marian knows more than she did in the beginning . . . ," writes Rigney. "[A]t least she has come to terms with something, has objectified her situation and apprehended it more realistically. The cake thus serves as a reflection, a way of seeing herself as in a mirror, and it expresses a truth not before perceived." In the view of Jayne Patterson, Marian's "fashioning and eating of the cake signifies her recognition and rejection of her former compliant self, culminating in her new ability to respond to her own inner feelings." "[B]y demolishing society's synthetic stereotype of femininity through the ingenious mirroring-device of the cake," argues Nora Stovel, "Marian frees herself to realize her own true identity." For Catherine McLay, the cake "feast" signals "the celebration of Marian's new freedom and even rebirth." At the end, according to McLay, Marian "has gained a sense of identity and a new knowledge of self." In the view of T. D. MacLulich, at the novel's end Marian "is a whole person again" and while her "fate is uncertain . . . she will face it squarely instead of trying to escape." And for Perry Nodelman, who finds Marian a "sympathetic" character, *The Edible Woman* is "a convincing narrative of personal growth." It is revealing that so many critics seem intent on rescuing Marian. For in the structured, controlled art of literary interpretation, critic/readers can reconstruct and rework the novel's closure and thus act out the rescue wish that the text generates but refuses to wholly gratify.

Although Atwood refuses to provide a definitive rescue in the closing scene of her novel, she does rescue her character from the traditional romantic and novelistic ideology that insists on marriage as the endpoint of the story of female maturation. "Feminist writers must engage with, and contradict, traditional narrative patterning in order to (re)construct texts capable of articulating their marginalized, oppositional positioning—both inside, described by, patriarchal ideology (as the idealist construct, Woman) and outside that discourse, experiential witnesses to its contradictions, its mystifications (as women) . . . ," writes Anne Cranny-Francis. Constructing a feminist reading position by both using and contradicting the conventional romance plot, *The Edible Woman* dismantles and demystifies the marriage ideal by laying bare what has long been naturalized—and hence ignored—in the traditional romance scenario: the painful objectification and self-diminishment of women in a male-defined order.

GLENN DEER

The Handmaid's Tale:
Dystopia and the Paradoxes of Power

Margaret Atwood has consistently written about women who are both powerful and vulnerable, strong enough to endure and retain a sense of self yet unable to elude the grimmer aspects of entrapment. Often Atwood's protagonists are writers or artists themselves and therefore have particular creative resources to help or even hinder them—Joan Delacourt in *Lady Oracle* (1976) is a writer of costume Gothics; Rennie Wilford in *Bodily Harm* (1981) is a lifestyle journalist; Elaine Risley in *Cat's Eye* (1988) is a painter. What will be considered here in greater detail is the voice of the most obviously entrapped artist-writer in Atwood's novels: Offred in *The Handmaid's Tale*.

This novel has received a great deal of critical and popular attention since it was published in 1985. Perhaps the popularity of *The Handmaid's Tale*, adapted into a film directed by Volker Schlondorff in 1989, can be attributed partly to the convenient opportunities it provides for teachers in the Canadian critical parlour to explain its generic inheritance from dystopian fiction (Orwell, Kafka, Zamyatin, Huxley) and to the postmodern design of the novel. Critics have been especially attracted to its metafictional elements and narrative frame. Among eight articles on *The Handmaid's Tale* published since 1987, four give prominence to the effect of the "Historical Notes" section on our reading. Out of these four, Amin Malak, Arnold

From *Postmodern Canadian Fiction and the Rhetoric of Authority*, by Glenn Deer. © 1994 by McGill-Queen's University Press.

Davidson, and Harriet Bergmann emphasize that the "Historical Notes" are an ironic treatment of the failure of male academic readings of the oral record left by Offred; the future historians fail to treat Offred's experience with compassion or emotional sympathy. As Davidson suggests, the Notes section is perhaps the most depressing part of the novel since it shows how little has been changed by Offred's discourse: the male oppression of women has persisted in a different form beyond the post-Gilead period, even into the aboriginal Republic of Denay. W.F. Garrett-Petts goes further and argues that the Notes section actually marginalizes and reduces the character of Offred to a mere shadow: he tries to show that her character is significantly deflated by the time we reach the end of the Notes. Constance Rooke, by contrast, asserts that Offred's character retains integrity and cannot be divorced from the politics of resistance.

Other tasks undertaken by various critics include the explanation of generic sources (Malak, Lacombe), the identification of motifs of nature and womanhood (Rooke, Rubenstein, Freibert), and the attempt to infer that Offred's metaphorically significant real name is "June" (Rooke, Rubenstein, Friebert).

Very little of the above criticism deals with the voice, ethos, or style of the narrator in *The Handmaid's Tale*. Only Lucy Freibert comments that the voice of Offred is the same "low-keyed" one that "B.W. Powe derides as 'virtually interchangeable' in all the previous novels." Freibert defends this monotonous voice by arguing that this "voice, approximating the limited scope of Offred's life symbolized by the blinkers on her veil, is precisely what makes *The Handmaid's Tale* credible."

Amin Malak says that although Atwood is writing in an Orwellian tradition, the novel "sustains an ironic texture" and is not filled with as many "frightening images" as Orwell's *Nineteen Eighty-Four*: "the few graphic horror scenes are crisply and snappily presented, sparing us a blood-curdling impact. Some may criticize this restraint as undermining the novel's integrity and emotional validity." I agree that Atwood's narrator does not present as many overtly "frightening images"; nevertheless, the narrator does consistently evoke a violent atmosphere that accords with the evil totalitarian regime. In fact Atwood's narrator is a powerful user of language, a poet and rhetorician who presents in a strategic way the true horrors perpetrated by the Gileadean state. Although in the "Historical Notes" we learn that the overall narrative arrangement is not Offred's, that her taped oral utterances have been transcribed and arranged by Pieixoto and Wade, the power of her rhetorical stance is distinctive and unusual.

Harriet Bergmann has recently written that "Offred was not, we can tell, a person who cared particularly about the written word before the establishment of Gilead." Actually, we don't know many details about the reading and writing habits of Offred before Gilead: we do know that she was university educated, that she loved books, and that she worked transferring books to computer disks. We should keep in mind that we are meant to read Offred's story as one composed retrospectively—and an extraordinary retrospective it is. Offred demonstrates immense skill in constructing her rhetoric; this "unskilled" storyteller pays expert attention to narrative point of view, to physical detail, and to remembered conversations. Indeed, Offred's discourse reflects a practised devotion to *written* rhetoric. And of course, one of the great compositional problems of the novel is that the *oral* qualities of Offred's taped discourse are always *imaginary* oral qualities: as we read the printed discourse, we attend to a complex syntactical and rhetorical play that is the product of the economy of writing, not speech. What we need now is an analysis of the paradoxical ways in which the language of the narrator scripts special footings of intimacy and authority with the reader.

In *The Handmaid's Tale* Atwood is caught in the dilemma faced by many creators of satiric dystopias: the author needs both to condemn particular social injustices and to portray the mechanisms of oppression as credible enough, as sufficiently powerful and seductive, to represent a believable evil, not an irrelevant or far-fetched one. While attempting to balance ethical interests with plausibility, the ambitious author risks falling into either transparent didacticism or a contradictory fascination with the rhetorical machinery of dystopic horror. Atwood's discourse is marked by stylistic and rhetorical features—habits of syntactic and lexical arrangement and strategies of managing point of view and addresser-addressee relations—that show she has succumbed to the latter: scenes of violence and horror meant to illuminate sites of oppression are also strategically designed to manipulate and horrify. Atwood's narrator is an authoritative and authoritarian storyteller, one who manipulates the reader as she tells her story but one who is also caught in the web of Gileadan power politics. Offred's powerful narrative skill conflicts with the powerlessness, the innocence, and the descriptive phenomenological cast of mind that also characterize her. It is as if Atwood's skill as storyteller continually intrudes, possessing her narrative creation. Narrative self-consciousness, in fact, does explicitly and strategically emerge.

To see *The Handmaid's Tale* as ideologically and rhetorically problematic is not a "politically correct" view, at least if one considers the majority of the above critical opinions, which aim at solidifying the conventionality of the text by inscribing it in an already readable canonical genre (dystopia, political satire, postmodern subversion), by deciphering allusions, or by weighing the effects of framing devices like the concluding

"Historical Notes" section. Only Frank Davey and Chinmoy Banerjee have recognized how the novel "participates not only in various literary conventions and bourgeois assumptions about the self but in various commercial formulas for capitalist book production" or how "Atwood is concerned with the aesthetic enjoyment of a particular kind of victimization, and not with a critical examination of its determinant relations." Atwood's politics in her earlier fiction have been cogently analysed by Larry MacDonald as bring fraught with contradiction (as are also, MacDonald points out, the fictions of MacLennan and Davies) because of the reduction of collective problems to "the psychic wounds of individual characters" and the tendency to undercut the possibilities of positive political change: "these novelists end by urging individual adaptation to a status quo which their fiction simultaneously urges upon us as intolerable."

The Handmaid's Tale is similarly caught in contradictory discursive impulses: it shows a world that is "intolerable," but it cannot avoid complicity in using the mechanisms or rhetoric of that very intolerable world. Hence, a trope that might characterize the rhetorical gestalt of the novel is *paralepsis*, the figure of verbal dissimulation and duplicity that asserts its lack of rhetoric while using rhetoric, that on one hand critiques authority and on the other is complicitous with that authority, that feigns powerlessness in order to wield power, that disavows deliberate arrangement while arranging words with great care: "I'm sorry there is so much pain in this story," Offred apologizes, then proceeds to make us wince with her sharp, "fragments, like a body caught in crossfire or pulled apart by force." By examining these and other instances of such discursive contradictions and paradoxes, I will provide a close reading of the novel and subject key sections to lexical, syntactic, and rhetorical analysis; I will try to get a grip on the authority and style of Atwood's storyteller while remaining close to the play of addresser-addressee relations, those social relations that metonymically reflect the implied storyteller's attitude to power.

The Authoritative Voice of the Victim

In *The Handmaid's Tale* the reader is addressed by a narrator whose authority is sanctioned by the implied author: she possesses an analytical intelligence that demonstrates her clear superiority over others. She is a reader of the social "signs" in her environment and in everyday objects. Offred is assigned the authority of an implied author; there is, in fact, no gap between implied author and narrator, no attempt to distinguish the voices. There is, however, a tension between Offred's narrative skill and the characterization of her as a Handmaid. This narrator wants the discourse freedoms and powers normally granted only to men; yet she is in the position of Handmaid:

The pen between my fingers is sensuous, alive almost, I can feel its power, the power of the words it contains. Pen is envy, Aunt Lydia would say, quoting another Centre motto, warning us away from such objects. And they were right, it is envy. Just holding it is envy. I envy the Commander his pen. It's one more thing I would like to steal.

The intelligence and wit of the narrator is but one of various rhetorical tactics that Atwood uses to induce our acceptance of the didactic authenticity of her satire. Its social and intellectual validity as argument is enforced by a narrator who shifts between readerly footings of intimacy and equality to footings of authority, superior insight, and impersonal detachment. In the opening first chapter of the novel we are guided through the world of Gilead by a narrator who surveys her surroundings with a highly developed analytic sense, who possesses a writerly skill in evoking shapes, odours, and images:

We slept in what had once been the gymnasium. The floor was of varnished wood, with stripes and circles painted on it, for the games that were formerly played there; the hoops for the basketball nets were still in place, though the nets were gone. A balcony ran around the room, for the spectators, and I thought I could smell, faintly like an afterimage, the pungent scent of sweat, shot through with the sweet taint of chewing gum and perfume from the watching girls, felt-skirted as I knew from pictures, later in mini-skirts, then pants, then in one earring, spiky green-streaked hair. Dances would have been held there; the music lingered, a palimpsest of unheard sound, style upon style, an undercurrent of drums, a forlorn wail, garlands made of tissue-paper flowers, cardboard devils, a revolving ball of mirrors, powdering the dancers with a snow of light.

There was old sex in the room and loneliness, and expectation, of something without a shape or name . . .

We yearned for the future. How did we learn it, that talent for insatiability? It was in the air; and it was still in the air, an afterthought, as we tried to sleep, in the army cots that had been set up in rows, with spaces between so we could not talk. We has flannelette sheets, like children's, and army-issue blankets, old ones that still said U.S. We folded our clothes neatly and laid them on the stools at the ends of our beds. The lights were turned down but not out. Aunt Sara and Aunt

Elizabeth patrolled; they had electric cattle prods slung on thongs from their leather belts.

The first chapter contains an odd mixture of clarity and obscurity, hard detail and shadowy impressionism. The plural subject of the first sentence—"We"—and the institutional gymnasium setting signal a makeshift group cohesion, the unity of refugees, the homeless, prisoners, or recruits in some military training camp. By the end of the third paragraph we understand that they are somehow all three. The second paragraph, drawing on a particular cultural stereotype marking women as the receivers of male sexual agency, hints that they are women; when they are named at the close of the chapter, we know their sex.

The narrator's language indicates that she has detached herself emotionally from any memories associated with the gymnasium. (The past tense, "slept," indicates that this is a memory.) The language that she uses to describe the gymnasium in the second sentence is unusual because it is a more elaborate or expanded description of the commonplace than we are used to: she isolates in separate "snap-shots" features of the floor—the "varnished wood," the "stripes and circles," the "hoops for the basketball nets"—in the language of a person who is culturally distant from the place and the events that the gym was designed to host.

The emotional detachment in the tone of the narrator, an emotional emptiness, matches her surroundings: the gym, a place formerly meant for players, activity, and spectators, is empty; the hoops are stripped of their nets (netting has a delicate, membrane-like sensual quality, a quality absent from the gym). The rather long third and fourth sentences that complete this first paragraph sustain a ghostlike atmosphere in which human activity has ceased and all that remains are inanimate forms like the balcony, which "ran around the room," and vague odours that set off memories of tastes, images, and sounds in the narrator's mind. However, we are not expected to read the tastes, images, and sounds in these sentences as mere mental projections: the narrator's tactic is to present these as if they are present in the very room, ghostly presences that can be excavated by a consciousness sensitive enough to do so. The faint smell is "like an afterimage," hovering in the gym air, and the adjective clause "as I knew from pictures" is subtly inserted after the image of the "watching girls, felt-skirted" in order not to disturb the immediate impact of it as a raw perception of a tangible presence. Of course, this presence is but a shadow of the original; its faded and intangible quality, however, is what Atwood's narrator could be trying to get us to apprehend. In the third sentence the narrator remembers the former fashions and changes in dating styles that the gym once was host to—basketball games give way to high-school romance; men and women playing competitively turn into different types of players. In the fourth sentence the sense that the gym is literally *haunted* by the past is even more forceful conveyed: the past-perfect verb cluster ("would have been held"), which suggests an already expired action, is followed in the second clause by an ongoing sound: "the music lingered, a palimpsest of undeard sound, style upon style, an undercurrent of drums."

As Atwood's narrator asyndetically tacks on modifying adjectival phrases, the language suggests both increasing action and increasing danger: the neutral "style upon style" shifts to the menacing "undercurrent of drums," then the surprising "forlorn wail," and finally the tragicomic carnival atmosphere of the death-dance suggested by the "flowers," "cardboard devils," "mirrors," and shadowy dancers powdered with "a snow of light."

Throughout this excerpt from the brief first chapter Atwood attempts to present the narrator as an innocent, a mere observer, a describer of her surroundings; this is a procedure that is retained in subsequent chapters. Chapter 2 begins "A chair, a table, a lamp." (The opening of chapter 2 and other meditations on physical objects and perception uncannily echo sections of Zamyatin's *We*, the obvious prototype for *The Handmaid's Tale*: "Are you familiar with this strange condition? You wake at night, open your eyes to blackness, and suddenly you feel you've lost your way—and quickly, quickly you grope around you, seeking something familiar, solid—a wall, a lamp, a chair".)

Offred just happens to "notice" things. But her innocent eye always manages to present us with ideologically significant comparisons, observations, and details; this may hardly be surprising if one grants that ideology is partly an extension of material circumstances. But there is an incompatibility between Offred's narration and the position of subjugation she occupies as a Handmaid. One might wonder why and how such a narrative intelligence could be subjugated in this way. Of course one could argue that Atwood is suggesting that if Offred can be enslaved, anyone can be. Atwood needs to convince us that this Handmaid was subjugated, that the oppression she experienced was evil: the rhetorical intelligence of the narrator is meant to emphasize the power of the regime and the changes wrought upon society. When we finally read the Historical Notes, we also learn that the tale is meant to be read as an experience remembered, as a story recollected in a rather different setting from that of Gilead. However, even before we acquire this contextualizing information, we apprehend that the first chapter contains the polish of arrangement and aesthetic management of a narrative originating from a position of literary sophistication.

What I am trying to suggest is that Atwood's narrator in this novel does not speak entirely in the voice of the victim, the writer who pleads "Mayday"; rather, she speaks in the skilled voice of the rhetorician and the fabulator who is purposefully telling a story. Atwood has the narrator move through her thoughts in a plain style, joining modifying phrases to the main clause on the right side of the sentence, as if to suggest syntactically the artlessness of the narrator. The co-ordinate structures and right-branching sentences, however, are filled with an abstract lexis, a lexis of contemplativeness that emphasizes the narrator's wisdom, her philosophical and emotional superiority over those around her: "We yearned for the future. How did we learn it, that talent for insatiability? I was in the air; and it was still in the air, an afterthought, as we tried to sleep, in the army cots that had been set up in rows, with spaces between so we could not talk." (The rhetorical question here is another indicator of the author's artfullness.) Here we encounter a paradox: the voluble narrator speaks confidently and precisely about the silence she endured. To increase the sense of the macabre sinisterness of the setting, Atwood's narrator plays on the tension between the domestic softness and military harshness, between the cozy flannelette sheets and "Aunts" and the rough "army-issue" blankets and menacing "electric cattle prods slung on thongs."

Orchestrations of Horror

The implied author's sanctioning of the narrator Offred suggests that the social world—its architecture, commodities, semiology—is open to systematic rational analysis: historical and political meanings are embedded everywhere; ideology is ubiquitously inscribed. Yet Offred is depicted as fascinated with the paradoxes of power. Offred's ethical assumptions would suggest that she is opposed to irrational modes of argument and persuasion; she is opposed to the tyranny of propaganda. Yet this ethical consciousness demonstrates its attraction to the rhetorical efficacy of violence, power, and the grotesque: Offred has, in her discursive practice, started to play the game of power politics like a true Gileadan.

Time after time Atwood's narrator demonstrates her ability to seize upon seemingly banal objects—a braided rug, the walls of a room, a pat of butter, a chair—and turn them into receptacles or symbols that have resonant metaphysical and political implications. Partly this is meant to illustrate the state of mind of an individual living in an ascetic and puritanically monotonous world: she is hungry for sensuous experience. Not only does this tactic supplement our sense of the repression and boredom in the Handmaid's life, but it also leads to an epiphanic moment—one of those moments that expose how Offred always knows much more than she says, that she possesses powers of apprehension that are impressive. Atwood has endowed this narrator with conspicuous gems of compressed wisdom:

I sit in the chair and think about the word *chair.* It can also mean the leader of a meeting. It can also mean a mode of execution. It is the first syllable in *charity.* It is the French word for flesh. None of these facts has any connection with the others.

These are the kinds of litanies I use, to compose myself.

In front of me is a tray, and on the tray with three slices of brown toast on it, a small dish containing honey, and another plate with an egg-cup on it, the kind that looks like a woman's torso, in a skirt. Under the skirt is the second egg, being kept warm. The egg-cup is white china with a blue stripe.

The first egg is white. I move the egg-cup a little, so it's now in the watery sunlight that comes through the window and falls, brightening, waning, brightening again, on the tray . . .

The sun goes and the egg fades.

I pick the egg out of the cup and finger it for a moment. It's warm. Women used to carry such eggs between their breasts, to incubate them. That would have felt good.

The minimalist life. Pleasure is an egg. Blessings that can be counted, on the fingers of one hand. But possibly this is how I am expected to react. If I have an egg, what more can I want? . . . I slice the top off the egg with the spoon, and eat the contents.

In the phenomenal world around her Atwood's narrator can find objects that remind her of her condition, that are models of the female life. It is important to note that the "litany" of chairs and eggs is in the "Birth Day" section, a chapter that presents the special birth ritual attended by the Handmaids: the pregnant Handmaid, Janine, literally gives birth—lays her egg—while seated in a special "birthing stool," a chair that allows the Commander's wife to sit behind and above the surrogate mother. The meaning of the word "chair" and the reflection on eggs takes on special significance in this context and contradicts the narrator's disclaimer that "none of these facts has any connection with the others," her need to retain an appearance of being artless, natural, spontaneous. The kinds of meanings that the narrator seizes on are connected to power and mortality—general concepts, to be sure, but concepts that are specifically linked to the exercise of power and the reminders of mortality that are dramatized when Janine gives birth. The birthing stool in retrospect is ambiguous. The mother can achieve prominence and power; or, if she fails to deliver a healthy child, a sentence of death.

The connection of birth to death, the fine line between power and failure, fertility and sterility, reflects the tendency of the narrator's mind to explore the ambiguities in her world, to delve under the affirmative and pull out the darker intimations of death. She utilizes this procedure when contemplating the egg: the two eggs, one on top of the other, are like a model of the Gileadean birth scene, with the Commander's wife seated up and behind the Handmaid. Offred begins with the neutral description "the egg is white"; she then moves into a figurative language that is resonant with female symbolism: the egg is compared to the moon; the moon becomes a desert; the desert, place of spiritual trial and of revelation. An alternating emphasis between fertility and sterility, energy and entropy, is played out— the egg literally seems to throb with temperature changes: "The sun goes and the egg fades. I pick the egg out of the cup and finger it for a moment. It's warm. Women used to carry such eggs between their breasts, to incubate them."

In this section the narrator's opening disclaimer would have us believe that her litany is artless, a stream of unconnected facts. Syntactically Atwood's narrator would have us perceive her thoughts as spontaneously stitched together: there are few logical connectors—however, moreover, therefore—that indicate argument. But there is a propositional cohesion here in the very juxtaposition of birth and death images. As I have already noted, one of the justifications for having the narrator produce these longish meditations—and displaying heightened sensitivity to the ordinary—is to portray the severe hunger for stimulation: Offred says, "In reduced circumstances the desire to live attaches itself to strange objects." At the same time, these meditations give us insight into the narrator's cast of mind: her values, fears, preoccupations. And what is highly significant in these preoccupations is that existing beside the analysis of the social condition of women is an attraction to pure power: "I slice the top off the egg with a spoon, and eat the contents" becomes an aggressive movement, a power signal.

There are times when Offred's discourses (or litanies, as she calls them) become redundant, a static piling up of grotesque descriptions. Unlike the previous examples, wherein the meditation upon the object yields a surprising turn, a transformation of meaning, a revelation of similarities, the presentation of the hanged men in chapter 6 involves the continuous reiteration of horror:

> We stop, together as if on signal, and stand and look at the bodies. It doesn't matter if we look. We're supposed to look: this is what they are there for, hanging on the Wall. Sometimes

they'll be there for days, until there's a new batch, so as many people as possible will have a chance to see them.

What they are hanging from is hooks. The hooks have been set into the brickwork of the Wall, for this purpose. Not all of them are occupied. The hooks look like appliances for the armless. Or steel question marks, upside-down and sideways.

It's the bags over the heads that are the worst, worse than the faces themselves would be. It makes the men look like dolls on which faces have not yet been painted; like scarecrows, which in a way is what they are, since they are meant to scare. Or as if their heads are sacks, stuffed with some undifferentiated material, like flour or dough. It's the obvious heaviness of the heads, their vacancy, the way gravity pulls them down and there's no life any more to hold them up. The heads are zeros.

Though if you look and look, as we are doing, you can see the outlines of the features under the white cloth, like grey shadows. The heads are the heads of snowmen, with the coal eyes and the carrot noses fallen out. The heads are melting.

But on one bag there's blood, which has seeped through the white cloth, where the mouth must have been. It makes another mouth, a small red one, like the mouths painted with thick brushes by kindergarten children. A child's idea of a smile. This smile of blood is what fixes the attention, finally. These are not snowmen after all.

The men wear white coats, like those worn by doctors or scientists . . . Each has a placard hung around his neck to show why he has been executed: a drawing of a human foetus. They were doctors, then, in the time before, when such things were legal . . .

What we are supposed to feel towards these bodies is hatred and scorn. This isn't what I feel. These bodies hanging on the Wall are time travellers, anachronisms. They've come here from the past.

What I feel towards them is blankness. What I feel is that I must not feel. What I feel is partly relief, because none of these men is Luke. Luke wasn't a doctor. Isn't.

The description of the executed men hanging on the wall exemplifies Atwood's narrator's penchant for the horrific. Presented as an innocent or guileless observer of her world, Offred in fact is an effective tale-teller; but

while seeking to condemn the violence around her, her protracted gaze
implicates herself, for she has made the vision and instruments of horror into
objects of voyeurism rather than symptoms that point to more complex
power problems.

This section is a skillfully orchestrated set-piece that begins tentatively
and builds to higher levels of shock. Each paragraph takes us gradually and
teasingly closer to the horror. Offred begins with a general declaration of the
purpose of this display, "so as many people as possible will have a chance to see
them." With the deft editorial camera eye of a Hitchcock, Offred avoids a direct
description of the bodies and instead focuses on the unoccupied hooks set into
the Wall. The pacing in this second paragraph is methodical and slow:
sentences are cohesively joined with lexical repetition—anadiplosis and
anaphora—as the narrator gradually moves from a plain description of the
hooks, "set into the brickwork of the Wall," then shifts to shocking comparisons
that carry an indirect hint of amputation and bodily injury: "The hooks look
like appliances for the armless." And the final figurative comparison in this
paragraph literally denotes the suspended questioning, the deliberately
suspended interrogation: "Or steel question marks, upside-down and sideways."

The third paragraph serves up images that are more calculatedly
grotesque: first the faceless "dolls," then the "scarecrows," and finally the
"sacks, stuffed with undifferentiated material." Atwood's narrator skillfully
intensifies the implied danger by keeping the face of violence just out of
sight. It is the tension between the *absence* of life and the dead *weight* of the
body that is effectively captured here; Offred's language is ponderous and
weighty, but spiritless.

The fourth paragraph continues Offred's carefully paced revelation of
the object of danger. The narrator begins to focus our gaze ever more closely
on the covered faces of the hanged men, "the outlines of the features under
the white cloth, like grey shadows." The metaphors in the last two sentences
here reflect a typical tactic of Offred's for evoking the grotesque: an
innocent, childhood image, a "snowman," metamorphoses into something
more sinister, more tragic. The climax of this progression is finally reached
in the fifth paragraph: "But on one bag there's blood, which has seeped
through the white cloth, where the mouth must have been." But Offred
continues to exploit the shock of the tension between childhood innocence
and the bloody evidence of the execution. The blood on the face of the
victim is "a child's idea of a smile. This smile of blood is what fixes the
attention, finally. These are not snowmen after all."

After this detailed description, how do we read and react to the
narrator's comment after she tells us that these victims were doctors who had
performed abortions in the years before the present regime? "What I feel

towards them is blankness. What I feel is that I must not feel. What I feel is partly relief, because none of these men is Luke. Luke wasn't a doctor. Isn't." The narrator asserts her "blankness," perhaps an emotionally protective measure to help her cope with the loss of Luke. But the presentation of her perceptions reveals much about her attitude to the reader and the scene she has witnessed: that she must orchestrate the feelings evoked by the scene in a deliberately shocking way, a rhetorically powerful way; that the impact of horror is as important as the reasons for it (and, after all, the Gilead authorities *are* setting the men up as human "scarecrows"); that a reader must experience the event's emotional impact before she or he can be introduced to its political or social background (i.e., the treatment of doctors as war criminals).

One might object that Offred is not meant to be seen as a character who is controlling the reader's perceptions, that the horror in her presentation is simply meant to illustrate how the authorities of Gilead have mastered the art of frightening its people: Offred is simply testifying to the effectiveness of the rhetoric of the Gileadan police state. However, the type of discourse that Offred uses does not simply inform us that the executed prisoners are frightful deterrents: Offred carefully constructs a narrative that makes the reader look at the objects of horror in a prescribed and suspenseful way, a way designed to increase the shock effect. Again, the evidence suggests to me that Offred is intensely aware of the power structures around her, that she is not naïve. When she compares the "one red smile" on the hanged man's mask to the "red of the tulips in Serena Joy's garden," she advances a disclaimer that we can barely accept is valid: the obvious pun that relates the red mouth to the "tulips" is irresistible. As a reader, I am compelled to read the narrator as the originary force behind the pun, that she is well aware of the connections, but that she is simply withholding her comments:

> I look at the one red smile. The red of the smile is the same as the red of the tulips in Serena Joy's garden, towards the base of the flowers where they are beginning to heal. The red is the same but there is no connection. The tulips are not tulips of blood, the red smiles are not flowers, neither thing makes a comment on the other. The tulip is no reason for disbelief of the hanged man, or vice versa. Each thing is valid and really there. It is through a field of such valid objects that I must pick my way, every day and in every way. I put a lot of effort into making such distinctions. I need to make them. I need to be very clear, in my own mind.

"I put a lot of effort into making such distinctions," Offred says. But what distinctions are they? She gives us a glimpse of the philosophical and analytical interest in her mind, then abruptly stops. This seems to be an instance of Atwood's standing too close to her narrator, then shifting to limit the character's knowledge so that it does not merge with that of the omniscient author.

I have been trying to argue that Atwood's narrator is a deliberate storyteller, one who manipulates the reader as she tells her story, and that this shows how she has become caught in the web of Gileadan power politics. This sense of narrative skill conflicts with the powerlessness, the innocence, and the descriptive phenomenological cast of mind that characterize Offred. It is as if Atwood's skill as a storyteller keeps possessing her creation. The storyteller's self-conscious power, in fact, emerges at the end of chapter 7, a chapter that begins with a night-time series of fantasies of the past. Offred remembers her friend Moira, her mother, and her daughter:

> I would like to believe this is a story I'm telling. I need to believe it. I must believe it. Those who can believe that such stories are only stories have a better chance.
>
> If it's a story I'm telling, then I have control over the ending. Then there will be an ending, to the story, and real life will come after it. I can pick up where I left off.
>
> It isn't a story I'm telling.
>
> It's also a story I'm telling, in my head, as I go along.
>
> Tell, rather than write, because I have nothing to write with and writing is in any case forbidden. But if it's a story, even in my head, I must be telling it to someone. You don't tell a story only to yourself. There's always someone else.
>
> Even when there is no one.
>
> A story is like a letter. *Dear You*, I'll say. Just *you*, without a name. Attaching a name attaches *you* to the world of fact, which is riskier, more hazardous: who knows what the chances are out there, of survival, yours? I will say *you*, *you*, like an old love song. *You* can mean more than one.
>
> *You* can mean thousands.
>
> I'm not in any immediate danger, I'll say to you.
>
> I'll pretend you can hear me.
>
> But it's no good, because I know you can't.

There is no hint of this narrative self-consciousness in the opening chapter of *The Handmaid's Tale*, no indication that the story is meant *to be read as if originally spoken;* only in the "Historical Notes" do we learn that the text is meant to be a transcript of a tape recording. But as well, there is no explicit signal in the introduction, such as the title-page to Richardson's *Pamela* ("In a Series of Familiar Letters from A Beautiful Young Damsel to Her Parents"), or the preface to Nabokov's *Lolita* ("The Confessions of a White Widowed Male"). Atwood's withholding of the contextualizing information creates a gap between our initial, heuristic reading of the book, a reading in which the narrator's authority is valorized through its writerly surface structure, and our retrospective reimaginings and rereadings that are informed by the "Historical Notes" (i.e., our retrospective reimaginings or our rereadings that postulate an oral consciousness rather than one originally cast in *writing*).

Offred's direct address to the reader emphasizes the artificial order that fiction imposes on reality: recognition of this artificiality is supposed to be consoling because "then I have control over the ending. Then there will be an ending, to the story, and real life will come after it." Yet Atwood's narrator wants her discourse to be *more* authentic than fiction, to have a privileged validity as a record of the *real*: "It isn't a story I'm telling." But if Offred's discourse is meant to be "like a letter," with a written sense of addressee, then why have the addressee markers been excluded from the earlier parts of the novel, especially in the introductory chapter?

I contend that Atwood's text compels us to see her narrator in two ways that are not entirely congruent: as innocent recorder and as a skilled self-conscious rhetorician and storyteller. Atwood needs to delay the revelation of this latter rhetorical self-consciousness because a self-dramatized narrator is immediately suspect, immediately prone to charges of unreliability and cunning artifice. And even when Atwood dramatizes the narrator in a self-conscious mood, as in the above, she inserts disclaimers, hoping to retain a sense of Offred's essential artlessness: the tale is a story she's telling "as I go along." Later, in the "Salvaging" section of the novel, Atwood has her narrator again profess that her discourse is artless and innocent: "I'm sorry there is so much pain in this story. I'm sorry it's in fragments, like a body caught in crossfire or pulled apart by force. But there is nothing I can do to change it." These apologies function to convey the ingenuousness of the narrator; but the stylistic evidence that we have gathered so far—her use of symbolic cultural objects, her deconstructions of them, her ingenious comparisons of images that connote power and mortality, her skilful rhetoric, which guides the reader to a special state of suspense and horror—these aspects of the narrator's discourse contradict her professions of artlessness.

The "Historical Notes" provide a significant shift in discourse. This is a peculiarly more comic section than the preceding narrative by Offred, and by being so is subject to ironic criticism. Ostensibly, these notes provide a gloss on the social, historical, and political origins of Gileadan society, as seen by a future society of scholars. The notes provide certain details that are not made explicit in the narrative (the escape of Offred to Canada, via Maine; the reasons for the extreme measures in the birthing process—disease, pollution, war, the President's Day Massacre). But more importantly, these "Historical Notes" are a further reinforcing of the *authority* of Offred's narrative: the academics are satirized as trivializers of history. They have turned Gilead into a matter of textual authentication and an occasion for levity and entertainment. The scholars are pompous cultural relativists; as Professor Pieixoto defends his objectivity, Atwood sets him up as hopelessly insensitive to Offred's story:

> Allow me to say that in my opinion we must be cautious about passing moral judgments upon the Gileadeans. Surely we have learned by now that such judgments are of necessity culture-specific. Also, Gileadean society was under a good deal of pressure, demographic and otherwise, and was subject to factors from which we ourselves are happily more free. Our job is not to censure but to understand. *(Applause)*

Pieixoto's attempts to "establish an identity for the narrator" are meant to be seen as demonstrative of his insensitivity to the text. Offred's story has not been understood by these scholars, who are rather poor readers of texts.

Since Offred's narrative is superior to that of the "Historical Notes," we should remind ourselves of how it operates, what kinds of discourses it contains, and whether these discourses are adequate to the task of exploring the power relations that she has targeted for criticism. I have tried to show how Atwood privileges the voice of her narrator in a paradoxical manner. The implied author attempts to suggest that Offred is ingenuous and artless. But she is unable to do this consistently because the intelligence and aesthetic knowledge of the writer, the storyteller, continually break through. Offred presents evil as both seductive and repulsive, an attitude that could be described as deriving from romanticism and the Gothic. Frank Davey, in *Margaret Atwood: A Feminist Poetics*, however, argues that "the Gothic element is a red herring" because it represents the distorted perspectives of Atwood's protagonists (specifically in *Lady Oracle*) who "lie and fantasize," "fictionalize on derivative models," and "exaggerate goodness and villainy, exaggerate the similarities between goodness and villainy" in order to escape from reality. We can remind ourselves, thus, that Gothic involves an element of parody and that an ironic poet like Byron or an ironic novelist like Jane Austen in *Northanger Abbey* deliberately undermines Gothic elements while using them. However, Davey also notes that there is a tension in Atwood's work between the objects of criticism and her own style, between the "rational, analytic, and male" mode of being and the "aphoristic, 'worldless,' and gestural" female mode: "Male order may constitute a travesty of female chaos and its gestural language, but only a wary appropriation of that order enables a speaking of either."

Satire is a form that cannot effectively manifest itself through "gestural" and cryptic language: the object of satire must be perspicuously framed. However, in *The Handmaid's Tale* there is a peculiarly ambiguous attitude to male modes of power and authority. Atwood's narrator is made to observe much that is politically repugnant, but her discourse contains a powerful rhetoric that derives from the ethos of Gilead: Offred is preoccupied with power and authority. What kinds of lexical collocations with power and authority are found in Offred's language? She tends to emphasize tactics and techniques: one of the most significant collocates of power is "vision," or the dynamics of observation—the power of the observing subject and the observed object.

Controlling the Observer

In *The Handmaid's Tale* the motifs of *vision* are an important part of the presentation of the politics of sexual control: these motifs connect masters to slaves, Commanders to Handmaids. The desires of both are controlled by state regulations: sex has been reduced to reproductive duty without contact and love; Commanders are forbidden to have contact with Handmaids in private. In Gilead even mere visual contact is severely regulated—Handmaids must not be looked at by men, nor may they look at men themselves. When Offred sees the Commander lurking near her room, she describes the act as a form of violation like "the signals animals give to one another: lowered blue eyelids, ears laid back, raised hackles. A flash of bare teeth, what in hell does he think he's doing?" Handmaids in Gilead have their vision obscured by the white winglike hats they must wear in public, making it "hard to look up, hard to get a full view, of the sky, of anything. But one can do it, a little at a time, a quick move of the head, up and down, to the side and back. We have learned to see the world in gasps." This presentation of the regulation of vision expresses the subjugation of the Handmaids (and their patient subversion, "in gasps"). No one is permitted to look at others freely, especially with desire; the exceptions are those agents of the state, Atwood's version of the thought police, the Eyes, who cruise the streets in the black vans "with the winged eye in white on the side. The windows of the vans are dark-tinted, and the men in the front seats wear dark glasses: a double obscurity."

In these visual motifs the power structure consists of the observer and a vulnerable object of vision. But this power structure is prone to reversal: the weakness of being observed is translated into the power of the controlling observer when Offred deliberately manipulates the Guardians:

> As we walk away I know they're watching, these two men who aren't yet permitted to touch women. They touch with their eyes instead and I move my hips a little, feeling the full red skirt sway around me. It's like thumbing your nose from behind a fence or teasing a dog with a bone held out of reach, and I'm ashamed of myself for doing it, because none of this is the fault of these men, they're too young.
>
> Then I find I'm not ashamed after all. I enjoy the power; power of a dog bone, passive but there. I hope they get hard at the sight of us and have to rub themselves against the painted barriers, surreptitiously. They will suffer, later, at night, in their regimented beds. They have no outlets now except themselves, and that's a sacrilege.

This use of the vision motif emphasizes the ambiguities of the power structure in Gilead and carries the implied author's belief that no matter how rigidly controlled master-slave or agent-object relations are, there will always be a point at which the observer is changed by that which he is trying to observe and control. Atwood thus questions the validity of the simple master-slave dichotomy: who really possesses power? The lover or the object of love? The desiring agent or the desired object? Can these agent-object relations be transcended?

Atwood presents Offred not simply as the object of subjugation but as possessing power herself: the power of the powerless, of the seductive prey. Atwood is continually tempted to endow Offred with the strength appropriate to a heroine, but instead she assigns the spectacular heroism to Moira, who mounts a daring escape from the Red Centre, an act of such dizzying audacity that it frightens Offred and the others, who "were losing the taste for freedom." Offred is not a Moira: when she is tempted to steal something from Serena Joy's living-room, or a "knife, from the kitchen," she admits that "I'm not ready for that." Offred, however, is assigned the kind of consciousness that both appropriates and transcends the power politics of Gilead. The implied author seems to privilege the female existential will, the realm of private consciousness, as an adequate recompense for her enslavement: "My name isn't Offred. I have another name, which nobody uses now because it's forbidden . . . I keep the knowledge of this name like something hidden, some treasure I'll come back to dig up, one day."

In a puritan society privacy is an important condition for retaining identity: the smallest bits of privacy can nurture the self's salvation and protect one's dignity. In Gilead private consciousness is all that is left; it cannot be regulated by the state. Offred may have lost most of the power to control others, to observe and control her world, but she still controls her private thoughts:

> I used to think of my body as an instrument, of pleasure, or a means of transportation, or an implement for the accomplishment of my will. I could use it to run, push buttons, of one sort or another, make things happen. There were limits but my body was nevertheless lithe, single, solid, one with me.
>
> Now the flesh arranges itself differently. I'm a cloud, congealed around a central object, the shape of a pear, which is hard and more real than I am and glows red within its translucent wrapping. Inside it is a space, huge as the sky at night and dark and curved like that, though black-red rather than black.

In this drama of power and powerlessness, Atwood clearly shows that certain types of oppression ensnare the oppressor along with the oppressed—power is always ambiguous. One of the explanations for the peculiarly ambiguous position of the implied author is her commitment to an essentially *romance* novel genre: she cannot help dramatizing horror and rhetoricizing violence, and she cannot help but make her "heroine" into a figure of compelling existential fortitude. This is not a negative judgment of the novel but simply an unveiling of its rhetoric's origins and intentions. Atwood has an ethical imperative, but she also has a rhetorical one—to create a convincing and suspenseful story. It is, of course, paradoxical that without imagining the dystopic situation, a conditional future of male tyranny, the implied author would not have a stage upon which to dramatize Offred's integrity.

I am suggesting that Atwood is experimenting with the deployment of compelling rhetorical form and with the rhetorical attraction of special conflicts. Take away the danger and repressiveness of Gilead—its Eyes, its Guardians, and its hangings—and you no longer have the persuasive climate that justifies Offred's quietly strident discourse:

Maybe none of this is about control. Maybe it isn't really about who can own whom, who can do what to whom and get away with it, even as far as death. Maybe it isn't about who can sit and who has to kneel or stand or lie down, legs spread open. Maybe it's about who can do what to whom and be forgiven for it. Never tell me it amounts to the same thing.

In *The Handmaid's Tale* we are guided by a cunning implied author, a voice that feigns weakness in the guise of Offred, her narrative mask; but this voice cannot help but advertise the control and strength of its origins: Margaret Atwood. The implied author plays a narrator who subjects her audience to a terrible nightmare in which she is the heroine. At one point she asks our forgiveness: "I'm sorry there is so much pain in this story. I'm sorry it's in fragments . . . Because I'm telling you this story I will your existence. I tell, therefore you are." But even this request is followed by a move that makes us conscious of the *writer's* power, for though this reader has participated and intervened in the critical reconstruction of this story, responsibility for its pain and power is shared with the rhetorical will of the author.

EMMA PARKER

You Are What You Eat:
The Politics of Eating in the Novels of Margaret Atwood

W hile literature is suffused with scenes of men eating, there is a conspicuous absence of images of women engaged in the same activity. Margaret Atwood displays a sensitive awareness of how images of women eating have been suppressed and erased. She remarks, "I think I first connected literature with eating when I was twelve and reading Ivanhoe: there was Rebecca, shut up romantically in a tower, but what did she have to eat?" (*CanLit* Introduction). Atwood probes the prohibitions on the public display of female appetite and the social taboos which surround women and food in terms of the politics of eating. For her, eating is unequivocally political. Atwood defines "politics" as "who is entitled to do what to whom with impunity; who profits by it; and who therefore eats what." Women are rarely depicted eating in literature because, as Atwood's comment implies, consumption embodies coded expressions of power.

Atwood displays a profound preoccupation with eating in her writing; she has even edited a cook book. In her novels eating is employed as a metaphor for power and is used as an extremely subtle means of examining the relationship between women and men. The powerful are characterized by their eating and the powerless by their non-eating. Eating is not the only, or the most predominant, metaphor for power; indeed, images of consumption seem so ordinary as to be insignificant. Nevertheless, they

From *Twentieth Century Literature* 41:3 (Fall 1995): 349–367. © 1995 by Hofstra University.

reappear persistently throughout the novels and, examined in totality, assume a potent significance. The domestic, the feminine, the inconsequential is, Atwood suggests, highly important. While *The Edible Woman* and *Lady Oracle* have been analyzed extensively in terms of food, particularly in terms of feminist theories of eating disorders, critics have failed to note the significance of the food theme in the rest of Atwood's fiction. An analysis of the politics of eating in all the novels provides a new way of reading Atwood and a new understanding of women's relationship to food.

All Atwood's heroines initially appear as victims, and they demonstrate their powerlessness through their relationship with food. In *The Edible Woman*, as Marion's wedding approaches and she subconsciously feels herself being absorbed by Peter, she stops eating. As she loses her identity and autonomy, so she loses her ability to eat. Her non-eating is a physical expression of her powerlessness and, at the same time, a protest against that powerlessness. Significantly, Peter's power is demonstrated by his ability to directly control what Marion eats. He chooses her order in the restaurant, and this is the moment from which Marion can no longer tolerate food. Duncan recognizes Marion's food refusal as a form of protest before she understands it herself. He tells her, "You're probably representative of modern youth, rebelling against the system; though it isn't considered orthodox to begin with the digestive system. But why not?" When Marion finally realizes what is happening to her, she bakes Peter a cake in the shape of a woman and offers it to him to symbolize how he has tried to consume her. Immediately after she ends her relationship with Peter, she regains her sense of selfhood and her ability to eat.

In *Surfacing* the narrator's sense of victimization by the father of her aborted child is symbolized by the way she imagines he controlled what she ate during her pregnancy. Anna's appetite is also controlled and repressed. She is a stereotypical woman who possesses all the traditionally feminine characteristics imposed by the process of socialization, and "isn't allowed to eat or shit or cry or give birth, nothing goes in, nothing comes out." The killing of the heron, in particular, highlights the relationship between eating and power. The way that killing is linked to eating and slavery suggests that eating, like killing and enslavement, is an expression of power:

> Why had they strung it up like a lynch victim, why didn't they just throw it away like trash? To prove they could do it, they had the power to kill. Otherwise it was valueless: beautiful from a distance but it couldn't be tamed or cooked or trained to talk, the only relation they could have to a thing like that was to destroy it. Food, slave or corpse, limited choices.

The narrator, Atwood suggests, faces similar choices. Her rejection of, and return to, society is reflected by what she eats. When she rejects culture and retreats into the wilderness to become a "natural" woman, she gives up eating processed food. Such food is contaminated in the same way that society is contaminated by patriarchal ideology. Both are unnatural, constructed, man-made, and both threaten to poison her. Instead, the narrator eats only the raw food that nature provides. However, as she runs out of food, she realizes she cannot live without physical sustenance just as she cannot live outside society. She must engage with life. Her return to the cabin to eat the food there signals her first step toward a tentative reintegration into society.

Food and control lay at the heart of *Lady Oracle*. The first part of the novel focuses on the power struggle between Joan and her mother, and this struggle centers on food. Joan's mother attempts to deny her daughter any sense of autonomy and tries to control her life and identity. She makes her diet and tries to assert her authority physically by reducing her daughter in size. Joan challenges her mother and takes control of her own life through eating. She retaliates against enforced diets by eating more and more:

> I was eating steadily, doggedly, stubbornly, anything I could get. The war between myself and my mother was on in earnest; the disputed territory was my body.

Eating empowers Joan, and she eventually vanquishes her mother. Although Joan decides to lose weight when Aunt Lou dies leaving her two thousand dollars on the condition that she do so, she capitulates only because the money will enable her to leave home. Money is a more powerful substitute for food. However, once slim, Joan remains powerless, because she remains trapped in a victim mentality. Like all Atwoodian heroines, she colludes in her victimization by accepting her subordinated status. The absence of power in her life is mirrored by her lack of control around food. Cooking and shopping are activities with which she has little success. Joan lives as she cooks and shops—chaotically. Significantly, she hides her automatic writing (writing over which she has no control) in a folder marked "Recipes." Nevertheless, the moments when Joan does attempt to exert control over her life are always accompanied by acts of eating. Just as she empowers herself through food in relation to her mother, her attempt to take control of her life in Italy is accompanied by an act of eating: "I sat at the white table with my hot cup, adding another white ring to the varnish, eating a package of rusks and trying to organize my life."

In *Life Before Man*, the relationship between eating and power is demonstrated by the three principal characters. Elizabeth is obsessed with being in control. She is confident of her own identity, independent and autonomous. Her power is symbolized by her hearty eating. However, power based upon the subjection of others (Chris and Nate) is precarious and dangerous. Chris's suicide has already indicated the unbalanced and unwholesome nature of a relationship not based on parity and mutuality. Elizabeth demonstrates that tyranny over others is eventually turned in upon oneself when there is nobody left to dominate and destroy. Her power indeed proves elusive and transient. She eventually loses control of the relationship between Nate and Lesje, which she has been attempting to manipulate to her own ends, and her marriage breaks down completely. Nate moves in with Lesje and he and Elizabeth discuss a divorce. Ultimately, Elizabeth's powerlessness is marked by the absence of food. The penultimate line of the novel reveals "There's nothing in the house for dinner."

Nate's subordinate position in his relationship with Elizabeth is epitomized by the fact that he does all the cooking. He even feels an impulse to nourish Elizabeth's lover, Chris. When Chris begs Nate to persuade Elizabeth to get a divorce and move in with him, "Nate wants to give Chris something, some food, what?" However, while Nate is powerless in relation to Elizabeth, he likes to dominate his girlfriends. When he asks Lesje to lunch, she orders "the cheapest thing on the menu, a grilled cheese sandwich and a glass of milk. She listens, eating in small bites, concealing her teeth." Whereas Lesje feels self-conscious eating, Nate voraciously devours his sandwich: "He bites into a piece of turkey, chews; gravy traces his chin." His choice of meat compared to Lesje's choice of cheese subtly suggests his predatory nature. This image is compounded by the way he sits looking at her picking a bread roll to pieces. Nate also insists on paying for the meal. The power he subconsciously reveals in his eating practice is reflected by his financial power. When Nate moves in with Lesje, his domination is signaled by his control over what she eats:

> At least she's eating better since Nate moved in. Nate is making
> her eat better. He brought some cooking pots with him and he
> usually cooks dinner; then he supervises while she eats.

Lesje is powerless in her relationships with both William and Nate. This is conveyed by the fact that she eats very little and frequently refuses food. She often misses lunch or just has a cup of coffee, and when she does eat she only has sandwiches or bran muffins (usually stale). Whenever food is on offer, "she herself doesn't feel like eating right now." This is epitomized in the dinner-party scene. Elizabeth invites Lesje to dinner because she suspects she is having an affair with Nate. She dominates the evening and deliberately tries to intimidate Lesje, who is so uncomfortable that she is unable to eat anything.

The significance of food in sexual politics is illustrated by the fact that most meetings in the novel take place over meals. The pervasive image of rotting food and the pervading aura of rancid decay it emanates powerfully evokes a sense of the unhealthiness of relationships based on the pursuit of power. The leftover *boeuf Bourguinon* destined for the garbage can symbolizes the decayed condition of Elizabeth and Nate's marriage, and when Chris, reluctant to accept the termination of his affair with Elizabeth, confronts Nate, he smells of "faintly rotting meat."

Rennie, in *Bodily Harm*, is another of Atwood's powerless heroines. Rennie is controlled by her boyfriend, Jake, who tries to change her to fit his ideal. He moves into her apartment, decorates it, hangs pictures of naked women over the bed, makes Rennie wear erotic clothes. He physically exerts his authority through sadomasochistic sex. Jake's power is reflected by food. He controls what they eat just as he controls everything else in the relationship. When he leaves, Rennie realizes, "From now on she would have to decide what to eat. Jake decided before: even when it was her turn to cook he decided."

While the scenes set in Toronto highlight the correlation between food and domestic power, Rennie's experiences in the Caribbean highlight the relationship between food and political power. Just like Jake at home, on the island those with power control the food. When Minnow tries to persuade Rennie to write an article on the political situation there, she is reluctant and tells him she only writes about "lifestyles," "what people wear, what they eat, where they go on vacation." He responds that this is exactly what he wants her to write about, confirming that the personal is political. Similarly, when one of Minnow's friends quizzes Rennie about her job, she tells him, "I just do food," to which he replies, "What could be more important?" The idea that food is political is borne out by Minnow's tale about the ham. When Canada donated a thousand tins of ham to the island's refugees, the food was diverted so that it never reached the people who needed it but instead turned up at an Independence Day banquet "for the leading citizen only." Guns in the novel also emphasize the connection between food and power. When Lora asks Rennie to collect a package from the airport, she tells her it contains food and medicine for her sick grandmother when it actually contains guns. "Food" becomes a suitable synonym for "gun," since both represent power. Paul, who carries his gun "like a lunch pail," offers the novel's most succinct comment on the relationship between eating and power:

'There's only people with power and people without power. Sometimes they change places, that's all!'

'Which are you?' says Rennie.

'I eat well, so I must have power,' says Paul grinning.

In prison, where Rennie and Lora have nothing to eat, this relationship is explicit. Rennie subconsciously associates food with freedom. She starts to fantasize about eating and her mouth waters as she repeats the names of different foods to herself.

In *The Handmaid's Tale* Gilead is a society in which women are denied any form of power. One of the main ways the system of oppression is enforced is through food. The handmaids have no choice about what they eat and are permitted to consume only that which the authorities consider will enhance their health and fertility. Caffeine, alcohol, and cigarettes are forbidden and sugar is rationed. Their meals are brought to them in their rooms and they eat alone. By controlling what they eat, the Gilead regime gains direct control over the handmaids' bodies. The connection between food and control is exemplified at the Red Centre, where women are prepared for their role as handmaids. They are indoctrinated with ideological justification of the government's aims and methods as they take their meals. Eating is accompanied by biblical exegesis. In addition, Offred suspects the food is drugged.

> *Give me children, or else I die. Am I in God's stead, who hath withheld from thee the fruit of the womb? Behold my maid Billah. She shall bear upon my knees, that I may also have children by her.* And so on and so forth. We had it read to us every breakfast, as we sat in the high-school cafeteria, eating porridge with cream and brown sugar. . . . For lunch it was the Beatitudes, Blessed be this, blessed be that. They played it from a disc, the voice was a man's.

Like Rennie in prison, Offred associates food with freedom. One of her memories of the pre-Gilead period is of being able to eat what she liked. Her reluctance to eat the food she is given suggests that she subconsciously realizes she is being controlled by what she eats. Her physical rejection of the food symbolizes her mental and emotional rejection of the tyrannical regime she lives under. As she recites the obligatory Lord's Prayer, she thinks, "I have enough daily bread, so I won't waste time on that. It isn't the main problem. The problem is getting it down without choking on it."

Recognizing that food is a form of power, Offred attempts to assimilate this power for herself. From her shopping expeditions she learns that oranges, which are rare and which Rita desires, are available. However, she chooses to withhold this information and subsequently denies Rita the oranges. Later, at a time that suits her, she decides to reveal the news about the fruit and "hold[s] out this idea to her like an offering." Food gives Offred the power to resist and deny. Similarly, when Moira is tortured to the extent that she can no longer walk, Offred and some other handmaids steal packets of sugar for her. They realize that the sugar itself is useless but because it is an illicit substance it becomes symbolic of rebellion. The sugar represents potential power. The subversive power of food is also symbolized by Offred's butter. Instead of eating the butter she receives with her meal, she saves it and later uses it as a moisturizer, which is an illicit luxury. The food which is intended to control becomes a means of subverting that control. When Serena Joy gives Offred a cigarette, she contemplates eating it. The cigarette, like food, represents power as Offred realizes she could use it to burn the house down, and her desire to eat it thus corresponds with her desire for power. Ironically, when Rita grudgingly allows Offred a match for the cigarette, she tells her, "Don't care if you eat it, or what." The subversive potential of food is similarly recognized in Offred's dreams of receiving a message from Luke. These fantasies focus on food. She wonders whether the note will appear, "under my plate, on the dinner tray? Slipped into my hand as I reach the tokens across the counter in All Flesh?"

The Scrabble scene perhaps best exemplifies how food functions as a metaphor for power. When the Commander instructs Offred to visit him in his study at night, she expects him to ask her to perform some perverted sexual act. What he wants, however, is to play Scrabble. The game is "forbidden," "dangerous," "indecent," "something he can't do with his wife," and hence "desirable." It is a particularly subversive activity for Offred because it centers on words, and reading and writing are illegal for women. Starved of any degree of control in her own life, Offred wants to absorb the power that Scrabble represents. This generates a desire to eat the letters. The control of words and food, both forms of power denied to women, are united in the image of Offred eating the Scrabble letters:

> What a luxury. The counters are like candies, made of peppermint, cool like that. Humbugs, those were called. I would like to put them into my mouth. They would taste also of lime. The letter C. Crisp, lightly acid on the tongue, delicious.

Like the other novels, *Cat's Eye* is centered on a power struggle. Here, however, Atwood focuses on the relationship between girls. Cordelia is Elaine's best friend. She is also her tormentor. With her accomplices, Grace and Carol, Cordelia tortures Elaine into believing she is "nothing" and sets her on a cruel program of reform. Elaine's powerlessness and her struggle to overcome the psychological hold her tormentors have on her is traced by her relationship to food. The relationship between eating and power is epitomized by Elaine's father. Whenever he appears in the novel he is eating voraciously and, as he eats, he speaks with authority on the subjects of science, philosophy, ecology, and culture. Elaine internalizes the association between eating and power that she sees operating in the world around her. She dreads going to school, where she cannot escape Cordelia, and in the mornings is unable to eat her breakfast. She identifies with her father's associate, Mr. Banerji, because, as a foreigner, he too feels alien and isolated. Like Elaine's, his powerlessness is reflected by his non-eating and the way he bites his hands. At the Christmas dinner he shuffles his food around his plate and leaves most of it. Elaine relates this sense of powerlessness specifically to food: "He's afraid of us. He has no idea what we will do next, what impossibilities we will expect of him, what we will make him eat." However, correspondingly, Elaine's power is also reflected by her eating. Her encounter with the Virgin Mary in the ravine induces a sense of protection which enables Elaine to defy Cordelia's control. Her act of defiance is accompanied by an act of eating. Leaving the house for school, Elaine ignores her friends and walks on alone. They follow her along the street insulting and criticizing her:

> I can hear the hatred, but also the need. They need me for this, and I no longer need them. There's something hard in me, crystalline, a kernel of glass. I cross the street and continue along, eating my licorice.

Henceforth, the balance of power begins to change between Elaine and Cordelia. The scene in which Elaine threatens to eat Cordelia contributes to this. Playing in a graveyard at dusk, Elaine teases her friend that she is a vampire and will suck her blood out. While Cordelia maintains a façade of disbelief, she is unnerved by the possibility this may be true. From this point on, the positions of power the two girls have assumed are irrevocably altered.

For all Atwoodian heroines the search for selfhood is symbolized by the search for something satisfying to eat. Initially, although Marian eats, she eats poorly. She lives on snack food, frozen meals, and TV dinners. Marion is hungry throughout *The Edible Woman* but cannot find anything to satiate her. Whatever she eats makes her sick. In *Surfacing* the narrator's search for physical sustenance in the natural world becomes symbolic of her lack of spiritual sustenance in the social world. At the end of *Lady Oracle* Joan has nothing to eat except some biscuits which are "hard as plaster and tasted of shelf" and "some cooked pasta, drying out already, and a yellowing bunch of parsley." She has failed to escape her old life and her old self, and the absence of proper, nourishing food indicates that, at the end of the novel, Joan is still trapped in the role of victim. In *Bodily Harm* Rennie seems to spend the entire novel searching for something decent to eat. All her food is awful. In hospital the food is "unbelievable. Green Jello salad and a choice of peas or peas"; on the plane the butter is rancid and the beef leaves a taste of rotting flesh in her mouth; in the hotel there is no choice and all the food is unappetizing and unnourishing. There is no fresh fruit or yogurt, the milk is tinned, the orange juice powdered, and the food is either uncooked, burned, or stale. In prison, the guards put salt in the tea. Throughout *Cat's Eye* Elaine never eats substantial or nutritious food. The sections of the novel set in modern-day Toronto trace her search for something to eat. When she wakes up in Jon's flat she finds the kitchen devoid of food. She decides she needs "to go shopping and get some decent food, organize. . . . I will buy oranges, yogurt without jam. I will have a positive attitude, take care of myself, I'll feed myself enzymes and friendly bacteria." Her intention to eat health food signals her desire for a positive sense of self. Nevertheless, she is never able to provide herself with the food she knows she needs. She wanders around Toronto moving from one location of food to another without eating. She goes shopping in Simpson's Food Hall but does not buy anything because she feels intimidated by the luxurious nature of the items. She eats leftovers and eggs mashed up in teacups. She eats "haphazardly now, snack[s] on junk food and take-outs without worrying about balanced meals." Because of her poor self-image, she is unable to nourish herself. She abuses herself with a poor diet. When she arrives at the gallery or the opening of her exhibition nobody is there because they have gone out to eat. Elaine stands alone and unnourished. After the party, Charna invites her to dinner but she declines. By the close of the novel Elaine has not rediscovered Cordelia and so has not been able to redefine her relationship with her old tormentor by breaking the strong bond between victim and persecutor. It is possible to interpret the scene in which Elaine returns to the ravine and conjures up a vision of Cordelia as a child as the point of reconciliation, the point at which Elaine finally forgives her old foe and the interdependent positions of victim and victor are transcended. However, the moment of epiphany is equivocal, and at the end of the novel Elaine is still eating mashed-up eggs in teacups.

All the heroines interpret the world in terms of food and negotiate their way through life using food. For women, eating and non-eating articulate that which is ideologically unspeakable. Food functions as a muted form of female self-expression but, more than that, it also becomes a medium of experience. Food imagery saturates the novels and becomes the dominant metaphor the heroines use to describe people, landscape, and emotion. As Sally Cline has pointed out, women appropriate food as a language because traditionally they have always been associated with food. In addition, food is one of the few resources available to women. As a consumer surveyor, Marion is constantly submerged in a food environment, and the other heroines have the major responsibility for cooking and shopping. Women control food, Cline insists, because they cannot control their lives. Given the patriarchal nature of language and its inability to accommodate female experience, it is unsurprising that women choose an alternative, non-verbal form of communication. The failure of language, the inadequacy of words as a mode of communication, is a recurrent theme in Atwood's work.

The significance of the politics of eating in Atwood's fiction is endorsed by images of orality. Extraordinary emphasis is placed on the mouth. Traditionally, as Rosalind Coward has shown, the mouth has been a site of vulnerability for women. In *Bodily Harm* Jake penetrates and polices Rennie's mouth as with every other area of her life and body: "You have a dirty mouth, Jake said. It needs to be washed out with a tongue." The power of the male mouth compared to the exploited nature of the female mouth is illustrated by Rennie's memory of being followed by Mexican men making sucking noises. In *Lady Oracle* the way in which Joan's mother always draws a bigger mouth around her own with lipstick mirrors her desire for power in the same way as her attempt to control what goes into her daughter's mouth. While Atwood demonstrates how women have been controlled through their mouths, she also presents the female mouth as a locus of potential strength. The mouth itself, like its uses, is a potential source of power. In *Cat's Eye*, before she meets Cordelia, Elaine feels comfortable with her mouth. She and her brother "practise burping at will, or we put our mouths against the inside of our arms and blow to make farting noises, or we fill our mouths with water and see how far we can spit." However, when she is bullied by Cordelia, Elaine starts to develop a problem with her mouth. Her emotional distress is expressed physically through her mouth via sickness. But just as her powerlessness is expressed through her mouth, so too is her rebellion. As the balance of power between the two girls changes, Elaine develops a "mean mouth":

> I have a mean mouth.
>
> I have such a mean mouth that I become known for it. I don't use it unless provoked, but then I open my mean mouth

and short, devastating comments come out of it. . . . The
person I used my mean mouth on most was Cordelia.

That the mouth is a locus of power is also suggested by Elaine's attitude
to her own mouth. In later life she worries that she is becoming senile because
she notices that she has started to walk around with her mouth slightly open.
Her worries about losing control of her mouth mask her real concern with
losing control of herself altogether. When Elaine imagines being old, she sees
the loss of control of her mouth as one of the main indignities to be endured.
She finds unbearable the thought of "shedding hair and drooling, while some
younger stranger spoons mushed food into my mouth."

The mouth also becomes an emotional center for Atwood's women. All
the heroines constantly experience their feelings in their mouths and their
stomachs. These places become the site of ingestion of both food and
feelings. When the narrator of *Surfacing* dives into the water to search for the
drawings and finds her father's dead body, she returns to the surface in shock,
"fear gushing out of my mouth in silver, panic closing my throat, the scream
kept in and choking me," and when Offred, in *The Handmaid's Tale*, sees Aunt
Lydia at the Salvagings, "hatred fills my mouth like spit." In *Lady Oracle* Joan
wonders "with a sinking of the stomach" whether Arthur likes her, and when
she meets Marlene, one of her former Brownie tormentors, she says, "I
suddenly felt sick to my stomach." When her mother warns her about bad
men in the ravine, she feels "doomed, and my oatmeal porridge would twist
itself into a lump and sink to the bottom of my stomach." The stomach has
a special significance for Joan, as her enigmatic first sexual encounter also
centers on this part of her body. In *Life Before Man*, when Auntie Muriel
inconveniently arrives at Elizabeth's house when she is in bed with William,
"she feels her wind go, as if someone has rammed her in the solar plexus, and
clutches the stomach of her dressing gown." Lesje, too, experiences her
emotions in her stomach. Upset by Nate's procrastination about leaving
Elizabeth, she feels "his absence is evidence, it's empirical. It has hardened
now to stone, a small tight lump she carries everywhere with her in the pit of
her stomach." In *The Handmaid's Tale*, as Offred watches a funeral procession
for a miscarried child, she notes that "Ofglen feels what I do, a pain like a
stab, in the belly." When she hears that Janine's baby is a "shredder," she feels
"an illness, in the pit of my stomach. Not an illness, an emptiness." In *Cat's
Eye*, Elaine feels sick every morning as she waits for her friends to call for her.
Her "stomach feels dull and heavy, as if it's full of earth" and when Grace
accuses Elaine of not praying in church her "stomach goes cold."

Teeth are another intrinsic symbol in Atwood's work. Ainsley's
anecdote about the woman who tries to murder her husband by short-

circuiting his electric toothbrush is humorous but simultaneously signals the power dynamic inherent in teeth. After all, you cannot eat much without teeth. Several of the heroines place particular emphasis on cleaning their teeth. Rennie is obsessive about oral hygiene, and Joan adamantly refuses to have her teeth removed in order to fake her death, as Sam suggests, by sprinkling them on a vat of lime. At Jezebel's, when the Commander takes Offred to a private bedroom, she knows he expects to have sex with her so she procrastinates in the bathroom. At this point, she desperately wishes she could clean her teeth. Just as the heroines experience a sense of unease around their mouths, so do many of them feel anxious about their teeth. Images of dentistry are particularly prominent and the images always convey a sense of fear and pain.

Teeth also reveal much about character. The teeth of predatory male characters are given specific emphasis. In *The Edible Woman* Peter has "teeth gritting" moods and when he takes the photograph of Marion at the party, "his mouth opened in a snarl of teeth." Len Slank's articulation of his philosophy about women, "You've got to hit and run. Get them before they get you and then get out," is accompanied by a dazzling display of teeth. In *Bodily Harm* Jake has particularly prominent canines and Paul constantly clenches his teeth. Jake, Arthur, and Joe all grind their teeth as they make love. Consummation slides easily into consumption; sexual and physical appetites converge. Conversely, all the characters that the protagonists like have nice teeth.

While the powerful display their power through their teeth, the powerless are toothless. In *Bodily Harm* the deaf and dumb beggar who chases Rennie wishing to shake her hand has a "gaping jack-o'-lantern mouth" which is "collapsing" because most of his teeth are missing. After being brutally beaten up by the police, he has no teeth left at all. Angela Carter argues that, symbolically, this is the condition in which women live:

> As a woman, my symbolic value is primarily that of a myth of patience and receptivity, a dumb mouth from which the teeth have been pulled.

Oral communication is another major theme in Atwood's work. Speaking, like eating, is a source of power. Diet and discourse converge in the mouth. Traditionally, women have been suppressed by being denied a voice just as their appetites have been repressed. When Joe tries to rape the narrator in *Surfacing* she tells him to stop, but he prevents her from speaking with his "teeth against my lips, censoring me." Trapped in the powerless role of victim, the narrator finds oral communication difficult: "I was seeing poorly, translating badly, a dialect problem." In the same way that her identity is molded by a patriarchal image of womanhood, she also finds that her speech is not her own. When Joe proposes, her response is clichéd and insincere: "The words were coming out of me like the mechanical words from a talking doll, the kind with the pull tape at the back; the whole speech was unwinding, everything in order, a spool." When Joe asks her if she loves him, she cannot find the words to answer. Because she is powerless, she is speechless. Worrying that she is turning senile, she repeats her name to reassure herself of her own existence. She finds it harder and harder to communicate through verbal language because "the English words seemed imported, foreign." She rejects language as a failed and inadequate form of communication. She also sees language as superfluous, and resolves never to teach her new baby any words. However, when the narrator returns to society she reverts to speech, realizing that "For us it's necessary, the intercession of words." As she rejects her role of victim and assumes a position of responsibility, she regains access to language and acquires the power of speech.

In *Lady Oracle* Joan is acutely aware of the power of words. Her memories of being bullied at school teach her that words are "not a prelude to war but the war itself, a devious subterranean war." Her persistent state of powerlessness at the end of the novel is symbolized linguistically by the fact that she does not speak Italian. She feels "deaf and dumb" and in the butcher's shop she is helpless because "I didn't know the words." In *Life Before Man*, after lunching with Lesje, Nate cannot remember anything Lesje said and wonders if she said anything at all. His domination and her powerlessness are indicated by her silence or, rather, his perception of her voice as insignificant and its erasure through his memory. In *Bodily Harm* the homeless, penniless, and victimized beggar is dumb. Rennie, in prison, thinks she will be all right as long as she keeps talking. In *Cat's Eye*, when Elaine is depressed she finds it an effort to speak and her powerlessness is symbolized by her inability to talk about her victimization. "Even to myself I am mute," she thinks. Later, Josef manipulates Elaine by controlling her speech: "He has taken to demanding speech of me; or else he puts his hand over my mouth. I close my eyes and feel him as a source of power, nebulous and shifting." Significantly, Offred's tale is an oral one.

The throat, the tract that connects mouth and stomach, is another important symbol in Atwood's work. As the vampire tradition illustrates, the throat has always been a particularly vulnerable site for women. Relationships between men and women in Atwood's novels are vampiric. The male characters live like parasites sucking the life, strength, and energy out of their female partners. In *Bodily Harm* the intruder who leaves a coiled rope on Rennie's bed makes himself a cup of Ovaltine before he departs. The Ovaltine acts as a substitute for her body. Jake, Arthur, and Joe not only grind their teeth when making love but like to bite women on the neck.

Strangulation is a recurring motif. In *Surfacing* the protagonist's sense of social unease manifests itself in the feeling that she is being strangled—"Again the strangling feeling, paralysis of the throat"—and when she rejects society and retreats into nature she feels "at once the fear leaving me like a hand lifting from my throat." Psychic strangulation results in a sense of physical strangulation. The image is chillingly appropriate, since the throat is often the site of physical subjection for women. At a time when strangulation is the most common method by which women are murdered, Atwood's presentation of the throat as a site of vulnerability is poignant. Joan's costume gothics create a threatening atmosphere which focuses on her heroine's neck. Redmond closes his hands around Charlotte's throat on several occasions, sometimes in an act of lust, sometimes in an act of rage. The two become indistinguishable. As often in Atwood, sex is murderous, and murder is supremely erotic. This connection is explicit in *Bodily Harm* and *Life Before Man*, when Jake almost kills Rennie, and William almost kills Lesje, while making love by placing an arm across the partner's windpipe so she stops breathing. Similarly, Nate experiences an intense desire to strangle Lesje. The young girl who is found dead in the ravine in *Cat's Eye* has been strangled. Strangulation seems particularly apt as a method of male domination, since by stopping the life-giving flow between brain and body it physically enforces the ideological dichotomy between mind and body which forms the basis of the hierarchical system of gender polarity which informs the whole of Western metaphysics and culture.

While Atwood explores the power dynamic of eating and non-eating, she simultaneously confronts the relationship between consumer and consumed. In her fiction, the powerful not only eat, they eat the powerless. Atwood's work is saturated with images of the body as food. She deconstructs the traditional metaphor of woman as food and explores the effects of symbolic cannibalism as a sanctioned cultural system. The appropriateness of the metaphor is endorsed by the present cult of cannibalism in the cinema. Peter Greenaway's *The Cook, The Thief, His Wife and Her Lover*, Jonathan Demme's *The Silence of the Lambs*, and Jen-Pierre Jeunet and Marc Caro's *Delicatessen* all suggest that cannibalism is currently a particularly pertinent metaphor.

In all the novels Atwood illustrates how symbolic cannibalism has become an institutionalized way of life and how the behavior this generates is perceived and socially endorsed as normal human behavior. The presentation of cannibalism as the governing social ethos exposes the disturbing underside of a violent relationship between the sexes that is only thinly disguised as civilization. The second epigraph of *The Handmaid's Tale*, a quotation from Swift's *A Modest Proposal*, hints at this. The epigraph itself reveals little, but points the reader to Swift's text, in which he sardonically suggests a solution to Ireland's problems of famine, overpopulation, unemployment, and poverty with the proposal that they export the children of the poor to the English as a gourmet delicacy. Atwood, like Swift, uses cannibalism for caustic political comment.

The cannibalistic nature of the relationship between women and men in Atwood's fiction is closely correlated with anthropological studies of cannibalism. Although it is a controversial question whether ritual cannibalism has ever actually existed or is merely a racist myth, many anthropologists base their studies on symbolic cannibalistic rituals. The focus on the symbolic makes such studies particularly pertinent to an analysis of Atwood. Peggy Reeves Sanday sees ritual cannibalism as a sophisticated means of regulating social and psychological categories in society, a way of maintaining the social balance of power. For her, cannibalism is about power and control. It is an act of domination motivated by subject/object polarities in which the person eaten is seen as the social "other." Her words strongly evoke Simone de Beauvoir, and this resonance strengthens the correlation between Sanday's social study of cannibalism and Atwood's fiction. Woman is the "other," and hence the eaten. Quintessentially, for both Atwood and Sanday,

> Cannibalism is never just about eating but is primarily a medium for nongustatory messages—messages having to do with the maintenance, regeneration, and, in some cases, the foundation of the cultural order.

Symbolic cannibalism is obviously a primary theme in *The Edible Woman*, but it is a phenomenon that Atwood also pursues relentlessly in her other novels. The narrator of *Surfacing*, noticing explicit sexual graffiti on the wall of a cave, realizes that men and women hunt each other like prey and metaphorically consume each other just as hunters once devoured animals. In the West, hunting is no longer necessary and has been superseded by the hunting of human enemies: "You draw on the wall what's important to you, what you're hunting. They had enough food, no need to draw tinned peas and Argentine corned beef." What disturbs her particularly is the realization that the way animals are treated, killed, and consumed is no different from the way people treat each other. Recalling her dissection classes at school, she realizes, "anything we could do to the animals we could do to each other: we practised on them first."

The cannibalistic nature of relationships in *Life Before Man* is epitomized by the lifeboat game played at Elizabeth's dinner party. Everyone is stranded in a lifeboat which has a limited supply of food, so someone has to be thrown overboard. To avoid this fate, each person has to justify his or her existence. Nate gives up and jumps overboard voluntarily, but Elizabeth, who threatens to drag others in if she is ejected, thinks the losers should not be thrown overboard but kept and eaten by the others. The strongest sustain themselves by eating the weakest. The monstrous nature of relationships based on this ethic is exemplified by Lesje's dinosaur fantasies. The voracity of the dinosaur's appetite is strikingly similar to the more covert cannibalistic tendencies expressed by men and women. Knowledge of the dinosaur's extinction creates a subtle sense of foreboding for the human race when men and women treat each other as meat in a fight for survival. The most disturbing image of women as food is created by Atwood's parallel between the way dead flesh is devoured by insects in the museum and the way women's bodies are devoured by the male gaze in society:

> In mammology, where the bones are real, they don't use dental picks. They have a freezer full of dead carcasses, camels, mooses, bats, and when they're ready to assemble the skeleton they strip most of the meat off and put the bones into the Bug Room, where carnivorous insects eat the shreds of flesh remaining. The Bug Room smells of rotting meat. Outside the door, several pictures of naked women are Scotch-taped to filing cabinets.

In *The Handmaid's Tale* Offred recalls her mother telling her that Hitler put the Jews in "ovens." She does not understand that they were gassed and thinks they were cooked and eaten, which, she decides later in life, "in a way I suppose they had been." By referring to the atrocities committed against the Jews, Atwood explicitly links eating with politics and symbolic cannibalism with megalomania and tyranny. In *Cat's Eye* Elaine learns that the historical identification of women with food is socially endorsed and celebrated through art. In her art-history course, she notices the constant re-emergence of certain themes and images:

> plates of food and cuts of meat, with or without lobsters. Lobsters are a favourite, because of the colour.
> Naked women.

> There is considerable overlap. . . . The naked women are presented in the same manner as the plates of meat and dead lobsters, with the same attention to the play of candlelight on the skin, the same lusciousness, the same sensuous and richly rendered detail, the same painterly delight in tactility. (*Richly rendered*, I write, *Painterly delight in tactility*.) They appear served up.

Throughout the novels women are constantly seen, and are taught to see themselves, as food. While this constitutes an unequivocal symbol of powerlessness, Atwood illustrates how women can use their bodies as objects of resistance against the system of oppression designed to control those bodies. Offred's persistent presentation of herself as food is a sign of her powerlessness, but she also uses the image of her body as food in a subversive manner. Conscious of the sexual frustration of the Guardians, as she passes them she sways her hips as if "teasing a dog with a bone held out of reach." This gives her a slight sense of power over those who have power over her. "I enjoy the power; power of a dog bone, passive but there." Even as she capitulates to the image of herself as food and the control this represents, she finds a way of subverting that control. What is a form of control and degradation becomes a form of power. Offred never overtly challenges the system that subordinates her by refusing the status of food, but she tacitly subverts it by using its own instrument of power against it. Her complicity is a survival tactic. She never glorifies her position of powerlessness, but explores alternative forms of power within, but not recognized by, the status quo.

While Atwood shows it is possible to subvert systems of oppression from within, she indirectly urges women to transcend such systems altogether. The images of women as food always convey a negative condition—unhappy, unwell, uncomfortable, or dead. Through such imagery Atwood demonstrates the debilitating effect this metaphor has on women's lives. The association of the food metaphor with such negative states subtly highlights how imperative it is for women to transcend this traditional association and forge a new, more positive relationship with food. Such a sentiment echoes Dworkin's insistence that "Women must serve herself instead of serving herself up like a turkey or a duck, garnished, stuffed, sharpened knife ready for ritual carving."

While powerlessness is primarily symbolized by non-eating, the body, that which food fuels, becomes a secondary site of powerlessness. The body politic is superimposed on the physical body. Because the body becomes a site of subjection for women, Atwoodian heroines experience a strong sense of unease about the body. This is reflected in the astonishing number of images of incomplete and mutilated bodies. In addition, because the female protagonists feel corporeally oppressed, they attempt to dissociate themselves from their bodies. They try to distance the experience of victimization and protect some aspect of their selfhood by psychically removing themselves from their bodies. Subsequently, all Atwood's heroines feel alienated from their physical selves and are unable to represent their own bodies. Marion does not realize she is crying until she feels the tears on her hand. She also dreams she is disappearing and imagines her body is dissolving in the bath. The narrator of *Surfacing* sees herself as only half a person and imagines the other half of her body locked away elsewhere. Elizabeth floats above her body as she lies on the bed. Rennie watches herself from the outside as someone else would watch her. During "The Ceremony" where she is forced to have sex with the Commander (and Serena Joy), Offred pretends not to be present: "One detaches oneself. One describes." Elaine learns to step out of her body by fainting in order to escape persecution by Cordelia. Such a phenomenon endorses John Berger's assertion that women are taught to survey themselves as objects of vision.

Eating expresses the ineffable. By writing about women and food, Atwood exposes one of the most subtle and subconscious ways in which power operates. Such articulation of the ideologies and mythologies which subordinate women implicitly suggests how to overcome them. Although, ostensibly, Atwood offers no alternative to the repressive social system she exposes, by highlighting the devastating effects of such a system, she brings into focus the need and means to transcend it. As Atwood illustrates how consumption embodies coded expressions of power which have served to subordinate women, she subtly urges women to reclaim the right to eat and to proudly re-inhabit their own bodies. Women have been driven away from their bodies as violently as they have been driven away from food. Atwood shows them a path back to both. By demonstrating how consumption is related to power, Atwood subtly urges women to empower themselves by urging them to eat their way into the world.

MOLLY HITE

Optics and Autobiography in Margaret Atwood's Cat's Eye

> The Panopticon is a machine for
> dissociating the seeing/being seen dyad.
> Michel Foucault, *Discipline and Punish*

> He died of an eye for an eye, or someone's
> idea of it. He died of too much justice.
> *Cat's Eye*

> This is the Watchbird watching YOU.
> *Cat's Eye*

More than any other of Margaret Atwood's fictions, the 1988 novel *Cat's Eye* raises questions about the relation of the autobiographical "real" to the meaning of a work of literature. Returning to events and characters form earlier novels and stories as well as from Atwood's own childhood, *Cat's Eye* plays with the implications of autobiography: advancing and withdrawing it as a mode of authorization; thematizing it as a strategy for simplistic interpretation or, conversely, as the hidden, damaged heart of a work of art; insisting with the fervor of its adolescent girls telling each other scary stories

From *Twentieth Century Literature* 41:2 (Summer 1995): 135–155. © 1995 by Hofstra University.

that this is true, this really happened, while at the same time demanding on both aesthetic and metaphysical grounds, What do you mean, *true*? What do you mean, *real*?

As a *Künstlerroman*, the novel seems to license a double substitution: for painter, read writer; for writer, read writer of *this* novel. Like Atwood's groundbreaking 1972 novel *Surfacing*, it takes the form of a first-person narration by a female artist, and in both works visual representation is an easy trope for the kind of literary representation going on in the book itself. But such apparently self-evident subrogations ultimately complicate rather than clarify, setting up two opposed accounts of the relations between artist and audience and leading to two opposed accounts of the relations between autobiography and meaning in a literary work. The oppositions are entailed by a fact central to the plot: neither art nor personal experience can be separated from the dynamics of power that structure social reality. Like *Bodily Harm* and *The Handmaid's Tale*, the two novels that precede it, *Cat's Eye* is set in an environment of extremity, where the central concern is not merely well-being but survival. As in *Bodily Harm* especially, issues of survival are mapped onto a number of levels, ranging from individual physical bodies to specific ethnic- or gender-based communities to national states. The death of Elaine's brother Stephen at the hands of terrorists, in many respects the climactic event of the novel, replays the gender-enforcing torture of the nine-year-old Elaine at the hands of her purported friends, a torture that leads at one point to their abandoning her to die and at another point to her attempted suicide. The recurrence of such incidents on different strata of the fictional universe underscores the political implications of conventionally personal events.

Such political implications inevitably inform the theme of self-representation in the novel. In this respect *Cat's Eye* is particularly controlled and self-conscious—Atwood hallmarks in any case—and it is especially guarded in its anticipation of readings seeking to catch "the author" somehow unaware, negligently half-dressed in some unacknowledged fold of her text. For visual art is not only a convenient displacement of literary art in this novel. *Cat's Eye* is also about visibility: about who sees and is seen, about evading or controlling the gaze, about the seeing that is the precondition and product of art. Like so many other things under scrutiny here, the portrait of the artist proves to be a metamorphosing construct. So much depends on how you look at it.

The environment of extremity in *Cat's Eye* incorporates a sense of radical contingency that has increasingly characterized Atwood's global vision. In *Bodily Harm*, people hurt other people "because they can," "because they can get away with things"; in *The Handmaid's Tale*, Offred's story is about the mechanisms of successful oppression, "about who can do what to whom and be forgiven for it." In both these novels, the motives for malignancy are far more systemic than individual. People are manipulated, mutilated, and killed because they occupy certain positions in the overall structure, due largely to generic or random factors rather than to anything they, in particular, have done. The question of deserving, and indeed any personal ethics of consequences, is radically reconfigured in this sort of political reality. There are oppressors and there is evil, but individual justice, especially the leveling of scores implied in the Hammurabic prescription of an eye for an eye, is largely inapplicable as a concept.

In *Cat's Eye*, Stephen is killed because he is a representative of the white, Western, male oppressor class, although as an abstract and abstracted physicist he seems singularly detached from any individual acts of oppression. In fact, he is so removed from human concerns that he does not seem to regard himself as vulnerable to any sort of attack and views himself as unassailable for exactly the reason he is finally killed: as Elaine suggests earlier, "He thinks he is safe, because he is what he says he is." Similarly, Elaine is a surrogate victim, representative of the category "girl" and thus a stand-in for the other girls, who use her as a scapegoat in order to displace their own suffering as members of a patriarchy, here literalized in the authority of their own fathers. Carol's whip marks reinforce the message that fathers have "real, unspeakable power," power that Cordelia attempts to appropriate for herself by applying to Elaine her own father's expressions of contempt, "Wipe that smirk off your face!" and "What do you have to say for yourself?" Elaine realizes later that Cordelia, unlike her Shakespearean namesake, will never please this father "because she is somehow the wrong person," but it takes her years to put together the corollary, that she herself was nearly sacrificed as a proxy "wrong person" in the symbolic economy of the little girls.

As a result of her experience as victim of this displaced oppression, Elaine turns away from the ghettoized lives of girls and women and toward the largely separate sphere of the masculine, which she apprehends as a relatively safe haven from female machinations. She sides first with the fathers of the neighborhood, then with the boys in her high school; then as an art student she arrives at an idealized image of "men" that reproduces the marks of paternal power and comes to life in the person of Josef Hrbik and his "experienced mauve bedroom," and finally reaches a tentative resting point with her caretaking second husband, parodically described in terms of Fifties fantasies about male protection.

This turn, however, also represents a deeply unsatisfying complicity with masculinist institutions that at points amounts to misogyny, prompted by an overwhelming fear that women "know too much, they can neither be deceived nor trusted." In a reactive newspaper interview arranged in conjunction with the retrospective exhibition of her paintings (and reminiscent of several interviews of Atwood herself), Elaine lashes out at the categories in which the young female interviewer attempts to contain her, finally maintaining that gender has nothing to do with either her work or its reception, although she also notes, "I am on dubious ground, and this enrages me." The interview suggests what aspects of conventionally female (and mass media-defined "feminist") identity she finds constricting and threatening, and in ways amounts to an etiology of an apparently antifeminist public stance. It is a public stance that is also complicated and undermined by many factors in her retrospective account of her life. For instance, she later narrates a version of the scenario she repudiates during the interview: "Male art teachers pinching your bum, calling you *baby*, asking you why there are no great female painters, that sort of thing," when she describes her near-simultaneous initiation into life drawing and sexuality. And the ostensible antifeminism is complicated in particular by the descriptions of her paintings, which appear both to document and to apotheosize the female universe she still imaginatively inhabits. The question of how to read these paintings is in many ways analogous to the question of how to read *Cat's Eye* as a whole. I will return to both in the closing discussion of autobiography.

Perhaps more than any other Atwood novel, *Cat's Eye* is preoccupied with detail, with a proliferation of social and cultural observations about the postwar era that, like Elaine's initial paintings of the domestic objects of her childhood, are "suffused with anxiety." As these details amass, they reinforce the imputation that growing up female, even growing up as a white, middle-class female in a relatively prosperous North American country, is different only in degree from living in a police state. *The Handmaid's Tale* was built on the observation that the implications of culturally constructed femininity, even femininity as constructed by a relatively liberal society, can be used in extremity to justify organizing women into slave castes based on various roles retroactively attributed to biology. *Cat's Eye* shows the more subtle means by which the relatively liberal society both marginalizes middle-class girls as a group and individualizes each girl, making her responsible for her own marginalization.

In this context, the *Künstlerroman* account of the making of an artist in this novel renders the whole idea of art problematic by making the artist one possible outcome of the process of socialization insuring the subordination of women as a group but reserving token "special" positions for a very few members of that group. Elaine manages to detach herself, albeit only to a degree, from the category of "women" by substituting an abstracted, observing eye for an engaged, interdependent I. That is, she achieves a quantum of power by self-division or self-synecdoche. *Cat's Eye* illustrates how such a mutilation is a precondition of agency in a society that maintains its identities through a rigorous separation of seeing from being seen.

This separation is at the heart of postwar definitions of masculinity and femininity, as these qualities are depicted in this novel. "Look" is always a pun, conveying at once the gaze that judges and the process of *being* gazed at and judged, as in "How do I look?"—or as in "I look like Haggis McBaggis." "I look like the Witch of Endor," or "I'd look like an old biddy." In these latter instances, to be object of the look is to look *like*, the trope of simile instantly invoking stereotypes of women who have aged past the point of being rewarding to the acquisitive gaze. Women look like, while in general men only look—unless of course they are less than men, "fruity clothes horses," in Stephen's "devastating" appraisal. In many respects, this distinction conditions the whole gender-segregated urban landscape of the novel's Fifties, defining the feminine episteme in terms of the arcana of twin sets and cold waves, and locating in the shameful invisibility of female underwear a correlative to the displayed male wound. For women, to be seen is both to have an identity and to be identified as vulnerable: both a requirement and a stigma. Fundamental to this definition is the premise that the female object of the look is also somehow guilty of it and thus susceptible as a consequence of her own instigation, a premise that lies behind the possibility of "making a spectacle of yourself"—"as if there's something wrong in the mere act of being looked at," Elaine reflects and leads to deep unease among the girls when another girl is found "molested" and murdered in a ravine: "It's as if this girl has done something shameful, herself, by being murdered." The prime female responsibility is to control the look so that it will not kill.

"Look at yourself!" Cordelia demands, handing Elaine a mirror, and Elaine learns to internalize the condemnatory gaze without discerning the means to "improve" herself that will remove her from the range of such judgments. Of course, the goal of improvement is part of the mechanism of condemnation and as such is unrealizable. Yet most of the women of *Cat's Eye* are obsessed with controlling how they look, with contriving all their appearances "on purpose." The adult Elaine still harbors a (not uncommon) desire to anticipate the impossible view of herself from behind. And when Cordelia falls in the snow by accident rather than by design, she needs immediately to displace onto Elaine her shame at being caught in an inadvertency and for this reason initiates an act of savage humiliation that verges on a murder attempt, demanding that Elaine go into the ravine and onto the ice of the creek to retrieve her hat, and then leaving her there. Cordelia tries, in other words, to reverse the direction of the gaze and thus the threat of attack, a tactic that she and Elaine use later as teen-agers when they "outstare" strangers on the bus. But the tactic has only limited efficacy because it is combined with a continued concern to control an appearance this is still female, to combine the dominating gaze with an awareness of being fashionably "cool" and "ultrasharp." The pose begins to crumble as Cordelia succumbs to her socialization and follows up her performance of "overly bright" chatter with the anxiously jokey question "But that's enough about me. What do *you* think of me?"

Elaine succeeds much better in reversing the direction of the gaze, but only by denying her inclusion in the category "women." The discovery that "boys are my allies" leads her to fantasize that boys do not view her in the same way as they view other girls, that she can "walk in the spaces between" the "silent words surrounding [other girls], *stunned broad, dog, bag* and *bitch*, pointing at them, reducing them, cutting them down to size so they can be handled." Later, in the company of male art students who speak of female models as "A cow," "A bag," "What a discard," she thinks she is "an exception, to some rule I haven't even identified." Her drawing instructor Josef's dicta that she is both an "unfinished voman" who needs to "be finished" and artistically "nothing. . . . We will see what we can make of you" suggest that insofar as she remains sexually female, she remains subject to the goal of "improvement." The difference is that she does not ultimately allow Josef to be final arbiter of her development, either professionally or sexually. The source of her ability to set limits to her desire to please him, unlike her earlier inability to say no to Cordelia, is wound up with her choice of the vocation of painter, a professionalized embodiment of the one-way gaze. As a painter, if not as a female body, she is in control of how other people look.

In other words, as a painter she occupies a position usually reserved for the dominant class of men in a patriarchal system: she can disengage seeing from being seen, and this disengagement gives her access to a key mechanism of what Michel Foucault has described as the modern disciplinary society. In such a society, power is dissociated, diffuse, and pervasive; as such, it is internalized, and thus self-policing. Foucault finds the emblem of this sort of society in Jeremy Bentham's model prison the Panopticon, designed to individualize prisoners by virtue of their physical isolation while rendering them completely visible to an authoritative viewer who himself remains unseen. The main operation of power in the disciplinary state is precisely this surveillance, this nonreciprocal seeing. The genius of the system is that while the power reinforces the existing hierarchy and institutions, the operation of power is not centralized in any one person or class of people. In principle, any member of the society can run the panoptic machinery: as Foucault notes, "In the absence of the director, his family, his friends, his visitors, even his servants" can carry on the monitory business. Eventually the prisoners internalize the gaze of the panoptic authority. They police themselves, self-surveillance becoming part of their identity as prisoners, just as in the "generalization" of the panoptic mechanism that results in the disciplinary society, surveillance, and finally self-surveillance, becomes both the origin and the definition of the citizen. The pervasiveness of the power, however, is no index of equality. People watch each other, but this watching guarantees first of all that everyone occupies a fixed place in a given hierarchy. As Linda Kauffman has noted in the case of *The Handmaid's Tale*, the invisible and omniscient institutional gaze is leveled first at gendered subjects whose visibility is by definition compulsory.

In *Cat's Eye*, as in *The Handmaid's Tale*, the subjects who are most evidently singled out for enforced visibility are female. The panoptic goal of individualizing subjects by partitioning them off in enclosures is insured by the institution of the nuclear family and its postwar containment in the single-family house, a unit that serves the disciplinary purpose of fixing hitherto nomadic populations like Elaine's own family. In particular, such houses pin down mothers, who are supposed to occupy them continually: "Daytime is rules by the mothers," as Elaine observes, although the real power comes with the nighttime return of the fathers. The function of insuring the visibility of subjects belongs to cultural institutions, in particular the institutions of mass culture, and the subjects who are supposed to be most visible are the women. The monitory figure of the Watchbird, who appears in women's magazines like *Good Housekeeping, The Ladies' Home Journal*, and *Chatelaine*, is an icon of the one-way gaze, directed initially at pictures that "show women doing things they aren't supposed to do," but then turned outward, toward the female reader: "This is a Watchbird watching YOU."

The role of the Watchbird is explicitly corrective, but at the same time it guarantees that correction is impossible. The women represented in the magazines, who "put germ killers onto germs, in toilet bowls; they polish windows, or clean their spotty complexions with bars of soap, or shampoo their oily hair; they get rid of their unwanted odors, rub hand lotion onto their rough, wrinkly hands, hug rolls of toilet paper against their cheeks," are fighting a losing battle. As the child Elaine sees, "There will be no end to imperfection, or to doing things the wrong way." Postwar women are fixed in their place by a process that amounts to a return to infancy, a process that renders them docile bodies, in Foucault's phrase, bodies that the preadolescent girls regard with terror: "Whatever has happened to them,

bulging them, softening them, causing them to walk rather than run, as if
there's some invisible leash around their necks, holding them in check—
whatever it is, it may happen to us too." The anxiety attendant on achieving
full feminine identity comes from the requirement that the adult woman
internalize a permanent belief in her need for improvement, a belief essential
to her primary role as consumer, as the magazine advertisements indicate.
The mitigating factor is that she can also align herself with the Watchbird to
police other women and female children. Mrs. Smeath relegates to herself
the task of attending to the spiritual improvement of Elaine, but with
apparent satisfaction finally judges her unredeemable, a "heathen." The most
successful product of female socialization among the girls, Grace Smeath,
does much of the actual surveillance of Elaine, both as an agent of her
mother and as an agent of Cordelia, who invents as an image of Elaine's
transgressions a stack of plates crashing noisily to the floor, a representation
of female domestic failure worthy of the Watchbird and strikingly at odds
with Cordelia's own character and concerns.

The obvious form of resistance to the one-way look is the look back, a
version of "outstaring" that apparently establishes parity by returning an eye
for an eye. "*So, Cordelia. Got you back,*" Elaine thinks near the end of the
novel, acknowledging the erasure of her former tormentor from the scene of
her return. But she goes on to gloss the apostrophe: "Never pray for justice,
because you might get some." Indeed, revenge has turned out to be as painful
as the events that motivated it. The reversal that put Cordelia in the place of
victim was the consequence of Elaine's partial self-erasure in substituting an
observing, judging eye for a gendered body susceptible to observation and
judgment.

The substitution represents an extreme form of denial, albeit a denial
warranted by conditions of extremity, the tactic of a body at risk. Modeling
herself on the cat's eye marble, a metonym for the one schoolyard game
played by both boys and girls, Elaine retreats "back into [her] eyes" to
avoid feeling too much of the pain inflicted by her "friends." Later she
intensifies the self-splitting by learning to faint on the playground,
discovering that she can watch herself lying on the ground or stand "off to
the side" of her own body. Still later, after her brush with death and her
repression of her memories of the "bad time," she encounters evidence that
she has separated herself from her own affective life, in the experience not
only of crying for no apparent reason but of not being able to "believe in
[her] own sadness," to "take it seriously." But she holds on to her hard-
earned status as someone who affects but remains unaffected: "I am happy
as a clam: hard-shelled, firmly closed."

In professionalizing this status by becoming an artist, she additionally denies her situation as a sexed female body, conventionally the object of the painterly gaze. The implications of this denial begin to come home to her when she witnesses the aftermath of Susie's life-threatening self-abortion and hears "a small, mean voice, ancient and smug, that comes from somewhere deep inside my head: *It serves her right.*" The judgment echoes that of Mrs. Smeath on the torture her daughter and the other girls inflicted on Elaine and anticipates the judgment Elaine visits on herself by painting Mrs. Smeath shortly after she learns that she, too, is pregnant: "Whatever has happened to me is my own fault, the fault of what is wrong with me. Mrs. Smeath knows what it is. She isn't telling." The assumption that misfortune is necessarily "the fault of what is wrong with" the person suffering it is intrinsic to the structure of the disciplinary society, in which the separation between watcher and watched is a sign of a separation between judge and judged and in which the physical isolation of the subjects who are watched and judged entails that guilt is individual and personal. The limitation inherent in the nonreciprocal gaze makes blaming a primary mode of interaction among people. In a disciplinary society, deserts are just, by definition.

Elaine has largely accepted this assumption. As a child, punishing herself for the unspecified transgressions the other girls darkly hint at, she peels her feet (Atwood here alludes again to Andersen's Little Mermaid, one of her favorite instances of the woman who suffers mutilation as a condition of entering an alien universe), bites her fingernails, and assumes confused responsibility for her lack of "backbone." As a teen-ager she adroitly shifts the blame for the consequences of not pleasing to Cordelia, demanding with oddly impervious self-righteousness, "How can she be so abject? When will she learn?" The device of blaming works for her just as it worked earlier for Cordelia, forestalling empathy, warding off any sense that the self might be implied in the other. These effects are most evident when Elaine seizes on blaming as a means to avoid information that might recall the "bad time" to consciousness: "I want to protect myself from any further, darker memories of hers, get myself out of here gracefully before something embarrassing happens." Protection succeeds because it takes the form of attack. "I harden toward her. . . . She has all kinds of choices and possibilities, and the only thing that's keeping her away from them is lack of willpower. *Smarten up*, I want to tell her. *Pull up your socks.*"

Here, as in many other parts of the novel, failure of "willpower" summons up slang injunctions to control appearance. Earlier, Cordelia's older sister taunted, "Pull up your socks, Cordelia, or you'll flunk your year again. You know what Daddy said last time." Like the more general condition of "letting yourself go," the specter of visibly drooping socks that need pulling up is a figure of feminine dereliction. Such figures specify the terms in which women monitor each other and demand "improvement." In the postwar society of *Cat's Eye*, women tell other women that they are letting themselves go, that they should pull up their socks. But behind these admonishing voices is the real threat, "what Daddy said last time."

The mechanism of blaming is essential to the disciplinary society and in its ultimate effects always insures the hegemony of the fathers. The contrary activity, forgiveness, is in many respects part of the same structure, in that only someone who is guilty can be forgiven—Cordelia sends Elaine into the ravine by urging "Go on then. . . . Then you'll be forgiven"—but in other respects it seems to translate subjects out of the structure, at least to some extent, by translating them out of their hermetic isolation. Most radically, forgiveness makes blame impossible by entailing comprehension of a whole context of influences and motives, as when Elaine observes, "Knowing too much about other people puts you in their power, they have a claim on you, you are forced to understand their reasons for doing things and then you are weakened." As this passage suggests, the mutilated self demands as its corollary a mutilated awareness of the other. In the disciplinary society, curtailment of knowledge is power.

As in *The Handmaid's Tale*, the people who can forgive are the least powerful, the most susceptible to control and judgment, the women. In *Cat's Eye* female forgiveness is embodied in the ambiguous figure of the lady. The little girls play gender-enforcing games with cutouts of women from the Eatons catalogue and call them "my lady." These pasted-down women serve as models of housebound Fifties femininity: like all the mothers but Elaine's own, they are fixed in place by the requirements of consumption and ownership while at the same time acting as the agents of such fixity in opposition to the men, who are "the outrageous, the subversive." In the girls' cryptic jump-rope rhyme, the lady is victim of "an obscure dirtiness. Something is not understood: the robbers and their strange commands, the lady and her gyrations, the tricks she's compelled to perform, like a trained dog." Yet the cry of "Lady" is also "the final word of appeal" when the adult Elaine encounters a drunk woman lying on the sidewalk. The word cues for her a refusal to blame, to reduce condition to culpability: "'She's only drunk,' a man says in passing. What does that mean, *only?* It's hell enough."

Elaine notes, "If you want something very badly you do not say *Woman, Woman*, you say *Lady, Lady*." The term seems to summon up longings for the pre-oedipal mother, a figure of primordial fulfillment whose gaze is not judgmental because it is not separate, the mother who is not other. Rejection by such a mother is for many women in Atwood's fictional universes the fall that is the origin of alienated individuality. "I know about you," the drunk woman says. "You're Our Lady and you don't love me." The charge evokes Elaine's childhood despair when her mother returned from the hospital after a traumatic miscarriage: "It's as if she's gone off somewhere else, leaving me behind; or forgotten I am there." Mothering is passionately imagined as the force that can reverse the partitioning, blaming structure of the whole society. Real mothers are inevitably failures, never enough. At the same time, the image of the lady marks the place of an alternative construction of intersubjective life, as when Elaine chooses, against the norms of the Smeath universe, to worship the Virgin Mary instead of the paternal God of the panoptic, "watchful" stars, who continually needs more "before he can be truly appeased."

The Virgin Mary is important as a reversion to a pre-verbal era—Elaine has not "yet learned the words to her"—who provides, at least in imagination, the encompassing aura of succor and concern impossible for actual subjects of a disciplinary society: "She knows already, she knows how unhappy I am." Her incarnations are the quasi-authoritative "ladies" of Elaine's experience who are salvific either in wish, as in case of the Princess Elizabeth, or in effect, as in the cases of Miss Stuart and Mrs. Finestein, whom Elaine "rewards" for their passing kindnesses in her painting entitled *Three Muses*. This Virgin Mary is above all an agent of restoration, a Virgin of Lost Things who redresses estrangement and truncation with the inaudible but somehow spoken words, "*It will be alright. Go home.*"

When Elaine recovers the cat's-eye marble and in the process recovers her memory of the "bad time," her relation to women undergoes a change. In recognizing what happened and forgiving her mother, she seems to comprehend for the first time both the necessary failures of all individual mothers and the context that makes visible hitherto unacknowledged strengths: "Against [my father's] bleak forecasting is set my mother's cheerfulness, in retrospect profoundly willed." In looking into the marble "and seeing my life entire," she seems to begin the process of relinquishing blame. Although women, especially in groups, continue to have the power to threaten her, she is also poignantly aware of the needs of female figures who are involved, as she is, in the reclamation of lost things—the bag ladies whom she resembles in her "collection of shreds" of time, the refugee woman who approaches her with the entreaty, "Please. . . . They are killing many people," a reminder of the war that "broke up into pieces and got scattered, it gets in everywhere, you can't shut it out," "the war that killed Stephen."

The refugee woman, especially, is a reminder of a universe of suffering that belies utterly the disciplinary mechanisms of individuation and blaming. "Every day there's more of it, more of that silent wailing, those starving outstretched hands, *need help, help help*, there's no end." Stephen was apparently killed somewhere in the Middle East, a region from which this woman apparently derives. But these appearances, connected as they are with motives of national identity and partisanship, are not reasons or causes and do not account for the logic that suddenly transforms a person into a representative, an emblem, and a victim. Families die, the lucky ones getting away to lives of begging in foreign countries, because they live on the sites of clashes that may have nothing else to do with them. Hostages die, the lucky ones rapidly, in midair, because they mark a point of disagreement between rival forces that may have nothing else to do with them. Recounting Stephen's death, Elaine asks, "Die for what? There's probably a religious motif, though in the foreground something more immediate: money, the release of others jailed in some sinkhole for doing more or less the same thing these men are doing." Motives, though inescapably hypothetical, are not inconsequential. At the same time they are not sufficient. They do not ultimately make sense of such facets as the refugees or Stephen's death by locating them in an economy of guilt and punishment. On the contrary, such an economy brings about its own unintelligible catastrophes. Elaine says of Stephen, "He died of an eye for an eye, or someone's idea of it. He died of too much justice."

In a world so much larger and so much more full of misery than an ethics of personal culpability can comprehend, Hammurabic justice is less to the point than the traditional feminine virtue of mercy. Giving money to the drunk woman, Elaine comments, "I'm a sucker, I'm a bleeding heart. There's a cut in my heart, it bleeds money." The "cut in my heart" suggests her resemblance to the version of the Virgin Mary to whom she first decided to shift her allegiance, Our Lady of Perpetual Help, who told her it was all right, she could go home. The bleeding wound is a stigma of femininity; it is also a sign of restoration and compassion. Similarly, the "bad heart" of Mrs. Smeath, which Elaine had imagined floating "in her body like an eye, an evil eye, it sees me" is not fully visualized until it is understood as also an organ of acceptance, and until Mrs. Smeath's own eyes are acknowledged not only to judge but also to reveal a suffering subject. In the paintings of Mrs. Smeath displayed in the retrospective exhibit, Elaine recognizes that the "self-righteous eyes, piggy and smug" are "also defeated eyes, uncertain and melancholy, heavy with unloved duty," and is suddenly able to see herself through these eyes, "unbaptized, a nest for demons: how could she know what germs of blasphemy and unfaith were breeding in me? And yet she took me in." The revelation supplements the original insight; it does not supplant it. Blaming falsifies vision by representing a part as a whole. Elaine sums up: "An eye for an eye leads only to more blindness." The revised maxim underscores the inadequacy of retaliation as an action and as an epistemological condition. It fails not because it is aggressive but because it is, in both senses of the word, partial.

Painting has served Elaine as a means of vision, and revision: "I have said, *Look*. I have said, *see*." The paintings of Mrs. Smeath suggest that the scope of vision depends on what is done with the look back: on whether it is countered or comprehended. Yet comprehension is also in crucial respects an impossibility. The project of recovery is also part of Elaine's goal as a painter, a goal served most obviously by the ability of a painted representation to fix bodies forever, so that they are not subject to the attrition of time. But this fixing is also part of the disciplinary project, intrinsic to the separation of seer from seen. "My love for them is visual," Elaine reports of the boys she dates in high school; "that is the part of them I would like to possess. *Don't move*, I think. *Stay like that. Let me have that*." Her tacit commands anticipate Josef Hrbik's treatment of the model in the Life Drawing class: "'Keep still,' he says to her. . . . He takes her arms and her sulky-faced head and rearranges them, as if she is a mannequin."

But these commands also articulate an impossibility. Even in a universe theorized by physicists like Stephen, in which time is a dimension and it is possible to exist in two places at once, there is no changing the past. If "nothing goes away," there is no real return, either; only successive reinterpretations of the gaze penetrating temporal strata that "like a series of liquid transparencies" are "one laid on top of another." Commenting on the painting of her mother entitled *Pressure Cooker*, Elaine says, "I suppose I wanted her timeless, though there is no such thing on earth. These pictures of her, like everything else, are drenched in time." The multiple images of her mother engaged in one of the earliest activities Elaine can remember, "cooking, in the ways and places she used to cook, in the late forties," do not bring her mother back from the dead, much less restore the pre-oedipal bond, the mother-child dyad in which seeing and being seen are experienced as the same. Representation can never be recovery; the represented is inevitably at a remove from presence.

The painting entitled *Unified Field Theory*, like the scientific enterprise to which it alludes, appears to be an ambitious attempt to encompass a whole within a condensed structure of symbols. Centered on the figure of the Virgin of Lost Things, who holds "an oversized cat's eye marble" in her hands, it sums up the theme of recovery through the intercession of a lady and through the assimilative gaze that can behold in one glance the vast and the infinitesimal, the living and the dead. But it is also and unavoidably incomplete, signifying finally a moment in time, one instant of recuperation that has itself passed into memory—and into the apprehension of other

people. Elaine reflects, "I may have thought I was preserving something from
time, salvaging something; like all those painters, centuries ago, who thought
they were bringing Heaven to earth, the revelations of God, the eternal stars,
only to have their slabs of wood and plaster stolen, mislaid, burnt, hacked to
pieces, destroyed by rot and mildew." The painting is only another object in
the world of objects it seeks to contain. And the painter has moved on with
the present, leaving the artifact as an element of detritus to be recovered,
reclaimed, and reinterpreted by the gaze of others. "Because I can no longer
control these paintings, or tell them what to mean. Whatever energy they
have came out of me. I'm what's left over."

The teen-aged Elaine had been uncomfortable with the loss of control
attendant on "knowing too much about other people," a situation in which
"you are forced to understand their reasons for doing things and then you are
weakened." But in the narrative development of *Cat's Eye*, this source of
disciplinary weakness emerges as a precondition for artistic strength, at least
according to the more comprehensive if perhaps utopian definition of art
that evolves from Elaine's own reassessments of her work. By this definition,
a work of art, whether a painting or a novel, involves understanding far more
about people than is consonant with a social structure of surveillance,
judgment, and blame. People's "reasons for doing things" make the processes
of representation and interpretation more complicated and more far-
reaching. Moreover, the increase in complexity and magnitude guarantees
that knowing "too much about people" is at the same time never knowing
enough. The more comprehensive the vision, the less its power to control.

One consequence seems to be that the painter must forego the project
of controlling the gaze of the other. A painting exists in itself and in the
present, leaving artistic intention behind as a piece of unreclaimable detritus.
The painting *Cat's Eye*, potentially a *mis-en-abîme* of the novel as a whole,
alludes to a famous icon of painterly authority, Van Eyck's *The Arnolfini
Marriage*, with its incorporation of the artist's signature "like a washroom
scribble, something you'd write in spray paint on a wall" as an assertion of
mastery comparable to the young Stephen's phallic inscription "in pee" of his
"girlfriend's" name or the names of the planets in the solar system. But the
element of Van Eyck's painting that Elaine appropriates is the pier glass
reflecting figures outside the frame of the main picture. This glass hangs
behind a self-portrait that shows only half of Elaine's head and incorporates
signs of aging that are also, in the tradition of self-portraiture, signs of
authority. Some of these signs are falsified because the marks of experience
appropriate to masculine dominance run counter to the demands made on
the sexed female body. Thus Elaine has painted "a few gray hairs. This is
cheating, as in reality I pull them out." She has produced, that is, "a public

face," but it is also only "half a face," not just in the obvious sense that it shows the top part of her head, but in the sense that it shows only the face prepared, the face under control, the appearance presented "on purpose," to meet the faces that it meets. The pier glass tells another part of the story.

The pier glass provides what by definition she cannot see, "a section of the back of my head," and in addition locates this spectacle in her past: "but the hair is different, younger." Furthermore, it represents the watchers who had this view in her childhood, "three small figures, dressed in the winter clothing of the girls of forty years ago." Yet this young Elaine is turned around, facing her erstwhile tormentors. The view of the back of the head is the view given to the public, the people outside both frames who look at the painting.

The extraordinary condensed symbolism of this painting seems at once a claiming and a relinquishing of control. The represented child Elaine looks back at the three girls; the represented adult Elaine looks back at the outside viewer. Yet the crucial element of the painting is the back of the head, which recalls the horrific power of "a mirror that shows you only the ruined half of your face" but also anticipates the recognition of what Elaine could give to Cordelia, and by extension what Cordelia could give to Elaine: "What you look like from outside. A reflection. This is the part of herself I could give back to her." In this latter realization, the gaze is transformed from an appropriation to a restoration, and *Cat's Eye* has established the basis for its final vision of alternative interruptions, summed up in the image of "something that will never happen. Two old women giggling over their tea." These women, old enough to be freed from the requirement to maintain appearance, have been released into the possibility of augmenting rather than truncating each other, of seeing and being seen at the same time, set apart from the estranging and mutilating operations of disciplinary power. The relationship is not a restitution of the maternal bond, but it draws on some of the same conditions as this pre-oedipal dyad and evokes some of the same inchoate yearning. And it is similarly impossible for Elaine, for the same reasons that the real Cordelia will never know it's all right, she can go home now. Elaine's retrospective gaze reinterprets only her own relation to the past and to Cordelia. Like the stay-at-home space twin of Stephen's (and Einstein's) thought experiment, she has moved forward while the other has not, and now she is wholly and irrevocably separated in time.

This poignantly inconclusive conclusion establishes *Cat's Eye* as a novel about loss and the impossibility of ever recovering what has been lost; about the extraordinary waste of human subjects, especially female subjects, in a society that defines personhood by radically separating people from each other and assigning them fixed places in a hierarchy; about surviving, aging, and coming to terms in such a society; and about the ultimate futility of blame and the correlative necessity for comprehensive vision. But *Cat's Eye* is also, and perhaps even more insistently, a novel about art and the artist, and in particular about Margaret Atwood's own art and its relation to Margaret Atwood's own life. The implications of all these other themes as they are developed in the novel make this relationship particularly complicated and problematic, setting up two opposed accounts of the relations between artist and viewer or reader, and leading to two opposed accounts of the relations between autobiography and meaning in an aesthetic work.

The most benign account of the relations between the creator and the consumer of the work of art is that the viewer or reader is as necessary as the artist, a co-creator who can develop and even perhaps complete the work. Atwood made some gestures toward this theory in her 1980 essay "An End to Audience?" although like Elaine later, she was inclined to bring in the viewer/reader only after the artist had left off, intimating not only that the artist was "what's left over" after the work was completed, but that the work of art was similarly detritus in the wake of the artist's own life. The quasi-parodic interpretations of Elaine's paintings offered throughout the narrative, however, combine to suggest that the eye of another person can provide the crucial part of the artistic work that, like the alienated "part of herself" which the other can "give back," is required for full compensation. For instance, Jody, who organizes the all-woman show in which Elaine first displays her work, says of the Mrs. Smeath paintings, "It's good to see the aging female body treated with compassion, for a change." In its immediate context this remark is a hilarious misreading of Elaine's avowed motives, but Elaine's subsequent recognition of Mrs. Smeath's suffering and relative generosity is provoked by these same paintings, which she comes to regard as having aspects that she was not aware of having rendered. Clearly, art can exceed conscious knowledge; most significantly, it may provide a more complete and more merciful representation than consciousness intends.

In the same way, the painting of Mrs. Finestein, Miss Stuart, and Mr. Banerji, *The Three Muses*, is glossed in the catalogue copy by Charna as a "disconcerting deconstruction of perceived gender and its relationship to perceived power, especially in respect to numinous imagery." Elaine comments with characteristic acerbity, "If I hold my breath and squint, I can see where she gets all that: all Muses are supposed to be female, and one of these is not." But the grouping obviously does signify interrelations of power and gender. The three muses, who are also in this depiction the three kings of Christian mythology, are all feminized inasmuch as all are racially and nationally other in terms of the hostile Toronto culture, at the same time as they are masculinized by the power of their largely fortuitous effects on Elaine's life, effects that associate them, in turn, with the redemptive female figure of Our Lady of Perpetual Help. Like Elaine's narrative as a whole, this painting, whether Elaine wills the interpretation or not, shows the contingency and fluidity of gender boundaries, especially within a framework of redemption by the mystically feminine, a framework in which the last is, paradoxically, first.

Another painting, the triptych *One Wing*, shows in its center panel Stephen falling, holding in his hand a child's wooden sword. The situation alludes to Stephen's death at the hands of the terrorists. Elaine comments, "This is the kind of thing we do, to assuage pain," and goes on to note, "Charna thinks it's a statement about men, and the juvenile nature of war." Despite the criticism implied by the juxtaposition, the two statements are not necessarily opposed. The World War II airplane and the luna moth of the flanking panels are both images of flight referring to situations in which Stephen was unable to see himself as endangered. The airplane recalls his childhood fascination with the war and his insistent command, "You're dead," a command reflecting his faith that war could have no real consequences for the real people of his experience: "He thinks our side is the good side, and therefore will win." The luna moth is part of a dense network of motifs connecting themes of flight, vulnerability, mutilation, and hope; in particular, it evokes the episode in which Stephen is arrested after chasing a rare butterfly onto a military testing zone, an illustration of his unawareness of the disciplinary system and of his own visibility within that system.

Throughout *Cat's Eye*, such ostensibly "wrong" readings of Elaine's work supplement and enrich the descriptions of the paintings themselves, which accrete meanings in strata, like a series of liquid transparencies laid on top of one another. These outside interpretations are layered over the autobiographical account of the events that motivated the work, although sometimes the autobiographical explication is formulated in pointed opposition to the external glosses, as in "But it was only my mother cooking, in the ways and places she used to cook, in the late forties." "But it was only" attempts to replace the reductive accounts provided by viewers—"Because of when it was done and what was going on in those years, some people thought it was about the Earth Goddess, which I found hilarious in view of my mother's dislike of housework. Other people though it was about female slavery, others that it was a stereotyping of women in negative and trivial domestic roles"—but succeeds in being similarly reductive. All the implications inhere in the description of the painting; all are revealed in the successive acts of interpretation in this passage, although each act of interpretation aims to cancel out all the others.

At the same time, however, *Cat's Eye* itself is built up of these autobiographical interpretations, inasmuch as the stories that motivated each painting are the key components of the narrative comprising the novel as a whole. In this respect, autobiographical information is crucial to understand the paintings wholly—and it is completely unavailable to the viewers who are posited as inside the novel. The fact that Elaine can no longer tell her paintings "what to mean" insures that they will never communicate as fully to these internal viewers as they do to the reader of the novel. Looked at this way, the creator's intention is the secret truth of the work of art. It is absolutely privileged and by the same token absolutely private, hidden within the artifact but discernible only when the creator chooses to reveal it through an explication that stands alongside the artifact; an explication which, unlike the work of art itself, carries the unambiguous guarantee, This is the truth, this is what really happened.

These two positions on the roles of authorial and outside critical interpretation enact a constantly shifting power imbalance between the creator and the consumer of the artistic work. In *Cat's Eye*, as in many other Atwood novels, the main source of this imbalance is the limited first-person narrator, who is unreliable inasmuch as she cannot *see* enough—either of her own motivations and desires and the forces conditioning them, or of the consequences of certain of her choices. Elaine Risley's development is a growing awareness of the implications of both her feelings and her actions, but like other Atwood narrators she never comprehends as much as is at least theoretically available to the reader, who can intervene at crucial junctures to fill in.

Of course, the narrator is not the author of the novel itself. Inasmuch as Elaine Risley is a figure *in* the text of *Cat's Eye* her limitation is one manifestation of Margaret Atwood's thematic and formal control. Evident control has been a distinguishing mark of Atwood's fiction from the beginning, and it is everywhere in this novel: in the complex patterning of images and motifs, in the careful piling of detail upon detail culminating in a neat turn into epigrammatic epiphany ("Up ahead there are huge oblong towers, all of glass, lit up, like enormous gravestones of cold light. Frozen assets", and in the ordinary words held up to the light and examined for traces of their origins or their alternative functions ("That word has been through a lot. Noble lady, Dark Lady, she's a real lady, old-lady lace, Listen lady, Hey lady watch where you're going, Ladies' Room run through with lipstick and replaced with Women"; "'Suck' is an especially satisfying word. . . . It suggests thumbs and babies. I haven't yet considered what else might be sucked, or under what circumstances").

The enactment of what Strehle calls "a feminist art that quarrels with its own grim origins" by deliberately insisting on its "lack of mastery over the subjects [that the paintings] show" thus conflicts with—and ultimately is comprehended by—an overmastering text that foregrounds its desire to control audience response. But both theories of art reflect ideologies that are in dialogue in the novel itself. The desire for control acquires a larger context—and an implicit self-critique—in the representation of the inevitably failed power to control the surveying, fixing gaze of the panoptic viewer. In this context, the writer is engaged in an ultimately futile battle to control what her reader sees. While this notion of art as power over the gaze is consonant with the project of revenge, Elaine's original intention in the Mrs. Smeath paintings and an intention that Atwood has discussed forthrightly with creative-writing students, the rereadings of the paintings in *Cat's Eye* suggest forcibly that the writer is as much a prisoner of the representational structure she creates as a monitory figure who can dictate how others look—in both senses of the phrase.

The second theory of art within the novel places the artist at a utopian remove from the disciplinary society and grants to her a capacity for comprehension that forgoes blame and derives its power from the intrinsic persuasiveness of its superior vision. The political and especially feminist twist that *Cat's Eye* gives to this familiar account of the artist as seer is the corollary that vision has as an essential component the possibility of the egalitarian coexistence of seer and seen in an intersubjective re-viewing that could entail a similar coexistence of audience and writer. But the marginal status, within the disciplinary society, of the "two old women giggling over their tea" intimates in turn how unlikely and how marginal will be any art that attempts to establish such a relation between author and reader. Many reviewers' responses to *Cat's Eye* have indicated how eagerly readers will seize on an opportunity to assign blame—most obviously, to blame female characters for Elaine's victimization, without taking into account anything of the political surroundings of this victimization. Reader participation inevitably carries societal conditioning with it, as indeed *Cat's Eye* has demonstrated. The idyllic freedom of two old women returning to pre-adolescence, and doing it right this time, cannot be assumed to be a possible relationship between writer and reader in a society constructed to perpetuate misogyny.

Yet the image has enormous pathos, freighted as it is with the grief over lost things that permeates the whole novel. Within *Cat's Eye*, art arises on the site of a loss for which it cannot compensate, a loss that it also cannot comprehend or even, in any direct way, represent. But *Cat's Eye* itself does better. It evokes this loss, marking the place of absence, of separation, by offering as a culminating image a representation *of* unmediated subjectivity—

"Two old women giggling over their tea"—that is doubly distanced because it is "something that will never happen." In the mode of the disciplinary society and of the masculinist art that Elaine equivocally embraces, this image isolates, distances, and freezes the object of desire, at one stroke denying the fulfillment of that desire and guaranteeing that the desire will be perpetuated. In what may be the most nearly autobiographical moment in Atwood's work, it points to the limits of Atwood's art and to what is lost because of these limits, although it also insists that the loss is necessary and that the limits are also what make the *acknowledgment* of loss possible. The oxymoron of "autobiographical fiction" in *Cat's Eye* finally authorizes not a transgressive glimpse into some pre-existing private realm of the "real," but a reminder that the "self" of self-representation is always seer as well as seen, and that both seer and seen are implicated in the social construction of how one looks.

HILDE STAELS

Atwoodian Gothic:
From Lady Oracle *to* The Robber Bride

Atwoodian Gothic is sinister and jokey, rather like the scary game which Atwood describes in *Murder in the Dark*, a game about murderers, victims and detectives played with the lights off. The only other thing the reader needs to know is that the victim is always silent and that the murderer always lies:

> In any case, that's me in the dark. I have designs on you. I'm plotting my sinister crime, my hands are reaching for your neck or perhaps, by mistake, your thigh. You can hear my footsteps approaching, I wear boots and carry a knife, or maybe it's a pearl-handled revolver, in any case I wear boots with very soft soles, you can see the cinematic glow of my cigarette, waxing and waning in the fog of the room, the street, the room, even though I don't smoke. Just remember this, when the scream at last has ended and you've turned on the lights: by the rules of the game, I must always lie.

This game is emblematic of Atwoodian Gothic; its aim is to scare, yet it is a sort of fabricated fright; there are rules and conventions and we enter into a

From *Margaret Atwood's Novels: A Study of Narrative Discourse*, by Hilde Staels. © 1995 by A. Francke Verlag Tübingen und Basel.

kind of complicity because we want to be frightened. Atwood suggests, 'You can say: the murderer is the writer' and then either the book or the reader would be the victim, which makes an interesting identification between Gothic storyteller and murderer, trickster, liar. We could take that one stage further with Atwood's female Gothic storytellers, Joan Foster in *Lady Oracle*, Zenia in *The Robber Bride* and Atwood herself, identified as sibyls, witches, supreme plotters all ('I have designs on you').

So, what is Gothic? At the core of the Gothic sensibility is fear—fear of ghosts, women's fear of men, fear of the dark, fear of what is hidden but might leap out unexpectedly, fear of something floating around loose which lurks behind the everyday. The emblematic fear within Gothic fantasy is that something that seemed to be dead and buried might not be dead at all. Hence the Gothic outbreaks of terror and violence as things cross forbidden barriers between dream and waking, life and death. It is easy to recognise a Gothic novel for it is characterized by a specific collection of motifs and themes, many of which come through folklore, fairytale, myth and nightmare. One of the most succinct accounts of the Gothic as a literary genre is Eve Kosofsky Sedgwick's critical study *The Coherence of Gothic Conventions*, which identifies two key terms to define the Gothic: the Unspeakable and Live Burial. Arguably those terms might be seen as different images for the same thing for they both relate to what is hidden, secret, repressed, and which is threatening precisely because it is still alive and blocked off from consciousness though ready to spring out, transformed into some monstrous shape—like Freud's *unheimlich*, both familiar and alien to us. It is this uncanny quality of Gothic which is embodied in its obsession with the transgression of boundaries and with transformations—'change from one state into another, change from one thing into another.' On the level of the supernatural, there is the phenomenon of ghosts transgressing boundaries between life and death, while on the psychological level there is the erosion of boundaries between the self and the monstrous Other. (What does a Gothic protagonist see or fear when she looks in the mirror?) In the borderline territory between conscious and unconscious, a space is opened up for doubles and split selves, which are not total opposites but dependent on each other and linked by a kind of unacknowledged complicity, like Dr Frankenstein and his monster. To return to that game in *Murder in the Dark*: Atwood reminds players that they may take turns to be murderer or victim, for one role does not preclude the other. Gothic finds a language for representing areas of the self (like fears, anxieties, forbidden desires) which are unassimilable in terms of social conventions. In relation to fiction, the major point to consider is how these transgressions are expressed through narrative, most obviously in the shifts from realism to fantasy signalled in dreams and hallucinations, when frequently the working out of dreams is crucial to the plot. There is also the difficulty any Gothic story has in getting itself told at all: Gothic plots are characterised by enigmas, multiple stories embedded in the main story, multiple narrators and shifting points of view, and mixed genres, where fairy tale may blur into history or autobiography. At all times the Gothic narrative suggests the co-existence of the everyday alongside a shadowy nightmarish world.

Not surprisingly, the Gothic romance has traditionally been a favourite genre for women writers, from Ann Radcliffe's *The Mysteries of Udolpho* (1794), Mary Shelley's *Frankenstein* (1818), the Brontës' *Wuthering Heights* and *Jane Eyre* (1840s), through to Daphne Du Maurier's *Rebecca* (1938), Jean Rhys's *Wide Sargasso Sea* (1966), and the contemporary fiction of Margaret Atwood, Beryl Bainbridge, Alice Munro. It is a devious literature through which to express female desires and dreads, and in Atwood it is easy to see the traditional forms surviving, updated but still retaining their original charge of menace and mystery, while balancing women's urge toward self-discovery and self-assertiveness with self-doubts, between celebration of new social freedoms and women's sense of not being free of traditional assumptions and myths about femininity. It is to this territory of Gothic romance that Atwood returns again and again, using its images and motifs and its narratives of transgression. To glance briefly at the pervasiveness of Gothic in Atwood, one would need to start with her early watercolours from the late 1960s where sinister knights in armour with hidden faces peer at damsels dressed in red, or dark male figures hold unconscious purple female bodies in their giant arms. *Surfacing* might be construed as a ghost story in the Canadian wilderness, a reading suggested by Atwood in an early interview when she explained that she was writing in the tradition of the psychological ghost story:

> You can have the Henry James kind, in which the ghost that one sees is in fact a fragment of one's own self which has split off, and that to me is the most interesting kind and that is obviously the tradition I'm working in.

The motifs of haunted wilderness and the split self are still there 20 years later in the story 'Death by Landscape' in *Wilderness Tips*, just as the werewolf image which was there in *The Journals of Susanna Moodie* recurs in 'Age of Lead' in that same collection. The title story in *Bluebeard's Egg* (1983) is a modern revision of fairy tale, while *Bodily Harm* (1981) and *The Handmaid's Tale* (1985) exploit traditional Gothic motifs in their

representation of classic female fears of sexual violence or imprisonment. In
Cat's Eye (1988) the protagonist is haunted by the past and by her
doppelganger Cordelia ('Lie down, you're dead!') who represents the other
half of herself, her dark mad twin. There is also a poem 'The Robber
Bridegroom' in *Interlunar* (1984), and it is interesting to note that 'The
Robber Bridegroom' was considered by Atwood as a possible title for *Bodily
Harm*. In this recirculation of images and themes, we note very repetitive
patterns which are the identifying marks of a literary genre. The same stories
are being retold, as the reader is constantly reminded through intertextual
allusions to fairy tales and old Gothic romances, so that versions that might
look contemporary and new circle around old enigmas. It is from this Gothic
continuum that I wish to single out *Lady Oracle* (1976) and *The Robber Bride*
(1993) in order to examine what transformations of Gothic conventions
Atwood has managed in novels that are nearly 20 years apart; to see how her
changing use of Gothic conventions reflects her responses to shifts in
cultural mythology, especially in her thinking about women. What we find is
the reworking of traditional Gothic motifs within the frames of realistic
fiction, for unlike her protagonist Joan Foster in *Lady Oracle*, Atwood does
not 'write with her eyes closed.' On the contrary, Atwood is an attentive and
often satirical critic of contemporary Canada, exposing popular myths and
social ideologies for Atwood has designs on us. But then, of course, so did
Joan Foster, and so did Zenia, the Robber Bride.

Atwood described *Lady Oracle* as 'a realistic comic novel colliding with
Gothic conventions—I give you *Northanger Abbey*', as she explained for a
lecture in 1982. It is also a fictive autobiography, told by a woman who is a
novelist and a poet, suggesting shadowy parallels with Atwood herself in her
early days of fame when she was becoming a cultural ikon in Canada. More
to the point because this novel is not autobiography but an autobiographical
fiction, there are strong parallels with *Cat's Eye* told by that other successful
woman artist, Elaine Risley the painter. In both cases a woman struggles to
find her voice, to define her identity through telling her life story in different
versions. *Lady Oracle* and *Cat's Eye* are curiously similar autobiographical
projects because the stories the protagonists tell offer multiple versions of
their lives which never quite fit together to form the image of a unified and
coherent self. Who is Joan Foster, who writes popular Gothic romances
under the pseudonym Louisa K. Delacourt? What is the significance of Lady
Oracle, Joan's other pseudonym when she writes poetry? The one thing the
reader can be sure about Joan is that she is a fantasist, and a trickster: 'All my
life I'd been hooked on plots'.

    Lady Oracle is a story about storytelling, both the stories themselves and
the writing process, for Joan offers us multiple narratives figuring and

refiguring herself through different narrative conventions. The novel is structured through a series of interlocking frames. First, there is the story of Joan's real life in the present, set in Italy where she has escaped after her fake suicide in Toronto, Canada. Enclosed within this is her private memory narrative of a traumatic childhood filled with shame, pain and defiance centering on her relationship with her neurotic mother, of an adolescence when she escapes to London and becomes a writer of popular Gothics, her marriage to a Canadian, her celebrity as a poet, to be followed by the threat of blackmail and her second escape from Canada to Italy. Embedded within this narrative are snippets from Joan's Gothic romances ('Bodice Rippers' as she calls them), which provide more glamorous and dangerous plots than everyday life in Toronto, or even in Italy, during the late 1960s and early 1970s. Then there is a fourth narrative thread, the curiously mythic 'Lady Oracle' poems, produced as Joan believes by Automatic Writing when she looks into a dark mirror in her bedroom in Toronto. These shifting frames generate a series of comic collisions, confrontations and escape attempts, but there are no clear boundaries between them as borders blur between present and past, art and life. Joan's fantasies of escape and transformation are always duplicitous and riddled with holes, so that one story infiltrates another and fantasy is under continual barrage from the claims of real life. Joan may adopt multiple disguises in the form of fancy costumes, wigs, different names and different personas, but 'it was no good; I couldn't stop time, I could shut nothing out.' Through this shimmer of different figures, the reader wonders if there is any chance of getting beyond the veils to the centre of the plot or to the enigma of Joan Foster herself. Do we ever get beyond the distorting funhouse mirrors? Joan is nothing if not a self-caricaturist as well as a parodist of Gothic romance conventions, as she switches between real life and fantasy roles in a continual process of double coding. All these fantasies are arguably distorted versions of herself, a process described by Paul de Man in his essay, 'Autobiography as Defacement': 'Autobiography deals with the giving and taking away of faces, with face and deface, figure, figurations, and disfiguration' in images of the self endlessly displaced and doubled.

It is arguable that Joan constructs the Gothic plots in her own life. From her point of view even her life story could be seen as a tale told by a ghost, speaking from beyond her watery grave in Lake Ontario: 'I planned my death carefully; unlike my life, which meandered along from one thing to another, despite my feeble attempts to control it.' Of course this 'death' is another of her contrived plots for Joan is not dead at all. One of the things that frightens her most in Italy is that people at home in Canada will think that she is really dead, and not even miss her. Having escaped from her husband Arthur in Toronto, Joan realises that the other side of her escape fantasy is isolation:

> The Other Side was no paradise, it was only a limbo. Now I
> knew why the dead come back to watch over the living: the
> Other Side was boring. There was no one to talk to and
> nothing to do.

Such reflection is a result of Joan's rueful recognition of the gap between real
life and fantasy, for she is haunted by memories of her visit to this same
Italian village the previous year with her husband and is now filled with
longing that he will come to rescue her from her own perfect plot which
begins to look 'less like a Fellini movie than that Walt Disney film I saw
when I was eight, about a whale who wanted to sing at the Metropolitan
Opera . . . but the sailors harpooned him'. Critics have been rather fond of
saying that Joan's real-life narrative and the Gothic novel she is writing in
Italy start off separate and gradually become entwined till at the end of the
narrative borders blur and Joan enters the Gothic maze in *Stalked by Love*.
That observation is true as far as it goes, but that is not far enough. Borders
between realism and fantasy are blurred from the beginning as Joan
continually slides from the embarrassments of the present into fantasy
scenarios and back again, for she is an escape artist who is beset by one
inconvenient insight, 'Why did every one of my fantasies turn into a trap?'
     However, before going any further into Joan's Gothic plotting, it is
advisable to look at the title *Lady Oracle* in order to see what it signifies about
Joan as a woman writer who faces the challenging questions: How do you
find a voice to speak for yourself, and what do you say when you do? The
most significant thing about an Oracle is that it is a voice which comes out
of a woman's body and is associated with hidden dangerous knowledge, but
that it is not her own voice. The voice of the Delphic Oracle was the voice
of the god Apollo, or earlier the voice of the Earth Goddess. Atwood's
research notes for her novel contain a significant amount of material on
oracles (from Robert Graves, *The Greek Myths*), on Pythia the priestess of
Apollo at Delphi (from Lamprière's *Classical Dictionary*), and on the Sibyl of
Cumae (from Virgil's *Aeneid*, translated by C. Day Lewis, and from Ovid's
Metamorphoses, Book XIV, in Loeb's Classical Library). Both Pythia and the
Cumaen Sibyl are described as 'possessed', the Pythoness speaking 'in a
convulsive state . . . the oracles of the god, often with loud howlings and
cries', and the Sibyl whose 'fey heart swelled in ecstasy . . . More than mortal
her utterance.' The role of prophetess is here in danger of being reduced to
the role of the hysteric, for the oracle is 'beyond herself' and not conscious
of what she is saying. Joan Foster presents herself as uncomfortably close
to this model—not only in the automatic writing of her Lady Oracle poems
but also in her costume Gothics. They too are a form of automatic writing,

for Joan is writing through Gothic romance formulas and she types with her eyes closed. The very name 'Lady Oracle' is not her own choice but is chosen for her by her male publishers: 'You write, you leave it to us to sell it.' When she becomes a celebrity, Joan even begins to feel a certain paranoia about her persona:

> It was as if someone with my name were out there in the real world, impersonating me . . . doing things for which I had to take the consequences: my dark twin . . . She wanted to kill me and take my place, and by the time she did this no one would notice the difference because the media were in on the plot, they were helping her.

In other words, Joan starts to feel like one of the victims in her Gothic romances written under her other *nom de plume* 'Louisa K. Delacourt' borrowed from the name of her deceased Aunt Lou. In her fiction, her poetry and her interviews, Joan refuses to take responsibility for what she says; though from another point of view her double identities also provide her with a kind of escape, for she cannot be defined by any statement made in her name and the name is always changing. There is Lady Oracle for whom Joan is merely the medium and Louisa K. Delacourt is the name of her dead aunt. Joan uses the names as alibis:

> The really important thing was not the books themselves, which continued to be much the same. It was the fact that I was two people at once, with two sets of identification papers, two bank accounts, two different groups of people who believed I existed. I was Joan Foster . . . But I was also Louisa K. Delacourt.
>
> As long as I could spend a certain amount of time each week as Louisa, I was all right.

Jean is a very slippery subject, parallel with Elaine Risley in *Cat's Eye* who does not take on the interpretative responsibility for arranging the paintings at her first retrospective exhibition but leaves it to the gallery directors and who says, 'I'm what's left over'. In turn, Joan and Elaine are like Offred in *The Handmaid's Tale* whose voice tapes are edited years after she is dead by someone else. All these women are 'missing persons'; they have no authoritative voice over their work, and they are all escape artists. Joan gives her readers multiple versions of the truth about herself, cultivating duplicity with an energy that suggests the forces of repression behind her performances:

> It was true I had two lives, but on off days I felt that neither of them was completely real . . . If I brought the separate parts of my life together (like uranium, like plutonium, harmless to the naked eye, but charged with lethal energies) surely there would be an explosion.

Indeed, Joan never does take the consequences for the minor explosion she participates in when she and her lover the 'Royal Porcupine' (whose less picturesque name is Chuck Brewer) stage an absurdly sixties happening in a snowy park using the sticks of dynamite which Joan is supposed to be carrying around Toronto for a crazy Canadian nationalist plot to blow up the Peace Bridge at Niagara Falls. She even uses those explosives as the basis for another of her fantastical plots, her fake suicide which is transformed in her absence into a real life murder mystery.

Joan assumes no responsibility for what she writes and yet through this pose she tells us a great deal about herself—her fears and ambitions and her forbidden feelings. It is through her memory narrative of a middle class Toronto childhood, that 'can of worms' as she calls it, that Joan reveals the sequence of humiliations and betrayals against which she has constructed her multiple self-defenses. Joan's life story is a tale of grotesques and monsters for Joan is an only child, the unwanted products of an unhappy wartime marriage, who cannot please her neurotic mother and who in a rage of adolescent defiance overeats till she looks like 'a beluga whale':

> I ate to defy her, but I also ate from panic. Sometimes I was afraid I wasn't really there, I was an accident; I'd heard her call me an accident. Did I want to become solid, solid as a stone so she wouldn't be able to get rid of me? What had I done? Had I trapped my father . . . had I ruined my mother's life? I didn't dare to ask.

For Joan, everyone is shadowed by their opposites. The most important and duplicitous figure is her mother, who 'puts on her face' with its larger-than-life lipsticked mouth, 'the real one showing through the false one like a shadow'. Her small daughter really believes her to be a 'triple-headed monster', and that mother returns to haunt her throughout her adult life. Joan's father, the benevolent anaesthetist also had a double career as a

French-speaking Canadian who had been an assassin for the Resistance during the war, a fact which causes his daughter as much bewilderment as the flasher in the ravines who might also have been the Daffodil Man who rescued Joan when she was tied up and left behind by her girl friends after Brownies. There is also her fat fairy godmother Aunt Lou, who leaves Joan enough money in her will to escape from home but only on condition that she loses weight. It is no wonder that Joan suspects everybody of having a secret life and that she sees herself too as a 'duplicitous monster' whose only means of expression is through disguise. Joan knows that value of this double coding when she becomes a self-parodist at the age of seven in a dance recital, where instead of being the fairy, the fat little girl is tricked into being a mothball in a furry suit. Her 'dance of rage and destruction' is interpreted by the watching parents as a comic entertainment to be applauded ('Bravo Mothball!'). Behind the performance Joan's anguished childhood self remains hidden. It is no wonder that as an adult Joan cannot bring herself to tell her raw-boned idealist husband that she writes costume Gothics for 'He wouldn't have understood' and she is afraid of losing his affection and respect. Indeed, Joan's primary motivating force is fear—fear of the past, fear of blackmail, fear of the loss of Arthur's love, and above all, fear of being found out. After all, 'when it came to fantasy lives I was a professional'.

In such a context Joan's insistence on the 'automatic writing' of the *Lady Oracle* poems begins to look like a psychological necessity, though Atwood's own comments on such a method of production are sceptical:

> In my experience, writing is not like having dreams . . . It's much more deliberate . . . You can shape your material into a coherent pattern.

An examination of the *Lady Oracle* manuscript material bears out this conscious construction, for in the Atwood Papers there is a letter to her research assistant in which Atwood asks for a map of Italy, an English–Italian dictionary, details of the water fountains in the Villa D'Este at Tivoli, 'especially; the sphinxes with water squirting out their tits and the statue of Diana of Ephesus which is covered with breasts', an Italian *photoromanze*, and a copy of *Jane Eyre*. 'Later, I'll tell you what all this is for'.

The connections between *Jane Eyre* and Joan's popular Gothic romances are plain, though we may question why anyone would write them and why so many women read them. Joan's short answer would be, 'The pure quintessential need of my readers for escape, a thing I myself understood only too well'. Joan explains and justifies her project to herself: 'The truth was that I dealt in hope, I offered a vision of a better world, however preposterous. Was that so terrible?' However, the fact remains that there is more anguish and violence than pleasure in these Gothic scenarios of *Escape from Love*, *Love My Ransom*, and *Stalked by Love*. As Atwood remarked when discussing *Lady Oracle* in an interview with Joyce Carol Oates in 1978:

> I've always wondered what it was about these books that appealed—do so many women think of themselves as menaced on all sides, and of their husbands as potential murderers? And what about that 'Mad Wife' left over from *Jane Eyre*? Are these our secret plots?

Janice Radway in *Reading the Romance* would seem to agree with Atwood when she argues that the appeal of popular romance fiction relates less to escapism than to women's fears about the loss of independence, male indifference and male violence. These issues are recuperated under the happy endings of romance, though women know such endings to be illusory. Possibly women read these novels out of lack and dissatisfaction, which is why they need to keep on reading them—or, in Joan's case, to keep on writing them.

How does Joan figure out her life (while stepping aside from her real life) through her Gothic plots, which are as grotesquely distorted as the fantasy of the discarded sodden clothes which come back to haunt her dreams in Italy, or the Fat Pink Lady fantasy of her childhood? This last is an extraordinarily interesting fantasy which is both reflection and sublimation for Joan, a grotesque fairytale image of 'The Biggest Modern Woman in the World' who walks across Canada on a tightrope, much to everyone's amazement, but who in real life is nothing but a circus freak. As Joan insists, it's all a trick, but like her other more sinister Gothic narrative tricks, 'it's still not so simple'. The Charlottes, Felicias, and Penelopes are all partial figurings of her fantasies of desirable femininity, while their persecutions are displacements of her own sense of inadequacy and dread. These Costume Gothics also allow Joan to indulge her New World fascination with Europe—its history, its decaying aristocracy, and its words for outmoded female fashions like 'fichu,' 'paletot' and 'pelisse'. It is no accident that her first lover was a Polish count who rescued Joan when she fell off a bus in London. It was Paul who encouraged her to write costume Gothics while he indulged his own fantasies by writing nurse novels under the pseudonym 'Mavis Quilp' a name he had found in Dickens. The titles of Paul's Nurse novels are as formulaic of that genre as Joan's Gothics: *Janet Holmes, Student Nurse, Helen Curtis, Senior Nurse, Anne Armstrong, Junior*

Nurse, and finally—after he comes to Canada, *Nurse of the High Arctic*. It is also symptomatic of Joan's imaginative transformations of real life that she would fall in love with Arthur Foster, a graduate student from the Maritimes, not in their native Canada but in Hyde Park, London, when she happened to bump into him while he was distributing leaflets for Ban the Bomb and she was walking the course for one of her costume Gothics. This chance encounter gives Arthur a Byronic tinge which is entirely imaginary:

> I looked at him more closely. He was wearing a black crew-neck sweater, which I found quite dashing. A melancholy fighter for almost-lost causes, idealistic and doomed, sort of like Lord Byron, whose biography I had just been skimming. We finished collecting the pamphlets, I fell in love.

Joan spells out her Gothic formula when she is looking over the proofs for her *Lady Oracle* poems:

> On re-reading, the book seemed quite peculiar. In fact, except for the diction, it seemed a lot like one of my standard Costume Gothics, but a Gothic gone wrong. It was upside-down somehow. There were the sufferings, the hero in the mask of a villain, the villain in the mask of a hero, the flights, the looming death, the sense of being imprisoned, but there was no happy ending, no true love. The recognition of this half-likeness made me uncomfortable. Perhaps I should have taken it to a psychiatrist instead of a publisher . . . and no one would understand about the Automatic Writing.

Joan does not understand it herself but Atwood does. There is a passage in an essay Atwood wrote in 1965 on Rider Haggard's novel *She*, which casts light on her attitude to Joan's psychological riddle. Haggard claimed that he had written his novel in a trance, and Atwood quotes one of his biographers as saying, 'Haggard was writing deep, as though hypnotized'; that biographer proceeded to connect *She* with Haggard's childhood traumas and his interest in myth—all of which sounds uncomfortably close to the psychological and mythic interpretations of *Lady Oracle*. However, Atwood's wry comment is worth noting: 'Haggard may have been writing "deep, as though hypnotized"; but if so the unconscious experience he was drawing upon was the creation of his [five] previous books.'

While this does not rule out psychological and mythic interpretations of the narrator's experience in *Lady Oracle*, it does point to the location of

Joan's sources of reference within her own real-life experience which is already written into this novel. Of special significance are her experiences with Aunt Lou and the spiritualists and her guilts about her mother—one of those terrible War Bride mothers, monsters with triple heads—who turns up again tripled, as three mothers in *The Robber Bride* and who are responsible for generating their daughter's insecurities and escape fantasies. The Gothic images of the 'Lady Oracle' title poem deriving from *She*, Tennyson's 'The Lady of Shallott,' Khalil Gibran and Rod McKuen, display an excess of signification which hints at complex energies incompletely understood by the subject herself for most of the novel. Joan's tormented relationship with her mother forms the 'unspeakable' subtext throughout her real life narrative, for even after she leaves home (where her mother in a fit of rage and frustration plunges a kitchen knife into Joan's arm) she is haunted by her mother's 'astral body' and her mother's face remembered from childhood 'crying soundlessly, horribly; mascara was running from her eyes in black tears'. More disturbingly this visionary visit to London signals her mother's death, which was apparently accidental but which Joan in her Gothic imaginings speculates might have been suicide or even murder by her father. The unacknowledged symbiotic relation between mother and daughter is signaled by a narrative switch from this memory of her mother's death to Joan's present forlorn condition in Italy suffering from her own fake suicide: 'I'm not really dead', Joan writes to Arthur on a postcard.

The 'Lady Oracle' title poem adopts traditional symbolism which both veils and reveals Joan's repressed memories of her mother, whose ghost she had failed to recognise as the figure standing behind her when she looked into the dark mirror during her occult experiments:

> She is one and three
> The dark lady   the redgold lady
> the blank lady   oracle
> of blood, she who must be
> obeyed   forever

Though the words which come to Joan in her automatic writing experiment cry out for interpretation with 'iron', 'throat', 'knife' and 'heart', they are sufficiently indeterminate for her to be able to repress any recognition of the dark figure who 'certainly had nothing to do with me'. Only near the end of the novel when she is at her wit's end and cannot think of any way out of her Italian escape fantasy does Joan realise that she too is capable of hurting people and so learns to recognise some similarities between them. She is able finally to forgive her mother's ghost and so to free herself from guilt:

> It had been she standing behind me in the mirror . . . My
> mother was a vortex, a dark vacuum, I would never be able to
> make her happy. Or anyone else. Maybe it was time for me to
> stop trying.

This revelation occurs at the same time as Joan's growing unease with
her Gothic plots, in real life and in fiction. Whereas up to this time her novel
Stalked by Love had been progressing according to its set formula while her
real life narrative spiralled and twisted, now Joan's novel also swings out of
control when she finds that she is identifying with the villainess rather than
with the heroine. Her fake suicide begins to have real life consequences when
reports reach her that the two friends who had helped her have been arrested
on a murder charge in Toronto:

POETESS FEARED SLAIN IN TERRORIST PURGE!

Joan finds herself trapped in a bizarre plot not of her own making: 'I'd have
to go back and rescue them. I couldn't go back.' As borders blur, the only
thing Joan knows for certain is that she is going to have to let her heroine
Charlotte go into the maze in *Stalked by Love*. 'She'd wanted to go in ever
since reaching Redmond Grange.' This is a classic piece of Gothic plotting,
but again 'it's not so simple' as Atwood reminded an interviewer when
discussing *Lady Oracle*:

> In Gothic tales the maze is just a scare device. You have an old
> mansion with winding passages and a monster at the center.
> But the maze I use is a descent into the underworld.

We are reminded of the winding passages which Joan encountered in her
walk into the dark mirror of her unconscious. Is this the maze into which
Joan must go to answer the sphinx's riddle in order to live? And who is Joan's
double—the Gothic heroine or the villainess? Is Joan an innocent victim or
is she a witch (as the Italian villagers believe her to be)? Faithful to habit,
Joan closes her eyes and follows Charlotte into the conventional Gothic plot
design, but much to her surprise, this time the plot does not conform to
stereotype: 'I'd taken a wrong turn somewhere.' When Joan resumes her
storytelling after some accidental disruption, there is a crucial shift which
infringes the Gothic formula, for this time it is not the heroine who enters
the maze but the villainess Felicia; now it is she who is determined 'to
penetrate the secret at last'. There is a further slippage of conventions in the

scenario of the plot so that Joan's book beings to look less like a Gothic romance than like a Fellini film, for Felicia finds herself confronting four women all of whom claim to be what she is herself, 'Lady Redmond'. There is no way out for Felicia—or for Joan—except through a door which looks the same from both sides. When this opens to reveal Redmond (husband or killer?) standing on the threshold, Felicia addresses him as 'Arthur', which is the name of Joan's husband. The final Gothic image is of Redmond–Arthur, the demon-lover, reaching for Felicia's throat. He undergoes a dazzling series of transformations which shadow all the men with whom Joan has ever been involved: her father, her lovers, her husband and the villain of the Lady Oracle poems, till finally they collapse into the figure of death:

> *The flesh fell away from his face, revealing the skull behind it; he stepped towards her, reaching for her throat . . .*

Romance fantasy, violence and death are telescoped in the final scenario but nothing is resolved, for Joan is interrupted by the sound of footsteps coming down the path. Does she think it is Arthur or does she think it is the figure of death? And are they the same? (Why do women see their husbands as 'potential murderers'?) In this crisis Joan acts with the energy of one of her Gothic protagonists, bashing the male stranger on the head with an empty Cinzano bottle when he appears at her door and knocking him out. This is the explosion which she had feared as real life and the shadows of fiction come into collision.

The ending is deliberately bathetic, for the man who Joan fears has come for her life has in fact come for her life story. He is a reporter and Joan tells him her story, which we realise is the novel we have just been reading. Joan decides to give up costume Gothics and to write science fiction instead, as 'the future is better for you', facing up to responsibility for her own life and returning to Toronto. Like *Northanger Abbey* this novel is about the perils of Gothic thinking, just as it is also about the heroine's moral education: 'Joan's gotten as far as saying, I am who I am—take it or leave it.' Through telling her stories and coming to recognise their distortions and limits, Joan seems to be on the point of finding her way back into real life with all its messiness; 'I don't think I'll ever be a very tidy person'. However, again like Jane Austen, Atwood gives her plot a mischievous twist at the end: Joan reveals that she has not yet returned to Toronto but that she is still in Rome looking after the man whom she knocked on the head, 'I've begun to feel that he's the only person who knows anything about me.' Like the surfacer on the edge of the wilderness about to step forward, this is a suspension bridge ending.

The Robber Bride could be classified as a mutant form of female Gothic romance with the return of a 'demonic woman' from the dead in a story about transgressions, magic mirrors, shape changers and dark doubles, betrayals and omens of disaster, until the final defeat of the demon by three women friends when her body is burned up and its ashes scattered over the deepest part of Lake Ontario. There is also a multiple homecoming and the restoration of social and family order at the end. Here we find the key Gothic elements of the unspeakable and the buried life, together with a whole range of traditional motifs like vampires, spells, soul stealing and body snatching. It could also be argued here that the traditional Gothic plot is 'upside-down somehow', for though there are female victims there are no rescuing heroes, just as there are no tombs, mazes or haunted houses; in this story the blood belongs to history and to metaphor. All of which highlights the fact that *The Robber Bride* is a postmodernist fiction which exploits the shock effects that occur when Gothic fairy tale migrates into totally different genres like the failed family romance, the detective thriller, and documentary history. Tony, the professional historian among the three friends, knows this technique and how it might be used to engage the interest of listeners and readers:

> She likes the faint shock on the faces of her listeners. It's the mix of domestic image and mass bloodshed that does it to them.

The novel is both like a fairy tale as the title indicates and like history, which—as Tony explains—is always 'a construct', being the combination of different kinds of textual evidence: social documentary, private memory narrative and imaginative reconstruction. History is a discontinuous text with crucial gaps, so that different interpretations of the facts are always possible. Tony's words recall those of the American historiographer Hayden White, who suggests that the narratives of history always reconstruct the available facts of the past for readers in the present according to congenial ideological perspectives and identifiable literary patterns like the quest of the hero or fables of decline and fall.

The Robber Bride is the story of Zenia, another of Atwood's missing persons like Offred in *The Handmaid's Tale* or Cordelia in *Cat's Eye*, told through the multiple narratives of her three friends, Antonia Fremont (Tony), Roz Andrews, and Charis. As each of the three tells her own life story, different overlapping frames of reference are set up through which Zenia's character and significance are given meaning, though Zenia never exists independently of the stories of others. It is through her relationships that Zenia's identity is constructed, but it is also transformed as it is refigured through the perspectives of a military historian (Tony), a successful businesswoman (Roz) and a New Age mystic (Charis). These women are all living in Toronto on 23 October 1990, a crucial date for the narrative as on that day they are having lunch together at a fashionable Toronto restaurant called the Toxique and 'Zenia returns from the dead'. Through the swirl of contemporary history which Atwood sketches as a globalised scene of disasters the novel focuses on this one particular event, the kind of 'definitive moment' so useful to historians—and to novelists—after which 'things were never the same again. They provide beginnings for us, and endings too.' The postmodern self-reflexivity of the narrative is signalled in the first and last sections, entitled 'Onset' and 'Outcome', told by Tony who has a 'historian's belief in the salutary power of explanations' while realising the 'impossibility of accurate reconstruction.' Yet for all its enigmas and secrets and dark doubles—traditional Gothic elements which we are reminded are also the features of historical and psychological narratives—the novel is structured quite schematically, moving out from the crisis of Zenia's Gothic reappearance in the restaurant five years after her memorial service, then scrolling back through the life stories of all three in an attempt to track Zenia down, only to return to the Toxique again about a week later where the final crisis occurs. Though the three friends have met to exchange stories of their confrontation with Zenia, whom they have all tracked down on the same day and to celebrate their resistance and her defeat, they discover something even more startling has happened: Zenia is dead, really dead this time. As Tony's husband West says, 'Again? I'm really sorry', and there is a second memorial service for Zenia a year later which is a replay of the earlier one, when the friends scatter her ashes and return to Charis's house to tell stories about Zenia all over again.

Within that contemporary frame the memory narratives of Tony, Charis and Roz all occur in chronological sequence charting the history of changing cultural fashions in Toronto over the past 30 years. Tony's section ('Black Enamel') recounts her memories of meeting Zenia as a student in the 1960s as it tracks back through Tony's unhappy childhood, and recounts Zenia's many attempts to rob Tony of her money, her professional reputation, and her beloved West. Charis's section ('Weasel Nights') focuses of her memories of Zenia in the 1970s, the era of hippies and draft dodgers, her American lover Billy and their daughter August, with flashbacks to her childhood as a victim of sexual abuse; it ends with Zenia's seduction of Billy and his disappearance. Roz's section ('The Robber Bride') recounts her meetings with Zenia in the 1980s and follows a similar pattern of recall: childhood memories, marriage, motherhood and a successful business career, up to Zenia's seduction of Roz's husband Mitch and his eventual suicide. Only Tony survives with her man, and it is left to her to give a narrative shape to the fragments of Zenia which exist in the multiple anecdotes of these women: 'She will only be history if Tony chooses to shape her into history.'

For all three Zenia is the 'Other Woman', and her existence challenges the optimistic assertion of the early 1970s feminists which Roz recalls with some scepticism in 1990:

> 'The Other Woman will soon be with *us*', the feminists used to say. But how long will it take, thinks Roz, and why hasn't it happened yet?'

Zenia represents a powerfully transgressive element which continues to threaten feminist attempts to transform gender relations and concepts of sexual power politics. It is the otherness of Zenia which is figured in her three avatars in this novel, identified in the different life stories told by the three friends. One avatar is from fairy tale: *The Robber Bridegroom* by the Brothers Grimm, which is here feminised by Roz's twin daughters and savagely glossed by her through the parodic mode of double-coding:

> *The Robber Bride*, thinks Roz. Well, why not? Let the grooms take it in the neck for once. The Robber Bride, lurking in her mansion in the dark forest . . . The Rubber Broad is more like it—her and those pneumatic tits.

A second avatar is from the Bible, the figure of Jezebel in the Old Testament (1 Judges: 21). This is prefigured in Charis's childhood when with her grandmother she used to choose revelatory passages from the Bible at random and once lit on the death of Jezebel; that 'message' is confirmed on the very day of her last confrontation with Zenia by her morning Bible reading:

> She realized it as soon as she got up, as soon as she stuck her daily pin into the Bible. It picked out Revelations Seventeen, the chapter about the Great Whore.

There is a third avatar advanced by Tony near the end, that of the medieval French Cathar woman warrior, Dame Giraude, who in the thirteenth century defended her castle against the Catholic forces of Simon de Montfort. She was finally defeated and thrown down a well. This is the most unsettling of Zenia's avatars because it introduces a new perspective on her otherness which extends beyond the demonic. Just as Tony very much admires the reckless courage of Dame Giraude fighting for a lost cause so too she has a sneaking admiration for Zenia as a guerrilla fighter, despite her own humiliations at her hands:

> Zenia is dead, and although she was many other things, she was also courageous. What side she was on doesn't matter; not to Tony, not any more. There may not even have been a side. She may have been alone.

This is a recognition of the 'otherness' of Zenia, which cannot be accommodated within the parameters of the friends' stories. Tony has always associated Zenia with war—or 'Raw' in terms of her own subjective life. As a result of having known Zenia, Tony contemplates writing a book about female military commanders: '*Iron Hands, Velvet Gloves*, she could call it. But there isn't much material.' It is also Tony who wishes to give Zenia's ashes a sort of military burial on Armistice Day: 'An ending, then. November 11, 1991, at eleven o'clock in the morning, the eleventh hour of the eleventh day of the eleventh month.'

Whichever way we look at it, the most interesting figure in the novel is Zenia, the 'demonic woman'; she is there in the title and it is her story which defines and focuses the narrative. How is it that this traditionally Gothic figure survives as such a powerful force in Atwood's novel about contemporary social reality in 1990s Toronto? I wish to suggest that Atwood herself has done a Dr Frankenstein performance here, reassembling the parts of old legends and fairy tales in order to create her female monster who strides through three Canadian women's stories from the 1960s to the 1990s haunting their lives and wreaking havoc. However, Atwood revises the *Frankenstein* ending for it is the monster who destroys herself and it is the three friends who survive, though their memories of Zenia will live on. This is perhaps putting it rather melodramatically, but what Zenia represents will always exceed the bounds of decorum. Her power is the power of female sexuality, and the figure of Zenia relates directly to contemporary social myths about femininity; it also relates to male (and female) fantasies about the feminine; and in addition it challenges feminist thinking about gender relations. In her reading from *The Robber Bride* at the National Theatre in London in 1993 Atwood offered an important clue to an interpretation of her new novel when she said, 'It's a book about illusion: now you see it, now you don't.' Through Zenia's story Atwood confronts the ideology of traditional female romance where 'getting the power means getting the man, for the man *is* the power' (a statement made by Atwood in Wales in 1982). In this novel Atwood is investigating the extent to which that old proposition about power still holds true in the feminist—or post-feminist—1990s. In answer to a question asked at the National Theatre, 'Why should women now mind much about having men taken away from them by other women?', Atwood replied, 'This is not ideology; it's real life.' I would add that *The Robber Bride* is also fantasy, for this is a fantastic tale which examines once again the fantasies that underpin real life as well as fiction. Female sexuality has always been a problem for real women and real men, just as it is a problem for feminism: 'Male fantasies, male fantasies, is everything run by male fantasies?' Have women internalised these fantasies to such an extent that as Roz fears, 'You are a woman with a man inside watching a woman'? Atwood answers Roz's rhetorical questions by investigating the effects of fantasies of desirable femininity on women themselves. Zenia inhabits that fantasy territory:

> The Zenias of this world . . . have slipped sideways into dreams; the dreams of women too, because women are fantasies for other women, just as they are for men. But fantasies of a different kind.

Who is Zenia? And what kind of fantasy is she for her three contemporaries? Zenia seems to be real but she has a double existence for she belongs to two different fictional discourses, that of realism and of fantasy. She is a very transgressive figure who exists both as a character in the realistic fiction and also as the projection of three women's imaginations. As the Other Woman, her identity is fabricated through their stories about her, which are all stories of seduction, betrayal and humiliation. She herself is an enigma. Indeed she derives meaning only within the signifying structures of other people's stories and then always retrospectively. Zenia is a liar, a floating signifier, possibly a void and certainly a fraud. There is no indication that she has any independent subjective life, unless it is her 'aura' which is savagely at variance with her glamorous appearance; it is according to Charis, 'a turbulent muddy green . . . a deadly aureole, a visible infection'. At least this is how Zenia appears to one of her victims, always on the loose and ready to rob them of whatever is most precious to them. Zenia is everything they want most and everything they fear, for she represents their unfulfilled desires just as she represents their repressed pain-filled childhood selves. She is the dark double of them all, having multiple identities but no fixed identity. As Tony discovers after systematic research:

> Even the name Zenia may not exist . . . As for the truth about her, it lies out of reach, because—according to the records, at any rate—she was never even born.

Indeed, there are three different versions of Zenia's life story which have been tailored to fit the lives of Tony, Charis, Roz. She is what they most desire and dread to be. They all think occasionally that they would like to be someone other than the persons they are; most of the time they would like to be Zenia. It is no wonder that Tony reaches this conclusion:

> As with any magician, you saw what she wanted you to see; or else you saw what you yourself wanted to see. She did it with mirrors. The mirror was whoever was watching, but there was nothing behind the two-dimensional image but a thin layer of mercury.

Why cannot the three women let Zenia go, when they believe she is dead and when they have been to her memorial service five years earlier? Having been tricked and robbed by Zenia of men, money and self-confidence, they keep on meeting once a month for lunch because of her. The positive outcome is that they become fast friends, and it is worth noting that this is the first time such a group of loyal friends has appeared in Atwood's fiction. However, the fact remains that they meet to tell stories about Zenia, and actually it is their collective need of her which brings her back from the dead—or would do so, if she were really dead. When she commits suicide the three friends stand looking at her, still needing to believe that she is looking at them:

> Zenia revolves slowly, and looks straight at them with her white mermaid eyes.
> She isn't really looking at them though, because she can't.
> Her eyes are rolled back into her head.

The switch in narrative perspective reminds readers of whose is the active needy gaze and it is not Zenia's. Even when they have scattered her ashes in Lake Ontario at the end, their stories will still be about Zenia. They need her, or their stories about her, in order to define themselves, for the 'good' women are shown to be as dependent on the 'Other Woman' as she is on them. Zenia is inside each one, for she represents their unfulfilled shadow selves: 'Was she in any way like us? thinks Tony. Or, to put it the other way around: Are we in any way like her?' The dark reflection in the magic mirror is still there, in that 'infinitely receding headspace where Zenia continues to exist'.

As Alison Light wrote of Daphne du Maurier's *Rebecca*, that story of another 'demonic' woman:

> It demarcates a feminine subjectivity which is hopelessly split
> within the bourgeois relations . . . [it] makes visible the tensions
> within the social construction of femininity whose definitions
> are never sufficient and are always reminders of what is
> missing, what could be.

Light's remark about a woman's novel of the late 1930s needs very little
updating in relation to *The Robber Bride* written nearly 60 years later where
the concept of split feminine subjectivity is shared by all three of Atwood's
protagonists. Signalled in their doubled or tripled names (Tony / Antonia
Fremont / Tnomerf Ynot; Roz Andrews / Rosalind Greenwood / Roz
Grunwald; and Charis, formerly known as Karen), it is commented on
explicitly in all three. Since childhood Tony has always been able to write and
spell backwards: 'It's her seam, it's where she's sewn together; it's where she
could split apart.' Similar comments are offered about Charis, who was 'split
in two' as a sexually abused child and about Roz, whose life was 'cut in two'
when her Jewish father returned to Toronto after the Second World War. All
three have a seam, a split, which is the space of repression occupied by their
'dark twins' and Zenia operates on this edge of desire and lack which is the
borderline territory of the marauding Gothic Other.

Zenia is a threat because of her flaunting sexuality, her deceptions and
betrayals, her ruthless contempt for others and her random destructiveness.
With her siren song she seduces men and pulls them inside out and then
abandons them, though as Tony realises there is nothing gender-specific
about this with Zenia:

> How well she did it, thinks Tony. How completely she took us
> in. In the war of the sexes, which is nothing like a real war but
> is instead a kind of confused scrimmage in which people
> change allegiances at a moment's notice, Zenia was a double
> agent.

The otherness with Zenia represents has to be construed as deviant,
dangerous and threatening, and it has to be annihilated again and again. Her
punishment is very like Rebecca's in the earlier novel when Rebecca suffered
murder, vilification and cancer of the womb; Zenia commits suicide—or was
she murdered?—she is discredited through the revelation that she was a drug
dealer and possibly an arms smuggler, and she is reputed to be suffering from
ovarian cancer. As Tony repeats, 'Zenia is history', which does not necessarily
mean that she is dead and out of the way but that her story will continue to

be retold in different versions and endlessly speculated upon. It is symptomatic that even her funeral urn splits in two and her ashes blow about all over her three mourners. In this Gothic fairy tale retold from a feminist perspective, Zenia is a very disruptive figure for she is the spectacle of desirable femininity, a beautiful façade which hides whatever is behind it. (Is it neurotic insecurity? or nothingness? or frigidity? or is it ruthless egoism?) The final image of Zenia is given by Tony in her ambiguous elegy:

> She's like an ancient statuette dug up from a Minoan palace: there are the large breasts, the tiny waist, the dark eyes, the snaky hair. Tony picks her up and turns her over, probes and questions, but the woman with her glazed pottery face does nothing but smile.

Always an enigma, Zenia is still present or as present as she ever was within her shifting figurations. During the narrative she has taken on all the pains of the twentieth century as the Jewish victim of Nazi persecution and of European wars, as displaced person, as victim of violence and sexual abuse, as suffering from cancer, AIDS and drug addiction—just as she has been the ikon of desirable femininity, Robber Bride, Whore of Babylon, and woman warrior. She remains un-dead, a vampiric figure desiring 'a bowl of blood, a bowl of pain, some death' for she derives her life from the insecurities and desires of the living.

The ending of *The Robber Bride* is not an ending but merely 'a lie in which we all agree to conspire'. We are reminded of Atwood's voice in *Murder in the Dark* whispering, 'I have designs on you . . . by the rules of the game, I must always lie.' Atwood takes Gothic conventions and turns them inside out, weaving her illusions 'like any magician making us see what she wants us to see', as she transgresses the boundaries between realism and fantasy, between what is acceptable and what is forbidden. Of course these are fictions; *Lady Oracle* and *The Robber Bride* are illusions created by Atwood's narrative art, but they speak to readers in the present as they challenge us to confront our own desires and fears. Atwood, like the old Gothic novelists, like Joan Foster and like Zenia, 'does it with mirrors'.

CORAL ANN HOWELLS

Cat's Eye:
Creating a Symbolic Space out of Lost Time

Cat's Eye has triggered off responses that echo some typical reactions to Atwood's earlier texts. Some reviewers and critics primarily focus on its so-called "feminist" content. Others try to detect facts about Atwood's life in what is supposed to be a fictional autobiography. Still others find proof of Atwood's so-called "bleak" world view, mistaking the stance of a protagonist for the viewpoint of the artist. By neglecting the essential formal features that underlie the narrative text, many of them fail to discover the richness of the novel and the complexity of the stance of its protagonist.

In *Cat's Eye*, the critical evaluation of the protagonist is not so much achieved by means of an ironic/parodic mirroring between verbal forms, but rather, as in *Life Before Man*, through the ironic mirroring of the behaviour of certain characters. This kind of ironic mirroring will be treated as an important strategy of the narrative text. It will also be made clear that the study of metaphors in the context of mind-style analysis is essential for a better understanding of the psychological stance of Atwood's protagonist.

In addition, there will be a discussion of the relationship between "normality" and "abnormality" or "sanity" and "insanity," a central theme in this novel and one that is closely related to the technique of characterization. For the first time, Atwood explores this theme in the relationship between two characters. As in her earlier novels, she treats the multiplicity of the

From *Modern Novelists: Margaret Atwood.* © 1996 by Coral Ann Howells.

subject both formally and thematically through the image of joined twins,
the mirror image, and the eruption of unconscious processes in dreams and
"madness," with a view to undermining the protagonist's illusory belief in a
coherent identity and in a given causality.

Cat's Eye is a moving novel, written in the form of a search for lost time.
It deals with girlhood, a subject that is seldom explored in literature for adult
readers. Margaret Atwood thus moves away from the overtly political
concern of *Bodily Harm* and *The Handmaid's Tale* to fictionalize the
retrospective journey of a middle-aged woman through the cultural
landscape of the past. A Canadian painter, Elaine Risley, undertakes a
spiritual journey through the space that shaped her identity in the nineteen
forties, fifties and sixties.

1. Creating a Symbolic Space Out of the Past

Cat's Eye is Elaine Risley's fictional autobiography, or the story told by
"Risley in retrospect." The narrative starts with Elaine's general reflection on
time, one that runs through the novel like a thread: "Time is not a line but a
dimension, like the dimensions of space." The first-person narrator
introduces the physicist's notion of time that is juxtaposed in the novel with
the individual experience of time. At regular intervals in the story, Elaine
refers to the nature of the universe from the perspective of her brother
Stephen, who became an astrophysicist. Stephen's scientific theories about
the origin and nature of the universe, in particular the interrelationship
between space and time, throw an interesting light on the narrator's creation
of a universe in discourse: "Time is a dimension," he says. "You can't separate
it from space. Space-time is what we live in. He says there are no such things
as discrete objects which remain unchanged, set apart from the flow of time."

During her introspective journey, which involves a travelling through
layers of space-time, the narrator creates a symbolic landscape, a psychic or
human space. Elaine colours events "with her own light" while she attempts
to make sense of her past experience.

The titles that serve as headings to the different chapters are solidified
images, firmly imprinted on the narrator's mind. The titles refer to objects
such as: "Deadly Nightshade"; "Wringer"; "Cat's Eye"; "Our Lady of
Perpetual Help"; "Half a Face" and "Bridge," which re-emerge at various
stages during the journey. They prove to be key metaphors that disclose the
psychological stance of the protagonist and that constitute the unity of the
narrative text. The different spatio-temporal contexts add new meaning to
these objects. They become richer in connotations as the narrative develops.
They reappear in dreams, in Elaine's symbolic paintings, revealing a

dimension of meaning that remains concealed in the realm of rational thought. Because these objects reappear in different spatio-temporal arrangements, the discursive landscape that the narrator creates gradually becomes heavily symbolic.

2. In Search of Lost Time

Elaine Risley travels from Vancouver, where she lives in exile from the past, to Toronto where she is expected to attend an exhibition of her "feminist" paintings, announced as *Sub/Version*. She intends to just pass through the city, like a transient. She does not return "home" to backtrack the past, but due to the contingency of events the object of her retrospective journey shifts to a rediscovery of lost time through anamnesis.

Elaine retraces how, when she was a child, she was initiated into the world of experience and how she developed the image of herself which she now has in relation to the outside world. The first eight years of her life, Elaine hardly lived in the city, and she never even spent a full year at school. The family used to travel up North in the summer to give her father the opportunity to pursue his research as a forest entomologist, and back South, heading for Toronto, when autumn began. During early childhood, when she was torn between spending time in the bush of Northern Quebec and the city, other girls regularly made Elaine aware of her social maladjustment. The good times in the city did not stand out in Elaine's mind as much as the "bad time." She remembers experiencing each separation from the idyllic, Edenic world as a loss of happiness, for the natural world was the place where other girls could not get at her. "I can be free of words now, I can lapse back into wordlessness," Elaine says. In nature, where there is no need for socialization, she did not suffer from a sense of being violated by words. The experience of crossing the border on the way back to Toronto coincided with a shift from happiness, security, freedom and peace to a sense of loss, pain, loneliness, humiliation and the threat of more pain. Elaine recalls that: "until we moved to Toronto I was happy."

She recollects the gradual process of socialization and conditioning, the children's winning-losing games at school, a microcosmic adult world, a foretaste of the rules that dominate adult life in society. While the second World War is going on in the background, the boys form gangs, they play war games, whereas girls are involved in mind games, or games of manipulation. In the school's playground, girls and boys play at marbles. The cat's eye marble, with its eyelike concentric circles, receives connotations of a reflecting glass or the transfixing gaze of the other. "For marbles you're either the person setting up the target or the person shooting," Elaine says.

The narrative establishes a metaphorical relationship between these marble games and the word games played between girls.

Elaine is punished by three girls, Cordelia, Grace and Carol, for her social awkwardness, for her lack of backbone and stamina. During the children's circle game, with its rules of inclusion and exclusion, Cordelia seems to take the lead. She torments Elaine by alternatively excluding her from the circle of friends, because she does not fit in, and taking her back in again. Elaine suffers feelings of guilt and humiliation, because she believes in her own abnormality. She feels unable to stand up to her friends in whose eyes she knows herself to be wrong, awkward, weak and helpless.

The cause of Cordelia's sadistic games is her unhappiness about the way she is herself treated by adults. When she breaks the rules of "civilized" behaviour, she is regularly subjected to severe punishments inflicted on her by her father. His disapproving judgments fill Cordelia with a sense of pain, humiliation and a deep fear of being unwanted and unloved. In her relationship with Elaine, she seeks retaliation for what is done to her. Unaware of the consequences of her actions, she imposes the norms of her father on other socially awkward girls out of a sense of frustration with her own social maladjustment.

In the city, Elaine feels a pressure coming from outside, the need to be improved or moulded into a proper, adapted form. The child is struck by a washing machine wringer, without consciously reflecting on its metaphorical significance. A person put through a wringer that squeezes out all the liquid would emerge in a "flat, neat" shape. Elaine thinks "This would hurt a lot first, I know that. But there's something compelling about it. A whole person could go through the wringer and come out flat, neat, completed, like a flower pressed in a book."

Elaine's experience of having been subjected to mind games for several years results in a lifelong insecurity about her identity. The adult protagonist, who reveals herself as a hypersensitive, tormented individual, accuses Cordelia of making her believe that she was nothing, of being at the root of a sense of social inadequacy and awkwardness that she has never managed to overcome. The small, mean voice of a nine-year-old girl remains embedded in Elaine's mind, the voice of a demonic accuser, an accusing memory, a tyrannical judge.

Around the age of nine, Elaine undergoes a traumatic experience that will lead to her knowledge of evil powers in others. Cordelia digs a hole in her parents' back garden. Elaine, expected to play the role of the beheaded Mary Queen of Scots, is put in the hole by her friends. The latter subsequently sneak away and abandon her. After this moment of betrayal, Elaine loses her blind trust in others. She sees them as evil in essence and herself as a helpless victim of their destructive power. This traumatic event brings about a deep sense of shame, guilt, terror and failure that will haunt Elaine for the rest of her life. She tries to repress the experience, but the pain mark will remain. "I have no image of myself in the hole; only a black square filled with nothing, a square like a door. Perhaps the square is empty; perhaps it's only a marker, a time marker that separates the time before it from the time after. The point at which I lost power," Elaine says. Gradually, Elaine's body will be "emptying itself of feeling" and the future will close on her "like a door." Convinced of her own nothingness, she moves away from daylight, entering a tunnel of darkness.

Cordelia strikes terror into the hearts of the other girls by recounting supernatural events that stem from folktales or legends. She informs then that one drop of the deadly nightshade berries "can turn you into a zombie." Significantly, this will prove to be a foreboding of Elaine's mental state during adolescence and adulthood.

Time passes, but Elaine does not participate in its process, at least as far as the life of affections and sensations goes. She suffers from mental and emotional immobility, as if life stopped at the age of nine, as if it came to a standstill. The metaphorical number nine, which returns obsessively in the narrative, is related in folklore to spiritual death; witchcraft; the Underworld, but also to the Great Goddess (see below).

Another traumatic event which Elaine remembers experiencing during early childhood is associated with the figure of the Protestant Mrs. Smeath, the mother of her friend Grace. As Elaine's parents do not go to church, Mrs. Smeath believes the child needs to be exposed to religion. Deep down, however, she is convinced of Elaine's sinfulness and wickedness, considering her to have no religion. During the manipulative games which Elaine is subjected to, Grace Smeath urges Cordelia to impose her mother's preconceptions or final judgments on Elaine. When Elaine finally realizes that the girls did nothing but apply the rules of Mrs. Smeath, she is filled with hatred against this woman, who from Elaine's perspective, represents the public eye that disapproves of her and that enforces punishments on her for being "wrong," "abnormal" and sinful. The memory of the destructive power of Mrs. Smeath adds to Elaine's sense of Toronto as Hell on earth.

After Elaine's second betrayal by her friends, when Cordelia sends her alone into the ravine and when Elaine falls into the water (see below "Beyond the Edge of the Past"), latent demonic powers rise to the surface. The cold marble or cat's eye that Elaine had thus far held onto in her pocket, as a protection against threats from outside, enters her heart. The fist that used to clench the marble makes way for a heart of marble, metaphorically speaking, or a heart like a closed fist. "There's something hard in me, crystalline, a kernel of glass," Elaine says. After this traumatic event, Elaine refuses to be involved with others who may cause her further suffering. She reverses the roles, the others will be her victims and she will be the victimizer whenever they become threatening.

Around the age of thirteen, Elaine has gained the "strength" of Cordelia who starts displaying signs of "weakness." Cordelia will indeed become increasingly vulnerable. Cordelia, named after the heroine in Shakespeare's tragedy *King Lear*, is the youngest of three sisters, who are also named after Shakespearean heroines. Elaine sees an analogy between Shakespeare's heroine and Cordelia in the sense that she is "the third sister, the only honest one. The stubborn one, the rejected one, the one who was not heard." Cordelia will lose the battle against the authority of her father. She suffers from a growing sense of insecurity and paralysis of the will, from a sense of being nothing in his, and therefore in her own, eyes. Elaine remembers Cordelia's attempts at normality, her desire to be "a lady" at the age of thirteen. Yet she fails at school and boys feel uneasy with her. In contrast, Elaine has managed to find a balance between internalizing the norms of family and society and being an individual in her own right; she is successful in finding her own way.

Elaine refuses to respond to Cordelia's call for a dialogue about whatever harm she may have caused in the past. She prefers to hold onto her protective shell, maintain her distrust of others and the version of the facts that she had constructed in the meantime. According to Elaine, "knowing too much about other people puts you in their power, they have a claim on you, you are forced to understand their reasons for doing things and then you are weakened." Elaine not only creates a discontinuity with the past, but she also closes the door to the future. She wants to stop the unpredictable process of time and keep herself, others and the future, under control. Like layers of skin that cover up the old wounds, new memories are superimposed on the earlier ones, which gradually fade away. On the surface, Elaine gives the impression of being able to cope. She has developed enough backbone, and her insecurity remains concealed, whereas Cordelia becomes gradually weaker and more and more spineless until she collapses.

When Cordelia can no longer cope, Elaine will deny her existence. Like Cordelia's father, she refuses to give love and recognition to the weak and helpless. She accuses Cordelia of bringing her failure upon herself, of complicating the lives of her family and friends, because of a lack of willpower. Cordelia's lack of steel and backbone and her demand for compassion fill Elaine with rage and contempt. Thus Elaine ends up doing to others what they did to her. The disapproving judgments that she hates in others, because they fill her with a sense of failure, become her own instrument of self-defense.

Elaine and Cordelia: Siamese Twins

Around the age of thirteen, as they are passing through a cemetery, Elaine tells Cordelia a horror comic story about the living dead, or about the dead who haunt the living like ghosts. She wants Cordelia to believe that she is one of a set of identical twins. She tells her that she is really dead and that the other half is walking around on the earth like a ghost or vampire. The story prefigures the relationship between the two main characters, for the memory of Cordelia, who is Elaine's double, will haunt Elaine like a ghost.

The narrative contains another significant horror comic about two sisters: "Cordelia reads a story about two sisters, a pretty one and one who has a burn covering half her face. The burn is maroon-coloured and wrinkled like a dead apple." The story embodies the *doppelgänger* motif, familiar from folklore: if you look into a mirror you do not see yourself but your soul. Soul and body relate to one another like two halves of a face. The ruined part of the face, the mutilated flesh, is but half of the human being.

The statement, "I never had a sister" applies literally to the protagonist, but not figuratively. Elaine's anxiety dreams reveal the existence of a repressed dimension of herself: "I dream that my mother has had a baby, one of a set of twins. The baby is grey. I don't know where the other twin is." By the end of her retrospective journey, Elaine reflects on the relationship between herself and Cordelia: "We are like the twins in old fables, each of whom has been given half a key." The two halves of the face relate to each other like the two halves of a key that one needs to open a door to the future.

As a child, Cordelia often threw herself backwards onto the snow. She would spread out her arms and move them up and down as if she were flying. She appeared to Elaine in the ambivalent image of a snow angel, "a stranger, shining with unknown, good possibilities," but also as a demon: "The snow angel has feathery wings and a tiny pin-head. Where her hands stopped, down near her sides, are the imprints of her fingers, like little claws." The ambivalent snow angel metaphor connotes the divine and the demonic aspects of human experience. By turning her back on Cordelia, Elaine cuts herself off from Cordelia's potentially destructive power, and also from her divine potential. Immediately after refusing to save Cordelia from the asylum, she has an anxiety dream about Cordelia in the image of a snow angel falling from a cliff or bridge, irrevocably lost. The dream revives one of Elaine's traumatic early childhood experiences, namely her descent into a ravine and her fall into a creek, an experience which caused Elaine's spiritual death. The dream also prefigures a turning point in the novel when Elaine returns to the ravine and restores the balance between destructive and creative power by bringing the forgotten part of herself back to the surface (see "Beyond the Edge of the Past").

Elaine and Cordelia relate to each other like Siamese twins, twins who dream of separation though they cannot escape the reality of being attached. This metaphor carries connotations of the multiple identity of the protagonist. One self is weak and helpless while the other self is fierce. One self stays in Toronto while the other runs away. Indeed, by escaping to Vancouver, Elaine tries to repress the knowledge of her mutilated inner space. Her attempt to silence a dimension of herself, to detach herself from the memory of Cordelia, leads to her static condition of living death. By consciously running away from the wounds she has suffered, she also further anaesthetizes the source of vital energy, or her grounding in natural energies. By repressing the pain of the past and by protecting herself against desires in the future, she remains encaged.

In Elaine's life, the head reigns, rather than the soul or the heart. In an attempt to cope with threatening forces that come both from inside and outside, she makes a choice in favour of rational control. A prominent metaphor in the novel is that of the severed, undamaged head. One of Elaine's paintings, presumably a portrait of the artist, represents a woman with a head like "a sphere of bluish glass." In Elaine's anxiety dreams, however, the repressed dimension of herself surfaces as a metaphorical decaying head.

The metaphor of the pumpkin Halloween heads that burst into pieces when they are thrown over the edge of a bridge and into the ravine that cuts through the city, comments on Elaine's emptied inner self. The image of the smashed Halloween mask reoccurs just prior to the protagonist's transition stage at the end of her journey, when it prefigures the disintegration of Elaine's established identity. Significantly, Halloween is the time "when the spirits of the dead will come back to the living . . . and the living will give them candy to keep them from turning vicious." As in *Life Before Man*, children, in the guise of witches, urge the adults to "shell out." Legends say that the dead become angry when they are forgotten. In *The Robber Bride*, Atwood will explore this motif extensively.

The novel's epigraph, a quotation from Eduardo Galeano's *Memory of Fire: Genesis*, mirrors two central leitmotifs, that of witchcraft and the split between body and soul. It provides a comment, among other things, on the importance of Indian religion and mythology in the novel. The epigraph is from a piece called "Witchcraft," a folktale about an old woman, a South American Tukana, who punished girls who refused to give her food. She took the bones out of their body and ate the marrow, so the girls were no longer able to walk. During early childhood, a frog had endowed her with the power to cure and to kill, to love and alleviate human misery, to hate and take revenge on other human beings. The rest of the folktale is quoted by

Margaret Atwood, and describes how the Tukana cut off the witch's head. In destroying her, they receive her soul.

The epigraph introduces the theme of the relationship between spirit or soul and body or outer form, which characterizes the relationship between Cordelia and Elaine. The one cannot live without the other, for a body without a soul is solidity without vital energy. Cordelia is the other, invisible side of Elaine, her shadow-self or the positive side of the self. She becomes an invisible power in Elaine's life, there and not there, as a potential dimension of Elaine. She has power over Elaine, for Cordelia's damaged face confronts Elaine with her own muted and mutilated inner self. Yet Elaine refuses to acknowledge Cordelia's existence as part of herself.

Elaine remembers Cordelia begging to be rescued from the asylum, where she is kept out of sight of her respectable family. Cordelia needs Elaine to rescue her from the imprisonment imposed on the so-called insane, on those who "lose their marbles," to pick up another image. Yet instead of recognizing Cordelia's existence, Elaine refuses empathy and avoids confronting Cordelia when the latter can no longer cope. Elaine refuses to give Cordelia back her reflection, that is to say, the reflection in the mirror that gives form to the shapeless. Human beings "have a tendency to exist," says her brother Stephen, implying they exist if others give them back their reflection.

Elaine's Outer Body: a Self-protective Armour

The cold glass surface of the cat's eye is a metaphor for the impenetrable protective shield which Elaine gradually develops, an image of the cold, disciplined surface that excludes interference with unpredictable life. Elaine shies away from the dangerous interaction between self and other, she refuses to be involved with those who demand too much from her. She has learned that openness and trust are dangerous and takes pride in being an expert at closing the door on others—she walks away, untouched and unharmed.

Elaine is largely responsible for her own isolation. She prefers enclosure, or the preservation of a hard core over which she has control. She says "I am happy as a clam: hard-shelled, firmly closed." Detachment, emotional numbness, a siding with nothingness is Elaine's response to the fear of being nothing in the eyes of the outside world. The image of an iron lung with only the head sticking out appeals to her, for she would love to retire into what she hopes to be an impermeable shell.

In an attempt to survive, Elaine chooses the peace and safety of a living dead person who survives indeed, though at the expense of joy and the fullness of life. She soon comes to a total emotional deadlock, which involves the incapacity to reach out for others, her own mother included: "I want to put my arms around [mother]. But I am held back." In a desire for rational control, Elaine represses the inner pain marks, and she sacrifices the fluid inner life. The recurring metaphor of the iron lung revives connotations of her entrapment in an emotional straitjacket.

Elaine shuts out others the way she was herself excluded as a child for being different. She can neither give warmth nor soothe the pain of others. She feels contempt for people who behave "irrationally," who display signs of anxiety or pain, or a lack of backbone: "The spectacle of [Mr. Hrbik's] suffering does not make me compassionate, but ruthless." The mean, pitiless voice with which she used to be judged by others, becomes her own. The puritan ethic that says people get what they deserve is a voice embedded in her head that she uses against others in revenge.

3. The Evil Eye

Elaine remembers her early childhood when Cordelia used to do an imitation of an unearthly creature who possesses the power of the evil eye. In folklore, the evil eye is a malevolent look, believed to be capable to inflicting harm on others, of bringing unhappiness, while those who have the evil eye remain unharmed. Elaine associates the eyes of Mrs. Smeath with Belladonna, the deadly nightshade with its red berries and its poisonous juice, destructive of life. In folklore, the Belladonna is related to witchcraft, and in the eyes of the narrator, Mrs. Smeath is like a witch whose eyes entrap living forms. The cat's eye metaphor receives connotations of a look that petrifies, like the stare of Medusa.

As a painter, Elaine directs her poisonous gaze against Mrs. Smeath, with the intention of hitting her very hard. Many of the "Life drawings," arranged chronologically on the wall at her retrospective exhibition, are arrested images of Mrs. Smeath. In her mind, this woman is a personification of the essence of Toronto. Elaine has fixed her in time as a flattened, unchanging image. She has created a picture narrative, a series of portraits, which give expression to Mrs. Smeath's effect on her mind. These portraits breathe ill will, "rancid hate." While she contemplates them during the exhibition, Elaine still struggles to discover why she hates this woman so much.

When she did the paintings, Elaine invested all her negative energy in them, tuning Mrs. Smeath into her main target, because in her mind she was the epitome of Toronto's intolerance and puritanism. Massive retaliation follows the ill treatment that she received as a child, and Elaine's portraits of Mrs. Smeath intend to be a final judgment on and a final victory over her enemy. This desire to take revenge, as she will realize at the end of her retrospective journey, has always hindered insight.

Mrs. Smeath, Elaine's negative shadow, becomes larger than life. In her works of art, Elaine hyperbolizes Mrs. Smeath to a malicious hag who has to be destroyed. Ironically, Elaine who sees in Mrs. Smeath the personification of Hecate, the goddess of witchcraft, has become a Hecate herself, namely a cold, wry old woman who cannot forgive. The image of the cold marble that encloses the dark nightshade is a metaphor for the cage-like circle or the perpetual Hell of Elaine's own mind. "I look into [the cat's eye], and see my life entire," Elaine says. The circular form of the marble connotes the mental condition of the protagonist, her entrapment in a (self)-destructive circle of aggression and accusation against others.

Mental immobility and circularity result from being stuck in one version of reality. Elaine causes her own unhappiness by remaining imprisoned in her resentment against the place in which she grew up, a resentment that poisons her life. Because of her negative sensations, she becomes her own emotional prisoner, someone who is locked into herself, and who limits herself. Put differently, in her coming to terms with the "inhumanity" of others, she has become one of them. She suffers from a diseased heart, a "flawed heart," like her image of Mrs. Smeath's "bad" heart. Elaine compares the heart of Mrs. Smeath to an evil eye. Yet Elaine's heart is itself metaphorically represented as an evil eye, as is clear from one of her destructive portraits of Mrs. Smeath, which has the revealing title "an eye for an eye."

In her art, Elaine presents Mrs. Smeath as "still alive" in "dim space" or with bloomers that give out a "dark stifling light." Ironically, this perspective on the living death of the woman who is supposed to personify Toronto mirrors Elaine's own condition. The perception of Elaine's Hungarian art teacher of Toronto's fear of life, its absence of "gaiety or soul," comments on Elaine's judgment of the city, but also on the fact that she shares its greyness.

4. The Solid "I"

In her fifties, Elaine still proves to be trapped in the nightmare of her childhood. Her response to other women, which she displayed as an adolescent, remains an ambivalent one. On the one hand, she obsessively reads in the eyes of women a disapproval of her, which involves a sense of violation and frustration that results in rage and malice. Feelings of rage spring up when she feels the judgments of others will make her lose control. "I am on dubious ground, and this enrages me," Elaine says. On the other hand, she knows herself to be extremely dependent on receiving the recognition of other women, on wanting to please. Elaine is torn between refusing and yet desiring "normality," between defiance and the desire to be included.

From childhood to adulthood, Elaine's "power" resides either in escape from the dangerous interference of others, or in aggression. She is always out to intimidate others, "I have a mean mouth and short, devastating comments come out of it . . . I know where the weak spots are." Part of her "strength" resides in negative impulses, in pent-up feelings of hatred, which hinder a positive and a creative development, both as a human being and as an artist.

"Home" is a foreign word in a place where the protagonist feels like a foreigner, where she felt and still feels out of place, isolated and excluded as if she were a member of a different culture or race. Despite the passing of time, Elaine keeps looking upon Toronto as the wrong place, as an oppressively small, because intolerant, puritanical city: "their watchful, calculating windows. Malicious, grudging, vindictive, implacable." Yet the wrongness, the darkness of the place resides in the unresolved conflict between the protagonist and traumatic experiences suffered in the past.

The failure of her first marriage fills Elaine with a sense of guilt and shame when she thinks of herself in the judging eye of others, and she decides to flee from Toronto to Vancouver. Toronto, which is killing her, represents an abhorrent world, as opposed to Vancouver, a place of refuge where she imagined she would be free of the past and would find happiness by starting anew. She believed in the potential warmth of Vancouver in contrast with the coldness of Toronto. The escape to Vancouver was an "evasion" or a flight from the familiar, an act of amputation, a choice of remaining at a distance from the dangerous memories of the past. By choosing separation, Elaine cancels a dimension of her subjectivity.

The Illusion of a Unified Identity

During the retrospective journey, Elaine is haunted by the memory of having tried to preserve her ordered identity by betraying her best friend, by denying their sisterhood. Elaine feels she needs Cordelia to save her from the confinement of "sanity" that she enforced on herself: "Get me out of this, Cordelia. I'm locked in. I don't want to be nine years old forever." Elaine needs the power to rescue the part of herself that is locked in, or sealed up in glass.

The ruined faces of the helpless confront Elaine with her own guilt and shame, with the powers in her that are destructive of her own humanity. During one of her walks through the streets of Toronto, Elaine refuses to be moved by the entreaties for pity of the needy and helpless on whom she projects the memory of Cordelia. They hope she will give them that part of her which the Virgin Mary offers, but she cannot give them any light or life. Elaine shows compunction, but also fear of begin invaded. She reads in the eyes of the weak and helpless an accusation of her own wrongdoing, which fills her with cold self-disgust. Toronto has the power of opening the old wounds. Elaine finds herself confronted with the memory of Cordelia, with the other, ruined side of her face, the knowledge of which is unbearable.

In her fifties, Elaine is obsessively preoccupied with mid-life and the deterioration of her body, or visible signs of the passing of time. On the surface, she wants to appear sane, normal, solid, to display no signs of social awkwardness and inadequacy. She does not want to make others feel she is in need of them, or give away other signs of weakness. She is terrified that if others detect signs of weakness, visible cracks in her solid facade, she will be an easy target. Like Elizabeth in *Life Before Man*, Elaine's fear of cracks is a sign of her anxiety about the unpredictability of life, "the thin edge of the wedge, the crack in the wall that will open, later, onto what?" Elaine lives in terror of being engulfed by the same shapelessness that invaded Cordelia. In a desire for self-preservation, she represses underlying impulses, desires and fears that are inconsistent with her adapted self. Yet she cannot escape the insistent threatening presence of a power that could easily make her fall apart. At unpredictable moments, she feels the rhythm of impulses coming from inside, the presence of a repressed dimension of herself. It is the weight of Cordelia pushing her towards an edge, a movement that endangers Elaine's established identity.

The Precariousness of Elaine's Ordered Versions of Reality

After the opening of the exhibition and before returning to Vancouver, Elaine realizes that there may be more to Mrs. Smeath than the frozen image of her paintings. Maybe Mrs. Smeath was not the monster which Elaine has always taken her for, but a human being who was fighting to fulfill her duty to God through the moral conduct of her day-to-day life. This must have been a cause of unhappiness and inner loneliness. If she were to see her from a different angle, in Mrs. Smeath's own context (Mrs. Smeath came from a small town in Ontario and she moved to Toronto, where she must have felt as much an outsider as Elaine), she might be no more than an ignorant imitator of the values and thought-patterns of the small puritanical community in which she grew up.

Elaine has created a human space, the only reality which she believed she could live with. At the end of her journey, she realizes that she needs to rid herself of her negative attachment to the image of Mrs. Smeath and

Cordelia if she wants to free herself from the hell of her own mind. Her emotions have always been far in excess of the situation. This thought seems to be summed up in the metaphor of an oversized cat's eye, held by the Mexican Virgin of Lost Things.

5. Beyond the Edge of the Past

The protagonist's second betrayal at the age of nine occurred when Cordelia snatched her blue knitted hat and threw it over the bridge, into the ravine. Then she ordered Elaine to fetch the hat. While Elaine descended into the ravine, the other girls once again betrayed her by leaving her behind, helpless. Elaine subsequently slipped halfway into the river that was covered with thin ice. A woman who resembled the Virgin Mary appeared to her at the edge of the ravine. Elaine heard the voice of the Mexican Virgin of Lost Things who brings comfort to the helpless. It was in fact the power inside herself that saved Elaine from death: "Then I can't see her any more. But I feel her around me, not like arms but like a small wind of warmer air. She's telling me something. *You can go home now*, she says. *It will be all right. Go home*." Yet after this painful event, which causes a break in consciousness, Elaine refuses to believe that she received a vision and heard the voice of the Virgin of Lost Things. By denying the latter's existence, Elaine negates the regenerative power inside herself; she denies the existence of the Great Goddess, the ancestral mother or Nature Goddess, who is the source of new life.

   Cordelia had told Elaine a folktale or legend about the dead who live in the river (Styx) that flows into the ravine. The tale turns out to be a premonition with respect to Elaine's life: "Cordelia says that because the stream flows right out of the cemetery it's made of dissolved dead people. She says that if you drink it or step into it or even get too close to it, the dead people will come out of the stream, all covered with mist, and take you with them." At the age of nine, Elaine leaves her spirit in the Underworld to return to the surface as an unfeeling person. The image of the fall not only refers to the loss of innocence but also to the season, which becomes a metaphor for Elaine's autumnal mental state.

   Just before going back to Vancouver, and once more turning her back on the past, Elaine goes through a transition stage while standing on the bridge over the ravine. In the novel, the bridge is a metaphor for the edge between the cold patterns of civilization and the cyclical process of nature. The sudden insight is an unexpected event that momentarily changes the structure of the action. Elaine had not expected that anything extraordinary would happen on the day of her departure, "The day feels vacant, as if everyone has moved out of it; as if there's nothing more to come." By returning to the bridge, Elaine retraces her footsteps to the place where her heart became a marble, where light and the joy of life seeped out of her. At first, while once more standing on the bridge, Elaine denies having heard a voice at the age of nine, the voice of the Heavenly Lady who saved her from death: "There was only darkness and silence. Nobody and nothing." In a similar vein, Elaine habitually associates interplanetary space, which is an image for the natural world, with silence and nothingness.

For many years, Elaine has superimposed the memory of the deadly nightshade ("darkness") on the voice of the earth mother ("light"). Similarly, her painting of a glass jar with a bouquet of nightshade, reveals eyes of cats that are "scarcely visible." In the context of her painting, the cat's eyes are those of the Great Goddess, or the eyes of the land's primordial inhabitants. On her final visit to the ravine, Elaine feels the potential existence of the invisible power of "something" buried under the bridge and of "someone" else standing beside her on the bridge. Shortly before the moment of revival, she remembers her brother Stephen who collected his cat's eye marbles in a glass jar and ritualistically buried the treasure underground: "Stephen's jar of light is buried down there somewhere." To him, they must have been like stars, like solidified light, remnants of the primal moment of creation. Stephen's cat's eyes are a metaphor for luminous stars, radiating energy, like "old light," remnants of the life-principle that he ritualistically returned to the origin. Significantly, Elaine once mistook the votive offerings that Mexicans pin on the Virgin's dress as signs of hope, for stars. In one of her paintings entitled *Unified Field Theory*, Elaine had imagined the votive offerings as stars: "Here and there on the black of her dress or cloak there are pinpoints of light."

A moment of anamnesia involves the recollection of something that was lost, the restoration of a broken current of memory. Elaine unexpectedly moves beyond her rigidified perspective. For a moment, she is convinced that the Heavenly Lady gave her protection, and brought comfort by expressing her love and compassion. The transitional stage is a momentary encounter with "something," with the secret treasure hidden in the subsoil. Elaine is thus reunited with the repressed dimension of the Triple Goddess, with birth and growth, with the spring season. In her painting *Unified Field Theory*, Elaine imagined the face of the Great Goddess "partly in shadow." The painter's lost shadow self, the submerged side of her life, is buried underground, and she unexpectedly touches the divine level of her existence, vital energy, the ground of being. She unites with natural space and primordial time, and thus gains the power of the earth mother as the source of regenerative power that can be reached only through the decomposition of her fixed identity, through a spiritual death-rebirth. The primeval realm of the Great Goddess, outer (interplanetary) space and the realm of creative imagination are metaphorically interrelated in this and other novels by Margaret Atwood, because each realm transcends spatio-temporal boundaries.

As said before, Cordelia inhabits a repressed dimension of Elaine. In recovering contact with drowned space-time, Elaine conjures up the spirit of Cordelia, that is, Elaine's departed soul. Elaine reaches out for Cordelia in a loving gesture, a warm embrace that affirms the existence of Cordelia as the lost part of herself. The gesture involves a moment of incarnation, when Elaine attempts to give a body to the formless spirit. Earlier, Elaine had contemplated that she could give Cordelia "something you can never have, except from another person: what you look like from outside. A reflection. This is the part of herself I could give back to her." As in *Bodily Harm*, the ritualistic gesture achieves what was previously unthinkable: the coldness and darkness, the negative sensations, make way for the opening up of her heart and the expression of love and warmth in open, outstretched hands. We read: "I reach out my arms to her, bend down, hands open to show I have no weapon. *It's all right*, I say to her. *You can go home now*. The snow in my eyes withdraws like smoke."

Elaine has dared to look back, open a door to something, the future, before it is too late. The visionary moment is a "revision," because the protagonist gains a new perspective that fills the landscape with a new dimension of meaning. The restored unity with vital energy, however temporary it may be, is a far greater achievement than rational understanding of past history. The protagonist still gropes in darkness with respect to the historical past, and the search for lost time fails as a discovery of the truth about the past. However, Elaine has learned that she had created for herself a bearable, self-justifying version of reality, a false peace, which she believed she could easily live with.

The flight back to Vancouver is a metaphor for the protagonist who heads for the future. The flight may also be a metaphor for her spiritual ascent, because in the airplane, Elaine is both up "here" as a solid "I" and down "there," united with the spirit of the land. She speaks of the latter in terms of "old" light, a voice of the past, an ancestral voice from a dark, forgotten matrix. The meaning of the "old light" metaphor may be derived from the similarity between Elaine's final reflection: "Now it's full night, clear, moonless and filled with stars . . . Echoes of light, shining out in the midst of nothing. It's old light. But it's enough to see by" and a scene during early childhood when Elaine is playing with her brother in the bush of Northern Quebec. There we read: "It's a clear night, moonless, filled with antiseptic stars . . . Stephen is teaching me to see in the dark . . . now I can see in the dark." In *The Robber Bride*, both Charis and her grandmother are also capable of seeing in the dark. Like Elaine, Charis is in close contact with the power of the Great Goddess, who is incarnated by the grandmother figure.

In this chapter, the main thrust of argument has tried to make clear that the study of metaphors in the context of mind-style analysis is essential for a better understanding of the psychological stance of Atwood's protagonist. As in most of Atwood's novels, *Cat's Eye* ends with a borderline event, a visionary experience that is expressed through metaphor. A close investigation of metaphors emerging during such a visionary moment contradicts interpretations that impose a downright pessimistic stance on Atwood's protagonist and, what is worse, on the writer herself.

KAREN STEIN

Margaret Atwood's Modest Proposal:
The Handmaid's Tale

Margaret Atwood begins her novel *The Handmaid's Tale* with two
dedications and three epigraphs: a passage from *Genesis*, a passage from
Jonathan Swift's "Modest Proposal," and a Sufi proverb. This abundance of
preliminary matter establishes a frame through which we read the novel, just
as a frame around a painting tells us to read the enclosed space in a certain
way, as an art object, an object re-presented in a way that calls attention to
its special relationship to surrounding objects. We look through—not at—
the frame, but its presence has already categorized the object within and
structured the way we will view it. Similarly, Atwood's interpolated texts set
up a frame that asks us to read the rest of the book in a particular way.

To frame means, among other things, to utter or articulate, to fit or
adjust to something, to enclose, to shape or fashion, to invent or imagine, to
plan or contrive, to devise falsely (to frame up); all of these meanings
resonate in *Tale*. In Gilead, women have been framed. Framed by their red
robes and wide wimples, the handmaids are clearly visible, marked and
delimited by their social status. For the wearer within the frame, the wimples
serve as blinders; to look *through* them is to see only straight ahead, a
narrowed view of the world. For us as readers, to look *at* the wimples is to
read the authoritarian practice of Gilead which attempts to control women,
and to permit only one view of reality. By decoding Atwood's framing texts,

From *Canadian Literature* 148 (Spring 1996): 57–71. © 1996 by The University of British
Columbia, Vancouver.

we can read the frame itself as well as reading through it. Such a reading may in fact expand our view, for it adds layers of inference and possibility. Many critics have discussed one of the framing texts, the Historical Notes section at the end. Indeed, this topic is the focal point of articles by Arnold E. Davidson and Patrick D. Murphy. Davidson considers the political implications of the Notes, while Murphy examines this section of the novel as a structural device. For other analyses of the Historical Notes, see, for example, Deer, Lacombe, LeBihan, Rubenstein, Stein, Tomc. Thus, while this section has received substantial attention, few critics have spoken about the prefatory material. Lucy M. Freibert addresses the dedication and all of the epigraphs, although she speaks in detail only about the material from *Genesis*. She remarks that the epigraph from Swift prepares us for political satire. Nancy V. Workman analyzes the Sufi proverb and its meanings for the novel. She mentions the Swift epigraph in passing, notes that it is "readily understood" and relates Swift's exaggerated satire to Atwood's exaggerated satire of American Puritanism and the Moral Majority. Linda Wagner-Martin discusses the novel's dedications briefly. Sandra Tomc explores in greater depth some of the ironic implications of the dedications. I will consider all of the prefatory framing matter here, and focus in particular on the Swift epigraph. I shall argue that this epigraph serves larger thematic and stylistic purposes in Atwood's novel. By examining these initial framing devices, I hope to ask useful questions about the narrative voice and to extend our readings of the novel.

Before considering the preliminary framing matter which will be our central concern here, it will be useful to sketch out the workings of the book's "Historical Notes," the concluding frame. This chapter, a report of an academic conference about Gilead held at the University of Denay, Nunavit ("deny none of it"), serves many functions. For one, the academic discourse satirizes academic pretension. More seriously, through its sexism and moral relativism it establishes ideological parallels between the dystopias of Gilead and the post-Gileadean society. Rhetorically, the speaker at the conference, Professor James Darcy Pieixoto, continues the process of ironic layering of texts which the multiple epigraphs have initiated. Pieixoto has in fact assembled Offred's story, rearranging and transferring her audiotaped oral narrative into the written text that is the eponymous story. Thus, through his editorial acts, and now, in the novel's narrative present, through his conference presentation, Pieixoto provides another narrative voice, another layer of interpretation to frame the handmaid's narrative. His narrative includes information about Offred's escape from Gilead and her recording of the story which, puzzlingly, she does not provide. Moreover, in bracketing her tale, his text reiterates the tension between Offred's words and patriarchal control of her story which forms the crux of her tale. We shall have more to say later about the ways in which Pieixoto misreads Offred's tale.

Additionally, the "Historical Notes" section furthers the satirical purpose of the novel. In describing the function of this frame, Patrick Murphy explains it as a device to solve a problem facing writers of dystopian speculative fiction: if the dystopian world is too far removed from ours, our reading may lead to "cathartic reduction of anxiety" with no impulse to act in our own world. The reader who is too comfortable may read for escape or to "reinforce smug assumptions." To reduce this distance, and induce a "discomforting" reading, the author employs a framing device "intended to reduce the distance between tenor [relationships in the empirical universe] and vehicle [relations in the fictional universe] and thereby further the fundamental purpose of this SF subgenre: to prompt readers to change the world. Murphy notes that while it has "historical precedents in the 'discovered manuscript' device used by Swift . . . and others, pseudo-documentary framing" is a more appropriate strategy for contemporary readers because it is closely related to "journalistic and academic writing conventions. . . [influenced by] 'new journalism' and the popularity of the 'non-fiction novel'." To Murphy's categorization of *Tale* as dystopian science fiction, I would append, as others have suggested, the label of satire (and also, the labels of journal, epistolary novel, romance, palimpsest). Satire, like dystopian science fiction, is a genre which addresses its exaggerated version of present evils to readers who have some power to act and, by this means, hopes to bring about social and political change. Offred's original text, recorded on audiotape, is presumably intended to inform a larger audience about Gilead and thus to serve the same purpose of bringing about action to extirpate the horrors of the dystopia.

This dystopian-science fiction-satirical-journal-epistolary-romance-palimpsest text then, this *Tale*, is the story of a rather ordinary, educated, middle-class woman who is framed by, but (presumably) escapes from, a dystopian misogynist society. How appropriate to frame (bracket) her story with a dedication to Atwood's ancestor, Mary Webster, who escaped hanging as a witch at the hands of the dystopian misogynistic Puritan Massachusetts. Because the rope broke and the law of double jeopardy saved her from being tried again, Webster escaped from death and subsequently moved to Nova Scotia, a more liberal society. Counterpoised to Webster, the novel's other dedicatee is Perry Miller, an American scholar of Puritanism (a teacher of Atwood's when she was at Harvard). Sandra Tomc demonstrates that the juxtaposed dedications posit the ironic relations between scholars and the texts they (mis)read, between the events of history and the historians who (mis)represent them. In explicating and valorizing the texts they interpret, both Pieixoto and Miller ignore the deeply misogynist strain of Gileadean and Puritan cultures. Pieixoto urges the conference audience to suspend moral judgment in studying Gilead; Miller was in the vanguard of American scholarship that celebrated the Puritan vision as quintessentially American. Observing that the ironic pairing of Webster and Miller at the start parallels the pairing of the handmaid Offred and Professor Pieixoto at the end, Tomc notes "the issue in both cases is the failure of the female object of study to fit the patterns of inquiry set out by her male scrutinizer." Moreover, because they do not fit these "patterns of inquiry," Offred and Mary Webster are able to escape from the traditional plots scripted for (or rather against) women, and thereby to elude not only the scholars who study them, but also the rigidly punitive societies that seek to destroy them.

Like the dedications, the epigraphs chosen as framing texts are drawn from the domains of history, literary history and religion, thus pointing to a wide scope of issues, to a seriousness of purpose and, also, to the persistence over time of the problems the novel will raise. These preliminary interpolated texts signal the reader that several discourses will be juxtaposed; several layers of meaning and language will be superimposed upon each other, and played against each other to produce ironic effects.

Because irony is a chief feature of the novel, and one of the components of satire, a brief discussion of its purposes is in order. A useful place to begin our understanding of irony is Linda Hutcheon's discussion. Describing the complex, multifaceted uses of irony, Hutcheon notes that its tone extends along a range that begins with the mildly emphatic and continues through the playful, ambiguous, provisional, self-protective to the insulting, the subversive or the transgressive. She offers a definition of "irony as the interaction not only between ironist and interpreter but between different meanings, where both the said and the unsaid must play off against each other (and with some critical edge)." Moreover, irony may be a device which creates a community of knowing readers who are complicit in their exclusion of the targeted groups, those other readers who do not comprehend the point of the irony. With this in mind, let us resume our readings of the prefatory matter of *The Handmaid's Tale* to discover how the ironizing frame of the novel is constructed.

Just as the double dedication suggests ironic possibilities, the biblical, Swift and Sufi epigraphs open up spaces for further ironic readings. Because others have addressed the biblical and Sufi material, we shall consider them only briefly here, and then focus our attention on the Swift text which needs further critical explication. In her analysis of the Sufi proverb, Nancy V.

Workman explains that punning, multiple meanings and paradox (discursive strategies central to *The Handmaid's Tale*) are central components of Sufi writings. She finds that the "inwardness and language play" important to the Sufi mystical tradition structure the novel and provide the narrator with "the power to shape reality." However, we must be aware that the reality Offred shapes is a private one; her world is a narrow cell-like room within which she is free to imagine and meditate as she chooses.

In contrast to Offred's constrained shaping of reality, the totalitarian government of Gilead appropriates biblical texts to institute and enforce harsh political control, to shape a political reality for its citizens. Lucy M. Freibert discusses the religious hypocrisy of Gilead and explores the comic implications of the biblical allusions and parallels, noting "humorous correspondence between the biblical account and Atwood's tale" and outright "high burlesque" in the prayer scene preceding the impregnation ritual. The epigraph biblical text *Genesis* 30: 1-3 suggests the importance of children to women and raises the issue of male control over women. Recontextualizing this passage, Gilead turns Rachel's anguished plea for children into the pretext for instituting a new domesticity based on the sexual triangle of a man and two women. In the guise of a re-population program, Gilead reads the biblical text literally and makes it the basis for the state-sanctioned rape, the impregnation ceremony the handmaids must undergo each month. In this recasting of the biblical passage, Gilead obliterates the emotional meaning of the story and, instead, turns a woman's desire into an instrument of male control.

Moreover, on a more figurative level, the choice of a biblical text for the epigraph suggests that spiritual as well as political significance is at issue in the novel. The state-controlled religion of Gilead, like the patriarchal Israelite society and the Puritan theocracy of Massachusetts, offers its adherents little spiritual sustenance. Its belief system is a harsh theology based on a judgmental father god rather than on a nurturing divinity. The state cynically selects the texts which it privileges to authorize its political control, and promulgates religious rituals (such as the Salvagings, Particicutions and Prayvaganzas) as "steam valve[s] for the female elements." Its written texts are subject to state control. Bibles are kept locked up, and only the men are legally allowed to read them. Computer-banks of prayer machinery print out prayer scrolls and intone them in metallic monotones, but no one reads or listens to the prayers: "you can't hear the voices from outside; only a murmur, a hum." Even worse, neither Offred nor her partner (and possibly no one else in Gilead) believes that the intended audience—God—"listens to these machines." Consequently, the computer prayers are voices which fall upon deaf ears, just as Offred's voice falls upon deaf ears, unheard or misheard. Since Pieixoto finds her audiotapes so many years later, hidden in a trunk in what was once the city of Bangor, Maine, we must assume they did not succeed in their purpose of conveying the story of Gilead to her contemporaries.

Another voice whose urgent, impassioned call to action was not heard by his contemporaries is the voice of Swift's Modest Proposer. Atwood's choice of an epigraph from "A Modest Proposal" invites us to explore thematic and stylistic parallels between her text and Swift's, and leads us to posit ironic readings of the narrative voices. The satire in each case depends upon an ironic narration, the "proposal" or "tale" of a supposedly artless observer who reports an appalling situation in a relatively flat style. The targets of satire are repressive governmental policies which produce worse harm than the problems they set out to solve. Swift, the brilliant Irish political satirist and clergyman, published his "Modest Proposal" in 1729 to expose the damaging consequences of British economic policy toward Ireland. Atwood, the brilliant Canadian novelist, published her *Handmaid's Tale* in 1985 to expose the damaging consequences of patriarchal misogyny in an imagined state, which Atwood alleges is not entirely fictional.

The passage which Atwood appends in her epigraph reads: "but as to myself, having been wearied out for many years with offering vain, idle, visionary thoughts, and at length utterly despairing of success, I fortunately fell upon this proposal." Whose is this voice? Is it the voice of Swift, the outraged public man who seeks to ameliorate the problems of a debt-ridden, colonialized Ireland? The Proposer, who frame—in a data-filled, matter-of-fact report—a most heinous solution to the problems of Ireland's poverty and overpopulation? Critics are still asking: How are we to read the connections between the voices of Swift and his Proposer? Swift chose the "Modest Proposal," a genre popular in his time, as his frame "to reduce the distance between tenor [relations in the empirical universe] and vehicle [relations in the fictional universe] and thereby further the fundamental purpose of this . . . subgenre: to prompt readers to change the world" (Murphy, bracketed text from Suvin). His satire is powerful in part because it is directed at its readers, both the educated business class of England and the oppressed Irish. English and Irish Protestant mercantile interests might speak in exasperated voices about the Irish poor, as does the Proposer. Or they might suggest policies as detrimental to Ireland as those of the Proposer, without realizing the tragic consequences of such legislation. On the other hand, many of the remedies the Proposer discounts as being ineffective or impossible to realize, such as the refusal to purchase foreign manufactured goods, are options available to the Irish themselves.

Whose voice(s) does the author of *Tale* mean to imply by the epigraph? Who are we to suppose is the equivalent of the Proposer? There are layers of authors: the imputed author, the handmaid Offred who narrates the tale, the archaeologist Pieixoto who pieces together the fragments of audiotaped oral narration to assemble the manuscript. Whose voices emerge from this layering, and with what degree(s) of innocence? And what are the targets of the novel's satire? What are we to make of the novel's use of romance story conventions? Should we conclude that because it uses the romance plot—the rescue of the helpless female victim by the mysteriously dark, silent lover—the tale is therefore retreating from politics and public life into romantic fantasy? Or is the tale satirizing the woman who would choose this plot for herself? Or is the tale satirizing those readers who do not see that the romance conventions are also a level of irony? Or is the tale satirizing all of the academics who attempt to pin down its voice and propound our own interpretations?

Swift's "Modest Proposal" and Atwood's *The Handmaid's Tale* share many stylistic and thematic features. Stylistically, both play with the range of possible irony. Both create characters (the Proposer, the Commander and the Professor) whose smug certainties are punctured by ironic narration. Thematically, both texts establish metaphorical links between women/animals/procreation/food. Both paint graphic pictures of the horrific consequences of misguided political policy. Swift's text demonstrates the tragic effects of English colonial policy which reduced Ireland to poverty & famine. Atwood's novel depicts the ravages of a fictional totalitarian regime (although Atwood insists, in an interview in *Quill & Quire*, that "there's nothing in the book that hasn't already happened"). In both cases, one social dilemma addressed is that of population. The "Modest Proposal" seeks to solve the problem of Irish overpopulation; the rulers of Gilead are obsessed with resolving their crisis of underpopulation, for industrial pollution and experiments in biological warfare have produced the sterility that led to underpopulation. In each case, the measures taken to rectify the population are draconian. Gilead resorts to the desperate remedy of enforced sexual servitude; the Proposer suggests another desperate remedy, cannibalism. The voice of the Proposer, like that of Gilead, is definitely hostile to women (note that the possibility that Swift was also a misogynist is a matter of some critical debate). Both the Proposer and the government of Gilead seek to control and appropriate women's sexuality and to commodify their children

In both texts, there are deprecating references to women as animals, especially breeding animals. Ofglen is a "trained pig," the handmaids are like "caged rats." Offred sees herself as a "prize pig," and "an attentive pet." She refers to the handmaids as two-legged wombs. She thinks of a Commander as a "rutting salmon." In "Modest Proposal," a similarly reductive perspective prevails. Women are compared to brood mares, calving cows or sows in farrow. Charles Beaumont finds that in its thirty-three paragraphs of text "Proposal" uses the terms "breed" or "breeders" six times, and "dam" (in the sense of female progenitor) twice.

Body parts of men as well as women (often exaggerated or grotesquely depicted) figure prominently in each text. In *Tale*, Offred sees worms as "flexible and pink, like lips"; she describes the Commander's penis as a "tentacle," "blind," like a slug. The sexual politics of Gilead foregrounds sexuality as reproduction, and leads the narrator to view the world in terms of reproductive functions. Offred perceives flowers as "the genital organs of plants." As a result of this distorted vision, as Roberta Rubenstein notes, "distinctions between human and non-human are grotesquely inverted or reduced." The hanged bodies of Gilead's victims are suspended from the walls of the former Harvard Yard like slabs of meat on meathooks. With bags over their heads, they are anonymous, featureless. Offred contemplates this process of dehumanization: "This is what you have to do before you kill . . . You have to create an it, where none was before. You do that first, in your head, and then you make it real." The "Modest Proposal" employs a similar strategy of dehumanization; the Proposer describes infants as "useless mouths"; Beaumont counts five uses of the word "carcass," and four appearances of "flesh."

Just as women in Gilead have become property of the state as child-bearing machines, the children they produce are commodified. In *Tale*, bearing a child insures the handmaid's survival, while handmaids who fail to produce progeny after three postings are exiled to the toxic waste colonies. Because of their enhanced value, pregnant handmaids flaunt their status. But they lose all rights to the infants after parturition: the babies become the property of the Commanders' wives. However, as a result of environmental pollution, many babies are born deformed and thus fail to actualize their commodity value: they are "Shredders" rather than "Keepers."

In "Modest Proposal," of course, the sole value of children is as marketable commodity. But market value here depends on weight and flavour. Children are described as "plump," "fat," or "fattest." Infants are reckoned up in terms of how many portions they will make: "a well-grown fat yearling child . . . roasted whole, will make a considerable figure at a Lord Mayor's feast, or any other public entertainment"; "a child will make two dishes at an entertainment for friends; and when the family dines alone, the fore or hind quarter will make a reasonable dish." Additionally, children are compared to venison or suckling pig, and recipes are offered.

The "Modest Proposal" continues to shock with its vitriolic satirical suggestion of cannibalism. But there are dark echoes of cannibalism in *Tale* as well, which it will be worth considering. Indeed, Atwood's first novel was *Edible Woman*, in which the narrator Marian MacAlpin perceives herself as a commodity that her fiancé Peter plans to consume. She thinks of herself as analogous to the rabbit he hunts and eviscerates; she runs away from the camera he seeks to "shoot" her with. In the conclusion, she bakes a cake in the shape of a woman and asks him to consume it instead of her. (For an exploration of the food imagery in *Edible Woman*, see MacLulich, who reads the novel as a version of the "Gingerbread Man" folktale.)

Atwood has clearly been fascinated with the idea of cannibalism. She has treated this subject playfully in at least one other context. In 1987 *The CanLit Foodbook: From Pen to Palate—a Collection of Tasty Literary Fare*, edited and illustrated by Margaret Atwood, was published. Written as a fund-raiser for Canada's Anglophone P.E.N., the book is a compilation of authors' favorite recipes, and selections from Canadian authors containing descriptions of food or meals. Atwood cautions her readers that this is not exactly a cookbook. Indeed, chapter nine is title: "Eating People is Wrong: Cannibalism Canadian Style." In her foreword, Atwood tells us:

> Chapter nine is devoted to cannibalism, metaphorical and actual, of which there's a surprising amount in Canadian literature. It appears to be one of those thrill-of-the-forbidden literary motifs, like the murders in murder mysteries, that we delight to contemplate, though we would probably not do it for fun, except in children's literature, where devouring and being devoured appears to be a matter of course.

In her selections for this chapter, Atwood includes the passage in which Marian MacAlpin bakes and decorates her woman-shaped cake. Atwood comments in the foreword that collecting recipes and "pestering writers" took a long time: possibly she had begun thinking about the *Foodbook* at the time she was writing *Tale*. Of course, the tone of the foodbook is much lighter than that of *Tale*. Alluding to cannibalism in connection with Hitler's policy of extermination establishes a much more serious context in *Tale* than in the tongue-in-cheek cookbook. Yet, this conflation of serious and comic is a recurring feature in Atwood's work. In fact, her playful *Foodbook* is a fund-raiser for the serious purpose of raising money on behalf of writers who are political prisoners.

Cannibalism, to the extent that it may ever have been actually practiced (apart from the desperate cases of stranded disaster survivors in extreme conditions), is an act of aggression against an other, a powerless, but somehow potentially dangerous and fearsome victim. We would apply the cannibal label only to alien others, whom we perceive to be savages beyond the pale of civilized humanity, for cannibalism is a powerful taboo, which has, as Atwood notes, the power to horrify and titillate readers. The cannibal theme is carried out in several ways in *Tale*. On some level, the foods the handmaids eat, symbolic representations of wombs and fertility (pears, eggs, chickens, bread described as baking in the oven), are analogues for their bodies. Additionally, one of Offred's flashback memories recounts her childhood fear of cannibalism. When her mother described the deaths of victims in Nazi concentration camps, she talked about people being killed in ovens. As a young child, not comprehending, Offred believed that these people had been baked and eaten. "There is something especially terrifying to a child in that idea. Ovens mean cooking, and cooking comes before eating. I thought these people had been eaten. Which in a way I suppose they had been." By means of this digression, Offred makes explicit the analogies between Gilead and Nazi Germany, and between her tale and "A Modest Proposal." In all cases, we have dystopian societies that are devouring their children.

Having explored some of the thematic parallels, let us now turn to the stylistic parallels between Atwood's and Swift's texts. These stylistic strategies hold the key to our readings of the texts, for through their styles the narrators establish their relationships to their texts and present themselves as subjects of the reader's interpretations.

Discussing the style of "A Modest Proposal," Charles Pullen writes that the Proposer "is quite capable of irony and anger: what he is incapable of seeing is how monstrous his marvelous solution is." Further, "The Proposer is . . . highly skilled, knowledgeable, imaginative . . . He is also a captive of his style which simply has no need or room for emotion, for morals, for human implication. Solving the problem is all: he possesses the rhetorical structure, the proper language and the necessary knowledge." This characterization of the Proposer's style applies equally to the first of the two male voices in *Tale*, the voice of the Commander (the state). The Commander, "highly skilled, knowledgeable, imaginative," is smugly certain that he has solved "the woman problem." But he is more sophisticated than the Proposer. Aware of the human implications, he is nevertheless pleased with his solution. In conversation with Offred, he lapses into cliché, thus signaling that his response is superficial, trivializing both the issue and the person he is answering. His response again relies on dehumanizing and cannibalizing the victims: "You can't make an omelet without breaking eggs." He also acknowledges that "better never means better for everyone. It always means worse, for some." Thus women become for him the eggs which are broken and consumed to create a better life for the patriarchal ruling class.

The Commander is evasive and trivializing about the human implications of his political revolution. On the other hand, we note that Professor James Darcy Pieixoto (the voice of the academy) who speaks in the Historical Notes section, is willing to remain oblivious to the "human implication" of Offred's tale, the story he has pieced together from fragments. His distanced, objective reading is at cross purposes with Offred's subversive political intent in recording her tale. Accordingly, his neutral stance highlights his links to the Commander, and serves to accentuate the satirical purpose of the novel. As Pullen notes in continuing his discussion of the Proposer's style: "Only a style of antiseptic distance could ignore the potential for horror in this." The last of the narrators of *Tale*, Professor Pieixoto prides himself on his "antiseptic distance," his fitting, proper, moral relativity. Ignoring the horror of Gilead, he warns his audience "we must be cautious about passing moral judgments upon the Gileadeans. Surely we have learned by now that such judgments are of necessity culture-specific. . . . Our job is not to censure but to understand." Thus, Pieixoto adheres to a reading practice that remains distanced from dystopian or satirical narratives, reading for escape or for comfort rather than as an impetus for action toward social change. It is this kind of distanced reading which perpetuates the dystopia of Gilead in its current avatar in Nunavit.

We now turn to the central narrative voice in *The Handmaid's Tale*. What are we to make of the voice of Offred, the handmaid whose oral narration has been transcribed by Pieixoto? Glenn Deer has analyzed the voice of the narrator, and finds her to be not as innocent as we might first suppose. Deer notes that Offred is a gifted storyteller; she does not remain an artless narrator. To some extent she is complicit in the story she tells, a story which foregrounds violence. "In *The Handmaid's Tale* we are guided by a cunning implied author, a voice that feigns weakness in the guise of Offred, her narrative mask; but this voice cannot help but advertise the control and strength of its origins: Margaret Atwood. . . [T]hough the reader has participated in the construction of this story, responsibility for its pain and power lies in the rhetorical will of the author." Deer argues that Atwood must create a skilled storyteller in order to achieve her rhetorical goals. I would like to push Deer's point somewhat further, to argue that the power of the novel comes precisely from the tension produced by just this layering of narrative voices. By reading the slippage between the voices of Offred and Pieixoto and the "rhetorical will of the author" we become aware of the layers of irony, "the interaction. . . between different meanings. . . with some critical edge." Similarly, it is in the slippage between the skillful speech of the

Proposer and the "rhetorical will" of Swift that the irony of "A Modest Proposal" resides.

A key stylistic feature of *Tale* is its use of layers of textual material to establish frames that set up ironic oscillations of meaning. The epigraphs, historical notes and dedications are part of this process, but even within Offred's narrative the novel employs this ironic layering device. First, we note that Offred's text, the main portion of the novel, is Pieixoto's piecing together of recorded fragments. Second, within the tale puns, digressions, flashbacks, asides, rewordings, abound. Offred sometimes retells the same event in different ways, reminding us that this is a "reconstruction" or an "approximation." Thus, Offred's words continue the pattern of layered texts, overlapping voices within the novel. Jill LeBihan notes that this textual layering functions to problematize the Gileadean notion that there exists one truth, one officially sanctioned version of reality: "the novel constantly reiterates its uncertain, problematic relationship with the concept of a single reality, one identity, a truthful history." Further,

> the dystopian genre and temporal shifts are ways of drawing attention to the frame, the arrangers, and the white space and flat surfaces which make perception . . . possible . . . *The Handmaid's Tale* is dystopian fiction, but also historiographic metafiction with a confessional journal-style first person narrator. The single identifiable generic frame is stretched to include as many different writing strategies as possible within its construction. But the story once in print . . . is not under the subject's control.

Thus, several narrative conventions exist in tension with each other, challenging the notion of a seamless reality and a unified narrative voice. Similar stylistic strategies are at work in "A Modest Proposal."

Returning to interrogate Swift's style, we find that its power stems from this very tension of layered voices. I quote at some length from Clive T. Probyn's discussion:

> [Swift] characteristically works from the margin inwards, leaving us with a false frame, or even several overlapping frames of discourse. . . . The background noise[s] (allusions, . . . genres, styles, . . . asides, . . . disconnections) are endless. There is no one voice for us to interrogate, and . . . [the] text

> . . . refuses to give us a definitive truth. . . [Swift situates] the
> crisis of interpretation within the narrative personality, *before*
> the text reaches the reader of print, when he or she recognizes
> that . . . to agree with Gulliver we must become horses, or that
> humanitarianism in Ireland depends on cannibalism. . . There
> is no solace or privilege for the critic in all of this. Swift's
> narrators are always their own first critics, analytically adept,
> logical to a fault, keen students of the literary text. . . Swift's
> solution to warfare between overlapping texts is to rewrite,
> recycle, and permanently distort one text by [another]. . .
> version of it. . . . The subversion of a given text by an incursion
> from the margin which rewrites either in part or whole . . .
> [adds] a further and implosive level.

The overlapping frames of discourse, the background noises (puns, allusions, digressions, memories, retellings, multiplicity of genres, disconnections); these are among the devices which construct *The Handmaid's Tale*. There are many voices, starting with the dedication, moving through the epigraphs and the journal-entry novel to the Historical Notes. The "crisis of interpretation" is situated within Offred and Pieixoto. To agree with Offred, we must become complicit in the voyeurism of Gilead and its sexual and political violence; we must reify the romance plot which engineers Offred's escape from Gilead. To agree with Pieixoto, we must acquiesce to moral relativism and patriarchal sexism. "There is no solace or privilege for the critic in all of this": we must interrogate our own readings; in the person of Pieixoto ("analytically adept, logical to a fault, [a] keen student of the literary text") we have already been subsumed into the text. Layers of overlapping texts "rewrite, recycle, and permanently distort one text by [another]. . . version of it." The incursions from the margins, the dedications and epigraphs which press in upon the text, the Historical Notes which rewrite the tale from a future time add "further and implosive level[s]." Atwood's scintillating satire appropriates and puts to powerful use the very strategies which built Swift's satire.

Let us now turn to the epigraph: "having been wearied out for many years with offering vain, idle, visionary thoughts; and at length utterly despairing of success, I fortunately fell upon this proposal." If we read this as the voice of the Modest Proposer, we see the man who considers himself a practical, decent person, exasperated by the folly and suffering of humanity, delighted to be able to offer a solution to the ills of Ireland.

Who is the equivalent of the Modest Proposer in *Tale*? Let us consider the options. Is it the Commanders of Gilead, who at last have fortunately come upon the solution to the political ills they addressed, and to the problem of women. In this context, we remember that the Commander tells Offred that men from the time before Gilead had lost the ability to feel, and believed "there was nothing for them to do with women." Or, is Atwood's Modest Proposer the voice of the somewhat obtuse, chauvinist historian Pieixoto who at this point in his professional career (after what previous encounters with ideas, what manner of "thoughts"?) "fortunately fell upon" Offred's narrative, which may lead to conference papers and publications, and thus insure his professional "success"? Perhaps it is Offred, who was "wearied out for many years" thinking her "vain, idle, visionary thoughts" in her cell-like room in Gilead, and has now "fortunately [fallen] upon this proposal" to dictate her memoirs as a way to communicate the horrors of Gilead to a larger audience which possibly has the power to intervene in Gilead, or at least to commemorate its history. Or perhaps we have here the gently self-mocking, ironic voice of the imputed author (or of Atwood?). This author has "been wearied out for many years" speaking publicly, writing novels and essays "offering vain, idle, visionary thoughts" and has despaired because the political changes her texts propose have not yet come to pass. However, she has now "fortunately [fallen] upon this proposal" as the cautionary tale which will at last bring others to see the light and to mend their ways. Or perhaps, dear readers, it is we, the scholars who, like Professor Pieixoto, "fall upon" our texts and read into them our own obsessions. Perhaps, it is we who commodify the texts we read and evaluate according to our standards; we who offer up recipes for consuming the texts.

PHYLLIS STERNBERG PERRAKIS

Atwood's The Robber Bride:
The Vampire as Intersubjective Catalyst

The turn away from Freudian psychology begun by the object-relations psychoanalysts in the 1920s has powerful implications for gender theory. As Suzanne Juhasz explains, early object-relations practitioners like W. D. R. Fairbairn in Britain and Harry S. Sullivan in the United States opposed the Freudian emphasis on "instinctual drives" and its privileging of the oedipal period as the dominant factor in child development; proposing that the infant's relation to other people (objects) is the motivating factor in human development, object-relations theorists focused attention on the child's earliest years and first relationship—with the mother. In the 1980s Daniel Stern and Jessica Benjamin extended this theory; denying traditional psychoanalysis's assumption of the infant's original undifferentiated oneness with the mother, they argued instead that the infant must paradoxically balance dependence and independence at each stage of his or her interaction with the m(other), a balance which facilitates both separation from and connection to the mother. This reseeing of infant-m(other) relations opens the door to new, non-oedipal ways of understanding the infant's growth into individuality, and thus creates new possibilities for mutual recognition and acceptance in male-female relations.

Margaret Atwood's novel, *The Robber Bride*, provides an intriguing "fairy-tale" site for exploring these new insights into child development and

From *Mosaic* 30:3 (September 1997): 151–168. © 1997 by The University of Manitoba.

gender relations. Indeed, in this novel Atwood seems deliberately to invoke the assumptions of the traditional Freudian/Oedipal schema and play them off against the new mother-child model. In particular she inverts or revises the Freudian/Oedipal emphasis on the dominance of the male in heterosexual love by embedding and deconstructing two classic versions of a gendered reading of sexual relations: one is the fantasy of erotic domination and submission acted out by the mythic figure of the male vampire in Bram Stoker's *Dracula*; the other is what Sharon Wilson calls the fantasy of "cannibalism and dismemberment of *females*" which is enacted by the bridegroom in Grimms' tale of "The Robber Bridegroom" who lures his wives-to-be to his remote house and eats them. In Atwood's realistic reworking of these texts, Dracula and the robber bridegroom metamorphose into Zenia, a clever and glamorous *femme fatale* whose mesmerizing stories, like Dracula's mesmerizing eyes, allow her to insinuate herself into the lives of the three modern female protagonists: Tony, a college-educated intellectual, Charis, a new-age spiritualist, and Roz, a wealthy half-Jewish business executive. Zenia's manipulative tactics also involve the seduction of the three protagonists' lovers/ husbands, whom she symbolically devours and discards.

Atwood had already used vampire imagery in her earlier novel, *Cat's Eye*, to suggest psychological control in friendships between girls and had hinted at the early childhood sources of these power imbalances. In *The Robber Bride*, I wish to argue, Atwood powerfully extends the vampire motif along the lines of Stern's and Benjamin's theories about the paradoxical relationship between dependence and independence in human development. Specifically, I wish to explore the way that despite its apparent insidiousness, Zenia's function is ultimately transformative, forcing the three protagonists out of submissive relationships and making possible new modes of self-other interaction. In order to establish the theoretical context for my discussion, I will begin by outlining the major differences between Stern/Benjamin and Freud/Lacan. In turning to Atwood's novel, I will first focus generally on the psychological dimensions of Zenia's fabricated stories and then examine in detail how her seductive interaction with each of the three protagonists enables them to overcome their stalemated heterosexual relationships and to discover new ways of relating to others.

According to classic Freudian theory, the infant's initial symbiotic attachment to the mother must eventually give way to a rejection of maternal closeness in order for the child to enter into the world of language, culture, and self-consciousness. Although this view continues to be subscribed to by Lacan, child-psychologist Daniel Stern has argued that the infant is never totally undifferentiated from the mother, and that he/she possesses from birth an innate capacity to organize experience and form an emergent sense of self. Taking "the sense of self as a developmental organizing principle," Stern goes on to outline "three different senses of the self and other . . . and three different domains of relatedness that develop between the age of two months and the second year of the infant's life." The domain of core relatedness, first achieved at about two to three months, concerns the infant's sense of a distinct, integrated physical self and of "other people as distinct and separate interactants." At about seven to nine months the infant first develops an awareness of his/her inner subjective states and first realizes that these too can be shared with another. This subjective sense of self allows the "mental states" of infant and mother to be "'read,' matched, aligned with, or attuned to" each other. Between eighteen and thirty months, according to Stern, the infant discovers the verbal sense of self, the domain in which he/she acquires the ability to use language "to create shared meanings." This domain both facilitates and obscures the child's interaction with self and others.

Unlike the Lacanian argument that language functions as a defense against regressive closeness to the mother, Stern presents language acquisition as increasing "enormously" the "possible ways of 'being with' another." Furthermore, the verbal domain gives the infant access to an objective sense of self and to the cultural world defined by language. Nonetheless, "language is a double-edged sword. . . . [which] drives a wedge between two simultaneous forms of interpersonal experience: as it is lived and as it is verbally represented." Finally, language gives the infant "the ability to narrate . . . [his/her] own life story with all the potential that holds for changing how one views oneself." Stern's most interesting contention— and the most helpful for my purposes here—involves his assertion that while these modes of knowing the self and relating to the other are originally formed during the sensitive periods outlined above, they "remain active, growing, subjective processes throughout life." In contrast to the Freudian and Lacanian models, for Stern "the infant does not grow out of any of [these modes]; none of them . . . get[s] left behind."

Building on Stern's work and on the gendered readings of the infant- mother relationship offered by Nancy Chodorow and others, Jessica Benjamin ties the relations between the infant and mother to the issues of "power and surrender in adult sexual life." According to Benjamin, the structure of domination associated with adult erotic relationships is an escape from the painful realization of the paradox of dependence and independence, of recognition and self-assertion that is first experienced by the infant with the mother. This paradox rests on the child's need not only "to achieve independence," but to "be recognized as independent—by the very people on whom he has been most dependent." Without recognition from the mother, the infant is unable to exercise his/her independence. Recognition "allows the self to realize its agency and authorship in a tangible way. But such recognition can only come from an other whom we, in turn, recognize as a person in his or her own right." Thus, paradoxically, our independence, our agency, rests on our dependence and recognition of an other whom we do not control.

The oedipal view of individuality of Freud and Lacan is built on the premise that the father's intervention is necessary to propel the child into independence. From this perspective, Benjamin argues, woman is the "contested point" in the "father-son rivalry," embodying the infant's regressive desire for oneness; she is "never [seen as] an other whose different and equal subjectivity need be confronted" by the infant. Furthermore, as Benjamin sees it, traditional psychoanalysis has not been able to distinguish between "two subjects recognizing each other . . . [and] one subject regulating another," so that infant-mother interactions are seen only in terms of a powerful partner taking care of the needs of a weak partner; since such a relationship can never lead to equality but "simply invert[s] itself," with the weaker partner fantasizing that he or she is the stronger, "the stage [is set] for domination." To overcome this dualistic notion of experience, what is required is a model based on "mutuality and sharing," in which it is possible "to share feelings and intentions without demanding control, to experience sameness without obliterating difference."

According to Benjamin, such a balanced model is particularly lacking in traditional discussions of women's sexual desire. Instead of the Freudian/Oedipal emphasis on the experience *within* the psyche ("the intrapsychic mode" of representation) in which the phallus is equated with power, separation and individuality and women are subsequently defined in terms of what they lack, Benjamin posits the relevance of the "intersubjective dimension" which considers "experience *between and within* individuals, rather than just *within*" and "where two subjects meet"; thus "not only man but also woman can be subject." Benjamin argues that this intersubjective view of women's desire can be better expressed "in spatial rather than symbolic representation" and builds on D. W. Winnicott's suggestive use of spatial metaphors to describe the relations between self and other. Winnicott proposes that the mother creates a "holding" environment for the child which meets the infant's needs while also leaving room for the child to discover his/her own feelings and desires. From Benjamin's perspective, what Winnicott calls "transitional phenomena," which define the space between separateness and union, expand into a "transitional *realm* in which the child can play and create as if the outside were as malleable as his own fantasy."

Here "the line between fantasy and reality blurs," creating a safe space that is essential for discovering one's own self-identity: "In the relaxation of this space it is possible to know one's impulses (drives) as coming from within, to know them as one's own desire." Applying Winnicott's theories of child development to women's desire, Benjamin observes that "the spatial metaphor repeatedly comes into play when women try to attain a sense of their sexual subjectivity," and that a woman's attempt "to find her own inner space can be . . . expressed as the wish for an open space into which the interior self may emerge, like Venus from the sea."

The psychological connections between domination and submission in erotic love, modes of infant-m(other) interaction, and the importance of narrating one's own life story are powerfully represented in *The Robber Bride*. The novel begins with the three protagonists in middle age suddenly re-encountering the supposedly dead Zenia. It then circles back to recount each of the protagonist's earlier traumatic involvements with the chameleon-like storyteller. Tony meets the strikingly beautiful Zenia while both are students in the 60s, and Zenia is living with West, a male classmate whom Tony silently loves. Zenia's lurid story of surviving a childhood in which her Russian emigré mother rented her out for the sexual use of various emigré officers, wins Tony's admiration and complete trust. Zenia repays Tony's adoration by blackmailing her (Tony has written a university essay for Zenia) and deserting West, leaving Tony to pick up the pieces. Later, when Tony has married West, Zenia returns, steals West away, deserts him, and again leaves Tony to repair the damage. Charis encounters a bruised and sickly looking Zenia in the 70s, when she shows up one day at Charis's Yoga class telling a grim tale of her struggles with cancer and her physical abuse by West. Soon after she moves in with Charis and her Vietnam draft-dodger boyfriend, Billy. In response to Charis's tender nursing, Zenia seduces, blackmails and makes off with Billy, leaving Charis pregnant and distraught. Roz befriends a glamorous Zenia in the 80s when she turns up at the restaurant where Roz is dining with her elegant but philandering husband Mitch, telling a story of having been saved by Roz's father from the holocaust. Deeply grateful for this positive picture of her wily father, Roz helps Zenia to become editor of the woman's magazine she owns, while Zenia responds to Roz's help by stealing away Mitch and eventually disappearing with a generous amount of the magazine's money. Shortly after, Zenia fakes her own death and Mitch commits suicide. Within each of these separate stories, the anonymous narrator plunges even further into the past to relate episodes from each protagonist's childhood, centering on her formative relationship with her mother (and in Roz's case also with her father) and its subsequent effect on her modes of relating. The novel concludes with each of the protagonists surviving one last encounter with Zenia before her mysterious death.

Zenia's means for establishing her powerful intersubjective exchanges with the three women center on her ability to create and inspire powerful self-narratives. She exists in what Benjamin calls "intersubjective space," the space across which, according to Stern, the infant first forms various kinds of relationships with the mother and develops corresponding modes of knowing the self. This is also the space in which, according to Benjamin, the adult woman engages in the dance of intimacy with an erotic other, her sexuality grounded in "the exchange of gestures conveying attunement" rather than in a particular organ. Always functioning in interaction with one of the other three protagonists, Zenia is never seen alone. Most often Zenia's interactions with the three women also take place in Winnicott's "transitional realm," a place of safety where it is possible to move freely between fantasy and reality. At the beginning of her relationship with each of the three protagonists, Zenia, like a therapist or the mother during infancy, seems to create this kind of safe space for the women.

Creating empathetic versions of her past and insinuating herself into the present of the three women, Zenia attunes herself to each woman's deepest patterns of subjective interaction. While each of the protagonists experiences all three of Stern's domains of relatedness, each has a characteristic style of negotiating intersubjective space that privileges a particular mode of self-other interaction. Neither Stern's theory nor Atwood's novel, however, is simplistic or mechanical and the modes overlap in theory and in the character's psychic lives. I shall be referring only to a predominance of one mode over the others in each character, in keeping with the way that Zenia responds most strongly to this dominant mode.

The woman whose perceptions begin and end the novel is Tony. Just as the novel's storyteller uses the gothic form to represent complex emotional experience, Tony uses her left-handed writing to reveal her inner world. This unconscious communication of her otherwise buried self is not understood until Zenia appears, recognizes and attunes herself and her story to Tony's left-handed or buried self and allows Tony, for the first time, to share her inner world and subsequently to begin to articulate a self-narrative.

Tony is the only one of the protagonists who is able to maintain an adult erotic relationship, to reclaim the man she loves from Zenia—twice—and to keep him. Her ability not only to survive Zenia's initial desertion but to gain from it her marriage to West is tied to her ability to acknowledge and use the left-handed dead-twin side of her self. This forbidden aspect of the self seems to figure as the gap between the conscious view of the self sanctioned by the (m)other and society—the self formed through normal language acquisition—and the pre-verbal and para-verbal self that is ignored, misattuned or rejected. In this case, Tony is able to bridge the gap between language and prior modes of relating by finding another form of language—a distorted or poetic form that figures the missing space between what she is taught to say and what she feels. Thus her left-handed writing figures the pre-verbal, Semiotic aspect of language referred to by Julia Kristeva which works to undermine language's purely Symbolic function.

Tony's ability to maintain her support for her denigrated left-hand with its odd slant on the world is tied to her ability to see the discrepancy between the words and feelings of her mother Anthea. Taken tobogganing, Tony knew by the way her mother was "pleating her lips" that, despite her mother's words of enthusiasm, "the scene before her was not exactly what she'd had in mind." Told by her mother that "she could dress Tony in a potato sack and Tony wouldn't notice," what Tony did notice was that it wouldn't "make any difference whether she wore a potato sack or not. Any difference to Anthea, that is." Thus, despite all the declarations that "Mother truly, truly loves you," Tony was aware that no amount of tea making or piano playing would win her mother's interest or love. Tony even intuited that the grammatical form of her mother's statement—using the third person rather than the first—signifies the gap between Anthea's decorous maternal language and her unverbalized but acted on feelings. This gap was most fully realized in Anthea's long good-bye note to her daughter, claiming that she would like to take her along, that she will write "lots," that Tony will understand when she gets older and that she "loves . . . [her] very much." All of these statements, Tony later realizes, were false.

Although as Tony Fremont she is outwardly docile and anxious to please, her inner world or the site claimed by "Tnomerf Ynot"—her name spelled backwards—is permeated with images of violence and war, and her childhood, like her engendering, is shaped by World War II. Called a war baby by her mother, Tony also recognizes the temperamental and cultural conflict between her parents, the family war that inscribes the outer war. As the smallest victim of this conflict, perceived as an alien by both her parents, having the wrong accent for her mother, the wrong gender for her father, Tony is aware at a young age that she is seen by her mother as belonging to her father's camp—emotionally a cold fish. Called a guppy at birth by Anthea, Tony opens and closes her mouth in the incubator, emitting no sound, or at least no sound that her mother can hear. This soundless crying, like her backward writing, figures Tony's relation to her mother—her needs are either inaudible or incomprehensible to Anthea.

The lack of recognition from her mother in childhood, a failure in the domain of intersubjective relatedness, leaves Tony as an adult unable to form close relationships or to believe that she can share her inner world with another. Never having had a friend, she is stalemated in her first significant relationship with an adult male, reduced to afternoon exchanges in beer parlors or coffee shops. Even the thought of going on a date with West overwhelms Tony: "She couldn't have handled the implications, or the hope."

It is at this juncture that Zenia appears and fixes Tony with her vampiric eyes—eyes that like Dracula's are capable of mesmerizing their victim. Presumably Dracula's power to entice his victims lies in his appeal to their suppressed and unacknowledged longings—in the unmarried Lucy Westenra a desire for sexual initiation, in the married Mina Harker for fuller outlets for her unused capabilities. Zenia also recognizes and responds to Tony's hidden self, asking her first, "What's [her] obsession?" and later questioning her about her mother. Both questions slip in under Tony's defenses and attune themselves to her inner world. Sharing that world with Zenia, Tony feels that "she's out of control. . . . These are perilous waters." In admitting Zenia into that lonely intersubjective space where mental states are shared, the space that she was never able to share with Anthea, Tony risks having her inner world invaded and appropriated by a powerful (m)other, i.e. being drained by the vampire. Like Mina Harker, however, she also gains for herself some of the vampire's strength—the strength that comes from intersubjective attunement—and begins to fit together the "shiny fragments" of her memory of her mother and to create for the first time a self-narrative of her painful childhood.

Calmly telling Tony a dark story of her own childhood horrors, Zenia creates an intersubjective space where Tony can imaginatively identify with the other young woman—seeing herself in Zenia's blue-black eyes "as she would like to be. *Tnomerf Ynot*. Herself turned inside out." Her hidden self acknowledged and responded to by the (m)other for the first time, Tony lets down her defenses and regresses to a child-like state where her normally sharp awareness of other people's insincerity is lulled asleep. She interprets Zenia's possibly mocking smile "as a touching gallantry," she writes Zenia's term paper, and she renounces her interest in West.

Zenia's manipulation, however, is not the real point of her friendship with Tony, *or not the only point*. Her attunement and recognition create an intersubjective space similar to Winnicott's "transitional realm," a space that provides the support and protection needed to explore the unknown dimensions of the self. In the security of this space Tony begins to reexperience and now share some of the lonely experiences of her childhood. After Zenia deserts her, forcing Tony back into adult reality, Tony is no longer satisfied to withdraw passively to the sidelines of life. She finds that she "has developed an appreciation for confidences." She shares her emotional inner world with Roz and is able to share her physical world with West, thereby discovering both that he truly needs her and that "she is bigger inside than out," and apt figure for her emotional as well as physical self.

In middle age, when the supposedly dead Zenia reappears like Dracula arising from his coffin, Tony thinks that to defeat her, she would have to become her. Tony, however, has already partially become Zenia: she has already been changed by her experience of a powerful intersubjective relatedness that can sustain and drain the self. Zenia has shown Tony how to relate in the domain of shared emotions, adapting herself and her story to the hidden self that Tony has never been able to share with anyone else. As a result of this experience of emotional attunement, Tony is able to share her inner world with West and her two friends, express her pain and anger, feel sexual pleasure and assert herself. Tony's experience of welcoming Zenia into her life during a crisis in an adult erotic relationship has allowed her to create with Zenia a transitional realm in which she can relive in a more satisfactory manner an early mode of self-(m)other interaction, and, after Zenia's desertion, retain some of Zenia's power, or rather discover her own feelings and desires.

Charis also befriends Zenia at a crucial point in her relation with a male lover. Although living with Billy in a tiny cottage on Toronto Island, Charis is unable to feel sexual desire or to assert her needs in this relationship. Playing the moon to Billy's bright sun, Charis passively complies to Billy's sexual demands, anxiously strives to feed and care for him, and even submits occasionally to being hurt by him without complaining.

Billy's domination and indifferences to her feelings are, in part, what Charis loves about him. Idealizing his sense of agency and autonomy, his ability to know and satisfy his desires, Charis seems to attain a vicarious sense of her own self-agency and independence through submerging her desires in his. As Benjamin points out, "The belief that the man will provide access to a world that is otherwise closed to [a woman] is one of the great motives in ideal love." Idealizing Billy's selfishness as a "shiny" "impermeable" surface against which, like hard rubber, other people's feelings just bounce off, Charis feels herself, in comparison, to be "covered all over with tiny feelers like the feelers on ants." While Billy has sharp clear boundaries between himself and the rest of the world, Charis is an open door, and "everything blows right through."

Charis's fluid sense of boundaries is only one of the many areas in which her sense of a core self is revealed to be in trouble. Indeed, she experiences disruptions in all the four areas that Stern identifies as constituting the core self: the sense of "being a nonfragmented, physical whole with boundaries," possessing an ongoing sense of "self-history," being able to experience the full range of "affectivity," and possessing a sense of "self-agency." Lacking a solid sense of boundaries, Charis not only experiences other people's feelings, she also bumps into objects because "she wasn't sure where the edges of her body ended and the rest of the world began." Her sense of "self-history" is also easily shaken; shocked by the sudden reappearance of the supposedly dead Zenia, she temporarily loses her on-going sense of life and must remind herself, "*I exist.*" Charis's inability to experience emotions is clearly obvious in the sexual area. Finally, and, above all, she has difficulty with "self-agency." On the one hand, objects never seem to stay where Charis thinks she has placed them; on the other, she lacks control over her own actions: she is unable to finish painting the bottom stairs of her house, to repair her broken sewing machine, or to pick up the thumbtacks after she drops them on the bedroom floor.

Charis's fluidity of boundaries makes her particularly susceptible to abuse, as we learn through a long look at her past, which details her painful childhood violations by family members. In a discussion of the relationship between the mother-daughter bond and incest in fiction by women, Paula Bennett links incest with "the mother's failure to protect her daughter or her self from invasion." Noting that the mother's close identification with her daughter often becomes the means through which the mother "transfers her own sense of deprivation and helplessness," Bennett shows how this includes the mother's self-hatred and inability to care for herself.

Charis's early experiences with her mother reveal precisely the transfer of feelings of deprivation and self-hatred analyzed by Bennett. Her mother's own inability to cope, her "bad nerves" and "hysteria" are translated into beatings for her young daughter Karen, as Charis was then called. Even while being beaten, however, Karen cannot simply respond to her own suffering but must keep her antennae attuned to the feelings of her mother: if she cries too little, she is "hard," and if she cries too long, she is making too much noise. Thus Karen is constantly taught to ignore her own physical feelings and respond to the feelings of the (m)other. In childhood she also sleep-walks like Stoker's heroine Lucy just before she is attacked by Dracula. The fluid boundary between her mother's identity and her own finally leaves the young Karen unable to identify clearly with her own physical needs and vulnerable to the feelings of others, a psychological condition that might also apply to *Dracula*'s Lucy.

As an adult, Charis (who has repressed Karen's name and the memory of her childhood abuse) continues to experience an extraordinary openness to the physical and emotional reality of others and a troubled core sense of self. Her sensitivity to physical stimuli totally dominates her personal relationships. Rarely interested in words, which "are so often like window curtains, a decorative screen put up to keep the neighbors at a distance," Charis watches instead people's body language or feelings. Meeting her friends for lunch, she responds, not to what they say, but to Roz's aura, "so golden and many-coloured and spicy," in contrast to Tony's "transparent coolness," like "a snowflake, so tiny and pale and fastidious, but cold."

When she meets Billy, Charis is especially preoccupied with trying "to get rid of the heaviness hidden deep within" her body, a heaviness which prevents her from responding to sexual intimacy. Unable to resolve this issue with Billy or to deal with her abusive past, Charis, like Tony before her, seems to be stalemated in her relation with an erotic other. Again like Tony, it is at this point that Charis meets Zenia, identifies with her story of being ill and abused, and invites her into her life. Whereas Tony had found in Zenia a (m)other capable of sharing Tony's inner subjective world, Charis finds in Zenia an abused child to whose basic physical needs she tends with sensitivity and care. Charis's care of Zenia on their first evening together suggestively captures the way that a mother creates a safe holding environment for an infant. Charis runs a bath for Zenia, gives her one of her own cotton nightgowns, wraps her in a blanket and sits her by the fire where she combs her hair and gives her hot milk and honey. Interacting with her at the most basic, core level of self, Charis provides Zenia with what Stern would call the sensitive, "self-regulating" physical mothering that Charis herself so terribly lacked.

For Charis, as for Tony, to invite Zenia in is to invite an unknown mode of knowing the self and relating to the (m)other. In Charis's case that unknown part of herself centers on her acceptance of her bodily needs and her ability to satisfy them. Gaining confidence in her physical agency and autonomy as a result of her ability to care for Zenia, Charis begins to experience herself as "competent and virtuous, overflowing with good will and good energy." For the first time, she sees Billy's lack of gratitude and starts to ask more for herself. Finally, shocked out of her idealization of Billy's sexual domination of her by Zenia's comment that Billy "wants to haul [her] into bed," Charis suddenly finds herself flooded with the memories of her earlier life as Karen. Just as she has provided a safe holding environment for Zenia, Charis is now strong enough to "hold" these feelings inside her and is able spontaneously and unconsciously to recover her past. Thus through the safe transitional realm created by Zenia's presence and her story, Charis is able imaginatively to repair her own experiences of early infancy by providing what Winnicott would call a "good-enough" mothering for Zenia.

Karen does not come back, however, in the same form that she left. She comes back grown up and "look[ing] like Zenia." A revisionist presentation of the way that in *Dracula* Lucy returns from the dead looking like a vampire, Karen comes back a hardened but also explicitly sexual being. The old, helpless and abused part of Charis's physical sense of self has been transformed into a stronger, more capable, Zenia-like physical self which can now acknowledge its sexual feelings. Incorporating this old-new identity into her sense of self, Charis no longer needs to cut off her emotional and verbal selves from her sexual experience: "Everything in her has been fused together."

Having relived imaginatively with Zenia the formation of her earliest core sense of self, Charis, like Tony, must cope with Zenia's defection with Billy in tow in order to solidify her new identity in the real world. Reexperiencing both the (m)other's appropriation of her physical sense of self through Zenia's lies about her sickness, and a recurrence of childhood physical violation in her discovery the morning that Zenia and Billy leave that all her chickens have been murdered, Charis feels that "Zenia has taken away the part of herself she needs in order to live." Pregnant with Billy's child, however, which embodies her fused senses of self and draws forth her new-found ability to mother, she finds the motivation to deal with her emotional pain and to mother herself. Receiving the help from her friends, who here seem to figure as the other domains of the sense of self, Charis eventually takes control of her life and, like Tony before her, asserts her autonomy by buying a house.

In emphasizing her protagonists' ability to acquire their own domiciles, Atwood seems to be re-envisioning *Dracula*'s entrapping patriarchal spaces— Victorian mansions which, despite their numerous rooms and plentiful servants, are still unable to provide Stoker's heroines with safe havens from the vampire's attack; instead these male-owned physical spaces leave them vulnerable to some one else's desire. Deconstructing this Gothic convention, Atwood instead accords with Benjamin's theory that women often need to find safe spaces of their own in order to experience the emergence of their sexual subjectivity. For both Tony and Charis, their houses become embodiments of their discovery of what Benjamin calls their "*own, inner* desire." Tony's fortress-style tower reflects her need for strong intellectual defenses to protect her from invasion by appropriating (m)others, as well as providing a safe habitat for her historical reconstructions, for West's "aural mayhem" and their mutually consoling relationship. Charis's tiny, shabby, slanting cottage embodies her dominant mode of being: her life rests on a fragile and permeable physical core self. Escaping both Billy's domination and Zenia's manipulation, Charis finds in her softly decorated and partially unfinished house a provisional but secure enough safe space, from which her new found ability to mother herself and her daughter can emerge.

While both Tony and Charis live out with Zenia the tensions surrounding pre-verbal senses of self, Roz becomes entangled with Zenia through her explicit concern with revising her narrative of her father's life and implicitly of her own. As Stern notes, the ability to create one's life story, which comes with the acquisition of language, allows the child to begin to construct a self-narrative which is very likely to reflect the distortions or judgments of self that are the product of her early experiences.

Roz's section, more than those of the other two protagonists, is explicitly concerned with this relationship between self-narrative and subjectivity. From an early age Roz weaves into her life-story a sense that she is inexplicably different from those around her. Aware that the nuns at her school give her funny looks when she asks too many questions, called a DP because of her skin color, told that her hair is too dark to play an angel in the school Nativity play, Roz feels that "an invisible barrier" sets her apart.

Her early sense that "She wasn't like the others" is dramatically increased and her life story is "cut in two" with the return of her father. While he provides Roz with a model for her bulky figure, loud voice, warm emotions, and sharp mind, her father also heightens her sense of being an outsider with his odd accent and clothes, disreputable friends and, eventually, his suspicious income. Nonetheless, Roz is immediately aware that her father has power, both over her mother and herself, and readjusts to her new position in the family. She identifies with her father as a way both to escape her mother's control—and the onerous duties that go along with it—and to punish her for pushing Roz to the outskirts of her affection. Sitting on her father's lap, not helping out, she watches her mother slave away "with gloating triumph and thinks it serves her right." In using her father to escape from her mother's power, however, Roz is also unable to balance her need for recognition from her mother with her need to assert her sense of difference. Denying her dependence on her mother while internalizing her judgments, admiring her father while feeling uncomfortable about his financial and sexual behavior, Roz comes to feel herself a "pastiche," not belonging totally to either camp.

Repressing her knowledge of her own powerful, father-spawned commanding nature, Roz constantly seeks acceptance. Labeling herself an outsider, Roz's need for recognition by the other involves her in what Benjamin calls a "dialectic of control: If I completely control the other, then the other ceases to exist, and if the other completely controls me, then I cease to exist. . . . True independence means sustaining the essential tension" between "asserting the self and recognizing the other." The excessive quality of Roz's attempts at gaining recognition, her too loud voice, talkativeness, pushiness and ostentatious use of her money, often occupy all the in-between space in relationships, leaving no room for the self-assertion or autonomy of the other. Unaware of the controlling or suffocating nature of her intersubjective behavior, Roz is prevented from getting the response that she wants: the mutual sharing of feelings and intentions of two independent beings who recognize and appreciate the independence of the other.

It is especially in her relations with her husband Mitch that Roz's split sense of self and problems with recognition take their most devious form. Drawn to Mitch by her feeling that he epitomizes the insider, Roz finds in the strikingly handsome, elegantly mannered scion of old money all the qualities she lacks in herself. Idealizing his charm, sophistication and physical attractiveness just as Charis idealizes Billy's independence, Roz hopes through Mitch's love finally to gain symbolic acceptance by the world—to be an insider herself. What Roz fails to understand, however, is that Mitch is more troubled over issues of control than she, sexually frustrating her in courtship and indulging in continual sexual conquests during their marriage to prove his self-worth and keep a sense of independence. Thus despite all her attempts at self-effacement and glorification of Mitch, Roz continues to feel rejected and lonely, grateful for Mitch's slightest recognition and over-generous with gifts and forgiveness.

It is at this point—the point at which Roz's life, like her sense of self, seems hopelessly divided between masochistic acceptance of Mitch's infidelities and confident assertiveness in her business endeavors—that Zenia comes into the picture. In an ironic inversion of the situation of Mina Harker—who is left exposed to the vampire's attack when Victorian sexual stereotyping prevents her from actively seeking out Dracula with the men— Roz consciously exposes herself to the vampire's power, assuming that she can control it. In giving Roz a heroic narrative of her father's life, and therefore of her own, Zenia seems to offer Roz the possibility of integrating the two halves of her split self-narrative: Roz can now identify with her dynamic father without feeling guilty; she can assert her difference from her moralistic mother without renouncing her; she can be both active and good. Identifying with Zenia's story of being a lonely outsider, living "on the edge," Roz offers Zenia an editorial position on *WiseWomanWorld*, and watches mystified as Zenia transforms the serious magazine into a vehicle for money-making beauty and clothing ads. Before long she also has Mitch leaving with her, leaving Roz devastated with jealousy and loss.

After Zenia's disappearance, Roz's pride and her misreading of Mitch's desperation as rejection prevent her from accepting Mitch back into her house and life when he shows up at her door asking to come back. A couple of months later, as Roz toys with the idea of trying for a reconciliation, Zenia's supposed death and Mitch's subsequent suicide destroy Roz's fragile attempt at wholeness and present her with the need to revise her split self-narrative and put all of herself in one story. For Roz, however, coping with Zenia's seductive power is a slower process than it was for either Tony or Charis, perhaps because her pride and strength of character make her more resistant to change, just as her vulnerability has not been fully acknowledged. Thus although she redecorates her expensive house after Mitch's death, this act is a superficial refashioning of her physical world rather than a sign of inner change.

Still trying to come to terms with the loss of Mitch, five years after his death, Roz's re-encounter with Zenia sends her down to the cellar of her home, and into the past to try again to piece together all the bits of information and form a new self-narrative that will somehow account for both her rejection of Mitch and her subsequent need for him. Her descent into the basement, like Tony's and Charis's purchase of their houses, represents Roz's move to a space where new dimensions of the self can potentially emerge. Rereading the Grimms' "Robber Bridegroom," Roz remembers listening to Tony read the story to Roz's twin daughters during a phase in their early childhood when they insisted on making all the parts female. The tale became "The Robber Bride," and the victims as well as the murderer were all women. This subversion of a patriarchal myth is the key to both Roz's split self-narrative and Atwood's gothic tale. Roz must rewrite the story of her life to include her attunement to and separation from both her parents. Roz, however, as Lorrie Moore notes, does not grasp the implications of the twins' transforming storytelling. She has not yet grasped that women play all the roles, vampire as well as victim—that aggression, power and neediness, independence and dependence, all belong in Roz's story.

In her final encounter with Zenia, Roz like the other two protagonists plays all the roles, each finally accepting the contradictory feelings she generates. For Tony and Charis, their final meeting with Zenia solidifies the growth in self that they have already undergone. Both are momentarily tempted to fall back under the vampire's spell, to slip into the transitional realm where they can play fantasized daughter to an ideal mother or vice-versa. Zenia's hypnotic tales, however, now no longer totally bind or blind them; both can now see how Zenia performs her tricks and, unlike the responses of Stoker's heroines to Dracula, both Tony and Charis catch the ironic gleam in Zenia's eye.

Roz's final encounter with Zenia, however, is more crucial and the outcome less clear than for the others. Learning from Zenia of the degrading role that Mitch played in their affair—his groveling, dependence, and sexual masochism—without appreciating his autonomy, Roz reexperiences her old doubts and fears about her father and herself. As Shannon Hengen points out, "Roz's belief that men are somehow powerless against competitive, antifeminist women prevents her . . . from seeing Mitch clearly," and the same point can be made about their son Larry. She projects onto him her childhood split between being an innocent victim-outsider and a powerful but corrupt insider, and assumes that Larry must be either victim or aggressor rather than a composite of strength *and* gentleness. Failing to appreciate his autonomy or to understand his homosexuality, Roz tries to fit him into her either/or gendered categories of active or good, masculine or feminine, independent or dependent. About to over-play her maternal role and fall victim to Zenia's lies once again (Zenia tries to blackmail Roz by claiming that Larry is her drug dealer), Roz escapes Zenia's power only by buying time. Sharing her story with Tony and Charis, she realizes like the others that they have not succumbed to Zenia and they have not killed her, "either physically or spiritually," and, therefore, they have not turned into her. They can recognize Zenia without succumbing to her regressive allure and can separate from her without destroying her.

Atwood's update of tales of vampiric power extends the possibilities of the female gothic to represent the growth of female subjectivity. The novel's conclusion—that the three protagonists will continue to tell stories and that "tonight their stories will be about Zenia"—suggests that to tell her story is to tell their stories of re-entering the shadowy transitional realm in which they imaginatively recreate their relationships with the (m)other. Each woman forms a close bond with Zenia at a time when her deepest vulnerabilities concerning self and (m)other are again aroused by a relationship with an adult erotic other. As in the case of Dracula and other gothic figures, Zenia seems to mirror the unknown and dangerous potentialities of intersubjective relationships, and in keeping with the gothic motif that the vampire must be invited in, the women do not just passively acquiesce to Zenia's overtones. Furthermore, in inviting Zenia into their lives at a crisis in their relations with a male lover, each of the three women seems unconsciously to act out her need to explore again the crucial domain of self-(m)other interaction that is responsible for her erotic stalemate.

     Charis acts out with Zenia the relatedness primarily associated with the core sense of self—discovering in Zenia's narrative of illness and abuse attunement for her tensions over physical agency and sexuality. Tony relates to Zenia most fully in the domain of intersubjectivity, finding in Zenia's story of stubborn survival in the face of maternal mistreatment and hardship a mirror for her defiant hidden self and unhappy childhood that enables Tony to create and share her own self-narrative of maternal misattunement and desertion. Roz interacts with Zenia primarily in the realm of verbal relatedness: she powerfully responds both to Zenia's tale of being heroically rescued by Roz's father as a baby and her story of living as a lonely outsider in her adult years. As a result Roz takes the first steps toward revising and integrating her own divided life-story to include a realistic acceptance of the strengths and weaknesses of both her parents and, eventually, of herself.

Strengthened by their immersion in the imaginative transitional space that Zenia inhabits, the three protagonists survive the vampire's desertion and their return to reality. Receiving communal support from the other two protagonists (and the other two senses of self), the three women learn to integrate their new modes of relating into their characteristic patterns of self-(m)other interaction, enabling them, finally, to celebrate the vampire's power because it is also theirs. Thus they expand the intersubjective possibilities available to women, and show that it is feasible in middle age to learn some new ways to navigate the in-between space that separates and joins us to the other.

Not only does *The Robber Bride* provide a fascinating fictional fleshing out of Stern's and Benjamin's theories, but their theories allow for a reading that surmounts the dichotomous moral judgments of Zenia found in numerous reviews of the novel in which, as Hengen points out, Zenia "is variously condemned or praised." Instead Zenia can be seen as the embodiment of intersubjective relatedness, inhabiting a number of different sites outlined in recent psychoanalytic theory.

Discussing the paradoxical quality of Atwood's narrators, Nathalie Cooke has noted that the more they "admit their unreliability, the more reliable they seem to become." In Zenia's case, the more she spins her various confessional tales, the less we believe her, and in the process the more firmly she entices her fictive listeners. While Cooke focuses on Atwood's "fictive confessions" as "rhetorical" and "ethical" strategies designed to force her readers "to confront their own expectations," Zenia's confessional tales can also be seen as intersubjective ploys, wherein she functions as an avatar of the author herself. Zenia is not only the storyteller whose tales enthrall the three female protagonists but also the catalyst for other readers to construct their own life stories.

JUNE DEERY

Science for Feminists:
Margaret Atwood's Body of Knowledge

Many powerful ideas of modern science have fallen on artistic deaf ears. Except for writers of science fiction, relatively few contemporary fiction writers have made natural science a central preoccupation. In fact, most authors ignore scientific developments altogether. An interesting exception is Margaret Atwood, who not only refers to science but also does so from a woman's perspective, something comparatively rare in literary evocations of science. Science is not Atwood's central concern, but she does suggest, albeit in a light and at times even whimsical fashion, that modern physics is suited to describing women's experiences. In so doing she produces a striking adaptation of a predominantly male discourse (natural science).

Despite an obvious display of science in her popular novel *Cat's Eye*, there has been little examination of this aspect of Atwood's work, with the exception of an admirable chapter in Susan Strehle's *Fiction in the Quantum Universe* (1992) which examines Atwood's use of physics in *Cat's Eye* as it relates to subject-object relations. In actual fact, as I will demonstrate, almost every major theme in Atwood's writing—the formation of feminine identity, the construction of personal past and cultural history, body image, colonization—all are at some point described in terms of the basic laws of physics. In particular, Atwood applies new discoveries about the interrelationship of time, space, energy, and matter to significant aspects

From *Twentieth Century Literature* 43:4 (Winter 1997): 470–483. © 1997 by Hofstra University.

of human experience, especially women's experience under patriarchy.

We know that for centuries science has been culturally coded as masculine as opposed to the more feminine arts and letters. At one point Atwood suggests, with some humor, that natural science originated in the male desire to avoid comparing penises, scientific measurements being a transfer of the male obsession with size. Yet physics, the "hardest" and most masculine science of all, has in this century become modestly aware of fundamental limits. Scientists have had to accept restrictions, uncertainty, and a certain degree of inscrutability. With the exploration of the subatomic realm, it now seems to students of Atwood's generation that "The universe is hard to pin down; it changes when you look at it, as if it resists being known," primarily because the observer affects the condition of the subatomic object under observation. To the extent that relativity theory and quantum mechanics recognize such limits, to the extent that they look at interrelationships and participation, Atwood has been able to use these bodies of knowledge to describe metaphorically women's constraints and their adaptive strategies. As we shall see, she also invokes scientific ideas to a limited extent in her role as a writer, in the forms her novels take. Of course, neither relativity theory nor quantum mechanics strictly applies to the macroworld of human experience; indeed, the way physics has gone off stage, so to speak, has been disturbing and alienating for laypeople this century. What Atwood does is demonstrate that scientific models can be used to describe figuratively the middle, human realm once we switch from the physical to the psychological. Her use of a scientific frame doesn't so much tell us something new about human experience as give us new terms in which to view our behavior—which is to partly create a new reality.

Atwood's references to science should not be altogether surprising, given the interest in science that runs in the family: Among immediate relatives, her father is an entomologist and her brother a neurophysiologist. Atwood herself enjoyed studying science at school, so much so that she believes that if she hadn't become a writer she would have gone on with science, and today she reads popular scientific accounts as a recreation. There is no evidence that Atwood possesses a thorough grasp of physics or that she has any serious intent to instruct her readers. Instead, she focuses on a few striking ideas and runs with them in her imagination. Her sources are already-mediated popularizations, not the original papers of Einstein, say, or Heisenberg. On the acknowledgments page of *Cat's Eye*, Atwood writes:

> The physics and cosmology sideswiped herein are indebted to Paul Davies, Carl Sagan, John Gribbin, and Stephen W.

Hawking, for their entrancing books on these subjects, and to my nephew, David Atwood, for his enlightening remarks about strings.

Clearly, this author is making no pretensions about having a profound understanding of science (even deferring to her nephew). She is offering her own "rendition," which can be heard by those outside the field, by those who have never read these men or the men who preceded them, a rendition that uncovers a similarity between science and other fields such as feminist thought. Atwood is not suggesting, nor am I, that feminism directly influenced science, nor that science has in this regard influenced feminist thinking. But one can see them as part of a common episteme where their consonance is intriguing.

Scientific ideas appear as theme, as metaphor, and as narrative structure in Atwood's works. There is a particular concentration of explicit references to science in *Cat's Eye* and a more implicit treatment in *The Robber Bride*. *Cat's Eye* tells the story of an artist, Elaine Risley, who returns to Toronto for a retrospective of her work and at the same time looks back on her own life, especially her relationship to Cordelia, who bullied Elaine as a child. Much of the science enters the novel through Elaine's brother, Stephen (named after Hawking), who becomes a top physicist before being murdered by terrorists. *The Robber Bride* follows three characters: Roz, the head of a successful business; Charis, a well-meaning New Age Psychic; and Tony, a diminutive history professor whose specialty is war. What they have in common is that each has been manipulated and betrayed by a protean and evil character named Zenia, who they at first think is dead but who returns to cause further pain to this group of friends before finally meeting her end. My discussion will focus on these novels and will highlight both explicit references to science and more latent possibilities for using science to describe women's experiences that Atwood's writing opens up by suggesting that apparently bizarre features of twentieth-century physics are already familiar to many women.

Energy-Matter

In Atwood's writing, matter is pictured as energy; for example, skyscrapers are described as "gravestones of cold light" or "Frozen assets" (*Cat's Eye*), and bodies as "pure energy, solidified light." Elaine, the protagonist of *Cat's Eye*, learned from her scientist brother that "matter and energy are aspects of each other." So "It's as if everything is made of solid light." She has also learned that "matter is not really solid. It's just a bunch of widely spaced atoms moving at greater or lesser speeds" (*Cat's Eye*). This subatomic picture is used by Atwood's heroines to express their everyday fears. Elaine voices her insecurity and lack of support as a fear of "the spaces between the atoms you could fall so easily through" (*Cat's Eye*). In *The Robber Bride*, when Charis fears she might lose track of Zenia, she speculates that "If you knew enough about matter you could walk through walls." An unsettling prospect.

There are several references in Atwood's writing to the apparent transformation of energy into matter and matter into energy. As an artist, Elaine is seen pouring her energy into her paintings so that they can materialize. "Whatever energy they have came out of me," she notes. "I'm what's left over" (*Cat's Eye*). Elsewhere there are energy transfers among women characters or between these characters and the material world. This is particularly prevalent in *The Robber Bride* where Charis, for instance, sets out to transfer her "positive" or "good" energy into the ailing Zenia. These exchanges often result in a change in physical appearance, usually with an inverse relation between energy and mass. Take the relationship between Elaine and her antagonist, Cordelia, in *Cat's Eye*. When Cordelia is lethargic, she gains "limp weight," which makes her "bloated and watery," whereas Elaine is trim and energetic. When Cordelia is on top of things again, she is thin and attractive, and Elaine is at a disadvantage. In the end, Cordelia is once more a defeated, bloated, and passive lump in a mental institution, with all the energy belonging to Elaine.

Forms of emotional energy also materialize in Atwood's writing. For instance, in *The Robber Bride*, Roz sees red when she's angry. And not just metaphorically. "She actually sees it, a red haze obscuring her eyes." Charis observes an even more variegated manifestation when Zenia is angry: "A dark aura swirls out from around her. . . . It's a turbulent muddy green, shot through with lines of blood red and greyish black" (*Robber*). Atwood has color-coded emotions before; for example, she describes a particular "pale-mauve hostility" among women in *The Edible Woman*. But in *The Robber Bride*, color has taken on material form, energy appears to have mass, and mass, energy.

A particularly sensitive character like Charis also claims to be able to detect characters' electrical fields (*Robber*). In a bad environment she feels "Ions are bombarding her, wavelets of menacing energy" (*Robber*), and when the evil Zenia enters, even Tony, a less-observant character, feels "Waves of ill will flow out of her like cosmic radiations" (*Robber*). Sexual abuse is also depicted in terms of bad energy. To survive her abusive uncle, Charis converted her body/matter into energy/spirit and escaped in an astral "body of light" (*Robber*). She dreamt she could in this way "change herself into energy and pass through solid objects" (*Robber*).

Quantum Women and Newtonian Men

Atwood's world is one of radical uncertainty, a continuation of the modernist angst famously encapsulated in Yeats's "Things fall apart, the centre cannot hold," which she cannot resist citing (*Robber*). For the historian, Tony, "everything has been called into question. Even in the best of times, the daily world is tenuous to her, a thin iridescent skin held in place by surface tension" (Robber; note the scientific "surface tension"). Atwood's heroines *experience* the world of quantum mechanics. Most of them are unknown, protean, inscrutable, treacherous—even to themselves. They have "a tendency to exist" (*Cat's Eye*). They appear and fade and reappear. They are hard to keep track of. They marry and change their names (*Cat's Eye*). They are, in Tony's words, "a bugger to predict" (*Robber*). For these women, things are not separate or well behaved. Things pour into each other, slip under their feet, interpenetrate. Things are not even things. The bemused narrators can only observe and wonder that Newton or Descartes or Galileo ever thought they could fix things down. And by observing they wonder also to what extent they create what they see. They wonder how responsible they are for their own unhappiness, or happiness. It's a burden. It makes them light (*Cat's Eye*). Gravity reduces them, atom by atom (*Cat's Eye*). Irony and duality blur their vision. Like wave/particles, characters appear to be enemy/friends and self/others—all of which breeds a mild paranoia.

The men, on the other hand, are mostly perceived as solid, fixed, linear, sterling, predictable. They are a still point, a calculable presence. Even their betrayal is predictable and forgivable, whereas female treachery is inexplicable. The women know enough about women not to trust them, and not enough about men to withdraw forgiveness. They choose, at least, to see men as reliable and secure. They continue, in other words, to identify them with the traditional Western subject: "he" who is coherent and stable.

Atwood suggests that some of men's solidity and predictability can be attributed to their inability to perceive others well. She portrays most men as being wrapped in unawareness and ignorance. When encouraged to be more sensitive, they become "trickier" and "more evasive"—that is, more like her female characters (*Cat's Eye*). Her male figures' apparent solidity may also be the result of Atwood's practice of not writing from the male character's perspective (except Nate in *Life Before Man*). Her men are simply more opaque as fictional characters.

Female characters are scrutinized more closely, and for them the uncertainty is profound. It affects every aspect of their interaction with the world, even their body boundaries. Part of the energy-matter transfer mentioned before is that Atwood's women physically intermingle with their environment, the extreme example being Charis who "wasn't sure where the edges of her body ended and the rest of the world began" (*Robber*). She is diffuse, like the quantum object, not hard-edged like the billiard ball model of previous science. Charis is "so penetrable; sharp edges stick into her," whereas "whatever slams into [her lover] bounces right off" (*Robber*). This diffuseness could be related to women's plural, multizoned sexuality, what Irigaray refers to as women's diversified geography of pleasure. A more soluble self-other boundary could also be said to reflect women's position in mother-child relationships: both a woman's ability to literally incorporate another in the womb when pregnant and the female child's close identification with the mother. The latter psychological attachment could also be a trait that male scientists and writers share with women. A longtime observer of literary artists and scientists, N. Katherine Hayles notes a similar blurring of boundaries in D. H. Lawrence's writing and in quantum physics, and suggests that Lawrence shares with scientists an anxiety that "is bound up with the drive to achieve an autonomous identity independent of the mother." From the mother's perspective, Atwood portrays a woman's body during pregnancy as frighteningly amorphous and "fluid" (*Robber*). The incorporation is disturbingly parasitic. Again, in *The Edible Woman*, Marian hardly recognizes her friend when she is released from pregnancy because:

> During the later, more vegetable stage of Clara's pregnancy she had tended to forget that Clara had a mind at all or any perceptive faculties above the merely sentient and sponge-like, since she had spent most of her time being absorbed in, or absorbed by, her tuberous abdomen.

In general, Marian feels suffocated by a "thick sargasso-sea of femininity," by the continual interchange between women and their environment, "the continual flux between the outside and the inside, taking things in, giving them out, chewing, words, potato-chips, burps, grease, hair, babies . . ." She wants something solid, a man apparently, to keep from being sucked into it.

More philosophically, Atwood relates this fear to women's epistemological and hence ontological subordination. Women's edges are uncertain and their self-definition blurred because, Atwood suggests, they do not know or see themselves—though they are beginning to. Her women characters, so long ignored or relegated as Other, still mostly see themselves as men do, as fragments, as fetishized and commodified erotic parts. They therefore fear self-disintegration, they fear being stretched and losing shape altogether. Since her first novel, *The Edible Woman*, Atwood has made it clear that a woman's tendency to intermingle and be diffuse is not an advantage but indicates a lack of power. The experience of fission also reflects the demands of women's positions in a social field where they are subject to contrary forces and are expected to play plural roles.

Atwood's male observers try to impose on women a definite and containable shape or shapes to their liking. Josef, her art teacher, at one point transforms Elaine into a Pre-Raphaelite figure so that she hardly recognizes herself. All her life Cordelia is shaped and misshaped under her father's observation. Elaine notes the patriarchal perturbation: "Dinners at Cordelia's house are of two kinds: those when her father is there and those when he isn't." When he is not there, everything is casual, and mother and sisters come and go randomly. But when her father is present, they set themselves and the table more formally, and everyone stays in her place (*Cat's Eye*). In other regards, the father does not have to be physically present to keep his wife and children in line. Like other fathers in the novel—and, by implication, like God, the Father of fathers—he is often invisible but strongly present. Atwood's point is that it is difficult to say what women are without male observation: Women have always been women-as-observed-by-men, just as the subatomic object is what it is because it is being observed. Outside this observation, it is difficult to say what exists. For example, light takes different forms, waves or particles, depending on the experimental apparatus used. So too have Atwood's female characters been determined by men. They feel the constant surveillance. Roz, a powerful CEO, describes "the ever-present watcher peering through the keyhole, peering through the keyhole in your own head, if nowhere else. You are a woman with a man inside watching a woman. You are your own voyeur" (*Robber*). Women have been taught to internalize this scrutiny and to enforce gendering on each other. This is Atwood's focus in *Cat's Eye*, a novel that painstakingly reconstructs how Elaine's friends/enemies instruct her in femininity. It appears to be an account of infra-female interaction, but the male voice is ever present. For example, Cordelia upbraids Elaine for not "measuring up," a key male and scientific term Cordelia would have heard from her father. That patriarchy has always depended on this kind of compliance is a point heavily underscored by Atwood's dystopian novel, *The Handmaid's Tale*. Atwood's social model is not a linear power hierarchy but a more complex Maxwellian, or Foucauldian, field of action.

The Matter of Space-Time

Where the male—and by extension, female—observation has had a huge, physical impact is on women's bodies. Atwood closely inspects the importance of the body as space and mass for women's cultural identity, highlighting the obvious relation between the individual body and the body politic. This is played out in *The Handmaid's Tale* where the association of women and body/matter reverts to an Aristotelian economy of procreation in which women passively supply the mass that is shaped by male force. Here and elsewhere in Atwood's writing, women are so closely identified with the body that a change in body shape, in space occupied, generally means a new relation to the rest of the world. Food is a quotidian example of energy-matter interchange to which women pay particular attention. When the body stores food (energy) as mass, it has dire consequences for women. A strong ideological image of femininity insists that women shouldn't be massive or occupy too much space, whereas Elaine observes of boys that "There always seems to be more of them in the room than there actually are" (*Cat's Eye*). Women are taught to be ordered and controlled. Diets are entered into like warfare and result in intimate battles fought by women against themselves; again we see this clearly in Roz, who pictures her body as "a besieged fortress" (*Robber*). This cultural pressure leads to all kinds of eating disorders, a perennial topic in Atwood's writing. Occasionally, there is a suggestion that body fat can be powerful. In *Lady Oracle*, as the protagonist, Joan, grows increasingly fat, she becomes invisible to men and to women, and this provides a certain power and protection. It also contravenes physics in that the more mass she has, the less observable she becomes as an object. However, ordinarily, occupying more space means a serious reduction in self-esteem for women and signifies defeat, not growth.

Space-Time in Literature and Science

In a lecture on "The First Pico-seconds and the Quest for a Unified Field Theory," Stephen reminds his audience, which includes his sister Elaine, that "time cannot exist without space and space-time without . . . matter-energy" (*Cat's Eye*). Elsewhere Atwood suggests, perhaps whimsically, that space and time are especially closely linked in women's minds. She speculates that men's brains separate space and time in a way women's don't: For men there is "Space over here, time over there . . . in their own sealed compartments," (*Good Bones*), whereas Atwood's heroines repeatedly conceptualize time in spatial terms. Elaine thinks of time "having a shape, something you could see, like a series of liquid transparencies, one laid on top of another. You don't look back along time but down through it, like water" (*Cat's Eye*). A more humble image emerges later when she thinks of herself as a bag lady picking up temporal shreds (*Cat's Eye*). In *The Robber Bride*, Charis domesticates the bizarre and unusual by explaining foresight in this way: "there is a fold in time, like the way you fold the top bedsheet down to make a border, and if you stick a pin through any spot, then the two pinholes are aligned, and that's the way it is when you foresee the future." Atwood's characters also recognize cosmic space-time relations, as when Elaine looks up into outer space and realizes that what she sees is the past because stars are echoes from another time (*Cat's Eye*).

As a novelist, Atwood likes to thematize and play with the space-time of the form in which she is writing. Her work reminds us that (written) literature has always spatialized time in that the book form spreads a narrative's beginning, middle, and end before its readers all at once: While the convention is to read the text sequentially, readers can dip in at any point. Atwood's narratives realize this potential for spatialization by interlacing past and present occurrences, so that even when reading sequentially the reader feels past and present events coexist (in space and time) together. In *Cat's Eye*, for example, we are driven through a series of temporal loops, from the fictional present back into past events that appear immediate by being described in the present tense. *The Robber Bride* extends this temporal spatialization to include even the future. This novel features not only prolepsis or novelistic foresight but also—contrary to current physics—a character's accurate foretelling of future events. As a child, Charis apparently could always tell when a telephone was about to ring, and she foresees both her mother's and Zenia's deaths. Her insight appears to be ratified by events in the novel, though since the narrative voice often merges with the characters' voices, it is not always easy to determine the author's opinion of these supernatural and scientifically heterodox powers.

Atwood's predominant interest is her characters' reconstructions of the past in the light of the present and their coming to understand the past's effect on their present selves. Both *Cat's Eye* and *The Robber Bride* are haunted books, books about haunting, about how space is drenched in time. In *Cat's Eye*, this is described in loosely relativistic terms. Elaine fantasizes about moving faster than the speed of light and so traveling backward in time, in what mathematicians as well as artists call "imaginary time." This is what she achieves in a sense, through memory, which allows us to be tachyonic (faster than the speed of light). In the novel's present, Elaine is in "the middle of her life," which is a time and a place (*Cat's Eye*). She is (in a variation of the French phrase) of an *un*certain age. She travels back to Toronto looking for herself, for certainty, for the elusive Grand Unified Theory, or at least for the cats' eyes on the road that will provide direction. She is convinced that she will find closure when she faces her old tormentor, Cordelia, her Einsteinian "twin" (*Cat's Eye*). She wants to know if Cordelia is moving through time at the same rate, or if, like Elaine's dead brother, her other twin (*Cat's Eye*), Cordelia has stopped existing in the present. In Toronto, where she and

Cordelia used to exist, the past is more real than the present, more real than her present existence in Vancouver, with its unreal-because-beautiful landscape. Elaine can't believe in the latter's postmodern hyperreality. She identifies instead with the past when things weren't post this or post that because they were "real enough to have a name of their own" (*Cat's Eye*). Toronto, the old Huron Indian name for "meeting place," fails to live up to its name. The meeting with Cordelia—which Elaine's narrative projects—never happens. She does not even know if Cordelia (like Schrodinger's cat) is alive or dead. If the vastness of Canada has a center, Toronto would be it. But now even Elaine doesn't feel at home there. The story ends with her literally in midair, flying back to Vancouver. The form of the novel thus remains uncertain, diffuse, and open. This lack of resolution Atwood elsewhere relates to the Uncertainty Principle in physics, which suggests to her that "There's something in the nature of things that's against closure." The lack of closure has caused dissatisfaction among reviewers of *Cat's Eye*, but it is wholly deliberate on Atwood's part and not an indication of her inability to orchestrate a more immediately satisfying plot. As Susan Strehle asserts, Atwood's point is that "The subject—even the artist—can't find an absolute frame from which to validate its perspective but floats without attainable certainty in relative space-time."

In *The Robber Bride*, it is Zenia, another tormentor, who haunts the other characters and, again, they are not always sure if she is alive or dead. While in *Cat's Eye*, space-time is explicitly discussed in scientific terms, in *The Robber Bride* it tends to come up under the discussion of history, the central idea being that what one discovers as a historian depends on one's viewpoint in time and space. Atwood has caught the contemporary academic excitement and anxiety over this and other discoveries of constructiveness in the social sciences. For example, she both supports and satirizes the historiographical debate in the epilogue to *The Handmaid's Tale*. Most constructivist accounts of history have come in the wake of new depiction's of scientific method, most notably the late Thomas Kuhn's *The Structure of Scientific Revolutions*. There is also some kinship between this view of history and essential features of modern physics: relativity's foregrounding of viewpoint and the quantum mechanical notion that the observer affects and is part of the observation. Atwood doesn't make these analogies explicit, but she does enact in her writing what both natural and social scientists have to say about epistemological subjectivities. *The Robber Bride* features a full-blown relativistic framework that demonstrates how knowledge is both temporally and spatially situated. Readers of *The Robber Bride* occupy three different characters' viewpoints, three constructions of the "same" past events. Interwoven are discussions of professional history making that highlight uncertainty and the uneasy relation between factual temporal knowledge and subjective agenda or memory. Atwood's professional historian, Tony, acknowledges that

> Every sober-sided history is at least half sleight-of-hand: the right hand waving its poor snippets of fact, out in the open for all to verify, while the left hand busies itself with its own devious agendas, deep in its hidden pockets. (*Robber*)

This applies both to personal and cultural memory. Private "battles" between Zenia and the others are counterpointed with discussions of larger military battles that Tony is studying. In each case, viewpoint is crucial. To better understand historical events, Tony spatializes them by constructing maps and material models that she can observe in total and from different angles. However, adding together the three characters' views of events in the novel does not provide the reader with as complete a picture as Tony hopes she enjoys when looking down on her models of famous conflicts.

Much of Atwood's writing explores history making in colonial and postcolonial situations. In this case, space-time formation affects energy. As a colony, Canada borrowed another's history, a faux past. At Elaine's school, stories of British monarchs and Scottish clans were superimposed on Canada's own history or histories to produce a blurring of reality and an uncertain knowledge. Students like Elaine had to struggle to orient themselves in space and time, and this blocked the energy needed to focus on self-identity. As Atwood remarks in an interview, "You can only indulge in the luxury of figuring out yourself when you're oriented in space and time. [As a colony] Canada was a country that lacked such orientation."

That history, of whatever kind, is something of a subjective narrative ought not to be altogether shocking. The concurrent discovery that science, too, resembles a narrative has been more disconcerting. To take a fundamental example, Newton's picture of Absolute Space and Absolute Time, twin pillars of the ordered universe, has now been revealed to be just that, a picture, and one that is no longer entirely useful. What scientists have discovered is that time can run at different rates, depending on one's viewpoint. As her brother, Stephen, reports to the incredulous Elaine, time runs faster in some places than in others and "can be stretched or shrunk" (*Cat's Eye*).

> Time is not a line but a dimension, like the dimensions of space. If you can bend space you can bend time also, and if you

knew enough and could move faster than light you could travel
backward in time and exist in two places at once.

The latter idea is still hypothetical. But what has been made
increasingly clear is that scientists, like historians, shape and measure time
for human purposes: In other words, science is another way to give time
meaning. For centuries, scientists have sought to order and calibrate time,
generally employing a spatial representation like a clock face. So accustomed
are we to think of time according to our conventional grids that we tend to
confuse instrument and object, as in Atwood's Relativistic joke: "Why did the
moron throw the clock out the window? To see time fly" (*Cat's Eye*). That the
actual measurement chosen is fairly arbitrary is something Atwood stresses
and has some fun with; for example, in *Cat's Eye* she refers to the "futon
dimension," the gentrification of neighborhoods, "best before" dates, and
classroom decorations as ways of calibrating time:

> At school we make Easter eggs out of construction paper, pink
> and purple and blue, and stick them onto the windows. After
> that it's tulips, and soon there are real tulips. It seems to be a
> rule that the paper things always appear before the real ones.

More seriously, Atwood observes how both art and technology are
employed to try to fix or stretch time: Museums, photographs, and
monuments are all seen as devices to halt its movement. One reason why
Atwood herself writes is "to stop or bring back time." She sees fiction as
providing a home for physical objects of the past, this being a primary
motive for writing *Cat's Eye*. But she also realizes that art doesn't exactly
capture the past. Nor does time freeze art. The past is gone, and art keeps
on changing. This is what Elaine discovers in her gallery retrospective.
Though we think of painting as a spatial mode, when she surveys her
pictures Elaine declares: "I walk the room, surrounded by the time I've
made" (*Cat's Eye*). Her paintings embody time past as she saw it then. They
also change through time because they are regarded from different
temporal viewpoints. Physical deterioration is not a large consideration
here, though elsewhere in the novel it is. Throughout Elaine's visit to the
city of her youth, she is struck by physical alteration, by time's ability to
dematerialize or reduce matter. The adult Elaine discovers that a window
ledge on which she used to sit is now "empty air" (*Cat's Eye*), doors she used
to enter she now enters only in her mind. Time, it seems, can make space
and matter a concept.

Scientific Imperialism

Nevertheless, materiality is still of fundamental importance. Atwood concludes that what links science, imperialism, and patriarchy is control of the body. Just as men have controlled and subdued the female body, so colonists have traditionally been depicted as conquering a nature identified as female. Atwood's usual fictional setting is a Canada emerging from British domination and facing the economic imperialism (if there is ever any other kind) of the United States. Women in such a situation are doubly colonized. Atwood makes the analogy between patriarchy and imperialism explicit when she remarks with characteristically dry humor:

> Canada as a separate but dominated country has done about as well under the U.S. as women, worldwide, have done under men; about the only position they've ever adopted toward us, country to country, has been the missionary position, and we were not on top.

In her suffering, the man Elaine most identifies with is one who has been feminized through colonization, Mr. Banerji, a native of the British Empire's subcontinent (*Cat's Eye*). She unconsciously detects a similarity between his position and hers. What both women and the colonized desire, according to Atwood, is to proclaim "We exist" and "We don't wish particularly to be defined by you." The difference is that while shaking off a feeling of inferiority can take more than one generation for the postcolonial, it is even harder to step out of global patriarchy.

But invading territories and putting down stakes are not the only ways of conquering nature. Western scientists, too, have traditionally been depicted as subduing nature-as-female. They share some of the same attitude as colonists: conquer, map, know, and sell. Thus, despite the new theoretical consciousness of limits, despite the recognition that objectivity and absolute knowledge are receding, Atwood's (male) scientists go on trying to make their mark, like young Stephen peeing the names of planets in the sand (*Cat's Eye*). The counting and the naming and the mapping continue, the hunt for the first picosecond, the great white quark, the distant stars. But the underworld of sifting objects, of unpredictability and evasion, this is the world of women. Men are protected by their unawareness. The "numbers men," as Elaine calls them (*Cat's Eye*), are beginning to discover it, but Atwood suggests that women know this realm already, from the inside. We see in her particularly feminine forms of *bildungsroman* the nascent self beginning to emerge and the observed object rising into a confused subjecthood. Science began the process of demystifying itself and its authority as (male) observer early this century and Atwood has taken a cue from there.

Bricolage

As we have seen, Atwood's recent novels suggest new possibilities for describing women's experiences in scientific terms. Several prominent postmodern themes appear under this guise and have thus reached a popular as well as an academic audience—for example, otherwise esoteric themes such as epistemological subjectivity, cultural inscription on the body, and the instability of the subject. Atwood is able to use intellectual concepts to reconnect the personal and the abstract, the local and the cosmic. This has always been an important function of the fiction writer, but particularly so in an era of disciplinary segregation and an increasingly formidable science. While most writers who invoke scientific ideas are male and write about men's encounter with science, Atwood looks at these matters from a woman's perspective. This is still, regrettably, a relatively novel idea.

Chronology

1939   Margaret Eleanor Atwood is born on November 18 in Ottawa, Ontario, Canada. She is the second of three children of Carl Edmund Atwood and Margaret Killam Atwood. Her brother, Harold, was born in 1937; her sister, Ruth, was born in 1951. Because Carl Atwood was a forest entomologist, the family would spend many months each year living in the Canadian wilderness. Margaret became an avid reader, particularly fond of Grimms' Fairy Tales.

1945   By age six, Atwood had become a writer of plays, poems, comic books, and a novel. Writes juvenile poems, "Rhyming Cats." Family moves to Sault Ste. Marie, Ontario.

1946–61   Family resides in Toronto, Ontario, where Carl joins University of Toronto faculty. Spends spring, summer, and autumn in Canadian bush.

1952–57   Attends Leaside High School in Toronto; writes for literary magazine *Clan Call*.

1957   Enrolls at Victoria College, University of Toronto, determined to become a writer. Her parents would rather she studied botany. Meets Dennis Lee; writes for *Acta Victoriana* and *The Strand*; begins reading poetry in public at Bohemian Embassy.

1959   Works as counselor at Camp White Pine, Haliburton, Ontario; meets artist Charles Pachter. "Fruition" is her first poem published in a major literary journal, *The Canadian Forum*.

1961   Receives bachelor's degree from Victoria College. Moves to
            Boston. *Double Persephone* published and awarded E. J. Pratt
            Medal for Poetry.

1961–62   Graduate studies at Radcliffe College and Harvard University on
            Woodrow Wilson Fellowship.

1962   Receives Master's degree in English from Radcliffe College

1962–63   Continues graduate studies at Harvard; meets first husband,
            James Polk.

1963–64   Moves to Toronto; works for market research company; poems
            published in *Poesie / Poetry 64*; writes libretto for John Beckwith's
            The Trumpets of Summer, broadcast on CBC.

1964–65   Moves to Vancouver; teaches literature at University of British
            Columbia. Writes poetry sequence "The Circle Game,"
            accompanied by Pachter's lithographs, published in limited
            edition.

1965–67   Returns to Harvard for doctoral studies with help of Canada
            Council grant.

1966   Awarded President's Medal for Poetry from the University of
            Western Ontario. Publishes collection of poems, *The Circle
            Game*.

1967   Receives Governor-General's Award for Poetry for *The Circle
            Game*; first prize in Centennial Commission Poetry Competition
            for *The Animals in That Country*. Marries James Polk.

1967–68   Teaches literature at Sir George Williams University, Montreal.

1968   *The Animals in That Country* published.

1968–70   Resides in Edmonton, Alberta. Teaches creative writing at
            University of Alberta.

1969   *The Edible Woman* published. Receives Union Prize.

1970   *The Journals of Susanna Moodie* and *Procedures for Underground*
            published. Meets novelist Graeme Gibson.

1970–71   Travels to England, France, and Italy.

1971   *Power Politics* published.

1971–72   *Surfacing* published. Writer-in Residence at York University,
            Toronto. Serves as editor and member of board of directors of
            House of Anansi Press.

1972   *Survival* published.

1972–73   Writer-in-Residence at University of Toronto.

1973   Receives D.Litt. from Trent University. Invited to tour Soviet Union as part of cultural exchange program; cancels trip in protest of USSR's expulsion of Alexander Solshenitsyn. Divorces James Polk. Moves, in September, to Allison, Ontario, with Graeme Gibson. Writes text for film *Grace Marks*.

1974   *You Are Happy* published; *Grace Marks* televised as *The Servant Girl* on CBC. Receives honorary LL.D. from Queen's University; awarded Bess Hopkins Prize for poetry.

1976   Daughter, Eleanor Jess Atwood Gibson, born in May. *Selected Poems* and *Lady Oracle* published. Translation of *The Edible Woman* published in Italy.

1977   *Dancing Girls and Other Stories* and a children's book, *Days of the Rebels*, published. Receives City of Toronto Book Award and Canadian Bookseller's Association Award for *Lady Oracle*.

1978   *Two-Headed Poems* and a children's book, *Up in the Tree*, published. Receives St. Lawrence Award for Fiction. Travels to Afghanistan and Australia.

1978–79   Resides in Scotland for the winter.

1979   *Life Before Man* published.

1980   Returns to Toronto. Receives D.Litt. from Concordia University, and Radliffe Graduate Medal. A children's book, *Anna's Pet* published.

1981   Chair of Writers' Union of Canada. Receives Molson Award and Guggenheim Fellowship. *True Stories* and *Bodily Harm* published; collaborates on film *Snowbird*.

1982   *Second Words: Selected Critical Prose* published. Receives Welsh Arts Council international Writer's Prize.

1983   Story collections *Murder in the Dark* and *Bluebeard's Egg* published. Receives Periodical Distributors of Canada award and the Foundation for the Advancement of Canadian letters Book of the Year Award. Writes text for *Speeches for Dr. Frankenstein: Soprano and Tape*, broadcast on CBC. Writes text for *A Night in the Royal Ontario Museum: A Theatre Piece*, recorded on Vienna Masterworks.

1983–84   Travels in England and Germany

1984–86   President of International P.E.N., Canadian Centre (English speaking).

1985   *The Handmaid's Tale* published. Writer-in Residence at the University of Alabama, Tuscaloosa.

1986   Holds Berg Chair in English at New York University. Receives Toronto Arts Award, Governor General's Award, and Los Angeles Times Fiction Award.

1987   *Poems: 1976–1986* and *The Can-Lit Foodbook: From Pen to Palate; A Collection of Tasty Literary Fare* published. Writer-in-Residence at Macquarie University, New South Wales, Australia. Receives Arthur C. Clarke Award for Best Science Fiction; Council for Advancement and Support of Education, Silver Medal, Best Articles of the Year; Humanist of the Year Award; Fellow of the Royal Society of Canada. Writes script for drama *Heaven on Earth*, produced on CBC and BBC.

1988   *Cat's Eye* published. Receives National Magazine Award for Enironmental Journalism, and YWCA Woman of Distinction Award.

1989   Writer-in-Residence at Trinity University, San Antonio, Texas. *Cat's Eye* named Coles Book of the Year.

1990   *For the Birds*, a children's book, published. Receives Order of Ontario; Centennial Medal from Harvard University.

1991   *Wilderness Tips*, a collection of stories, published; receives Trillium Award.

1992   *Good Bones* published. Returns to Toronto, where Atwood currently resides with Graeme Gibson and their daughter, Jess. Atwood is Lecturer of English at the University of British Columbia, Vancouver,

1993   *The Robber Bride* published; receives Trillium Award. *Heaven on Earth* produced on PBS.

1994   *Good Bones and Simple Murders*, a collection of stories, published. Receives French Government's Chevelier dan l'Ordre des Arts et des lettres, and Commonwealth Writers' Prize.

1995   *Strange Things: The Malevolent North in Canadian Literature*, a collection of lectures published; *Morning in the Burned House*, poems, published and receives Trillium Award; *Princess Prunella and the Purple Peanut*, a children's book, published.

1996   *Alias Grace* published; awarded Giller Prize.

Contributors

HAROLD BLOOM is Sterling Professor of the Humanities at Yale University and Henry W. and Albert A. Berg Professor of English at the New York University Graduate School. He is the author of over 20 books, including *The Anxiety of Influence* (1973), which sets forth Professor Bloom's provocative theory of the literary relationships between the great writers and their predecessors. His most recent book, *Shakespeare: The Invention of the Human* (1998), was a finalist for the 1998 National Book Award. Professor Bloom is a 1985 MacArthur Foundation Award recipient, served as the Charles Eliot Norton Professor of Poetry at Harvard University in 1987–88, and has received honorary degrees from the universities of Rome and Bologna. In 1999, Professor Bloom received the prestigious American Academy of Arts and Letters Gold Medal for Criticism.

JUDITH McCOMBS is the author of *Margaret Atwood: A Reference Guide* and *Against Nature: Wilderness Poems.*

ARNOLD E. DAVIDSON is research professor of Canadian studies at Duke University. He is coeditor of *The Art of Margaret Atwood: Essays in Criticism*, and author of *Seeing in the Dark: Margaret Atwood's* Cat's Eye, as well as books on Mordecai Richler, Jean Rhys, and Joseph Conrad.

ANNETTE KOLODNY is Professor of English at the University of Arizona. She is author of the award-winning studies *Lay of the Land* and *The Land Before Her*, as well as numerous articles on women writers and feminist theory. Her most recent works include *Dancing Through the Minefield.*

241

SHARON ROSE WILSON is a Professor of English and Women's Studies at the University of Northern Colorado. She has pulished articles and essays on romance, film, and modern literature, and is the author of *Approaches to Teaching Margaret Atwood's* The Handmaid's Tale *and Other Works*. She is past co-president of the Margaret Atwood Society.

J. BROOKS BOUSON is the author of *The Empathic Reader: A Study of the Narcissistic Character and the Drama of the Self.*

GLENN DEER is the author of *Postmodern Canadian Fiction and the Rhetoric of Authority.*

EMMA PARKER studied her doctoral research at the University of Birmingham. Her thesis examined the theme of women, food, and power in writing of contemporary women writers.

MOLLY HITE is Professor of English at Cornell University. She is author of two book-length studies on contemporary authors, two novels, and a number of articles and essays.

CORAL ANN HOWELLS is the author of *Alice Munro, Jean Rhys, and Margaret Atwood*, and *Love, Mystery, and Misery: Feeling in Gothic Fiction.*

KAREN STEIN is Professor of English and Women's Studies at the University of Rhode Island, and Director of Graduate Studies in English. She has written essays on Atwood, Toni Morrison, and other women writers, and is the author of *Margaret Atwood Revisited.*

PHYLLIS STERNBERG PERRAKIS teaches English literature at the University of Ottawa. She has published essays on Doris Lessing, Margaret Atwood, and Alice Munro. She is editor of *Spiritual Exploration in the Works of Doris Lessing.*

JUNE DEERY is Assistant Professor of Literature and Science at Rensselaer. Her publications include *Aldous Huxley and the Mysticism of Science* and articles on technology, gender, and cyberspace in twentieth-century fiction in *Extrapolations* and *Utopian Studies.*

Bibliography

Banerjee, Chinmoy. "Alice in Disneyland: Criticism as Commodity in *The Handmaid's Tale.*" *Essays in Canadian Writing* 41 (Summer 1990): 74–92.

Bignell, Jonathan. "The Handmaid's Tale: *Novel and Film,*" *British Journal of Canadian Studies* 8:1 (1993): 71–84.

Carrington, Ildiko de Papp. *"Margaret Atwood," Canadian Writers and Their Works: Fiction Series,* Vol. 9. Toronto: ECW Press, 1987. 25–119.

Christ, Carol P. "Margaret Atwood: Surfacing of Women's Spiritual Quest and Vision." *Signs* 2 (Winter 1976): 316–30.

Davey, Frank. *Margaret Atwood: A Feminist Poetics.* Vancouver: Talonbooks, 1984.

Ewell, Barbara C. "The Language of Alienation in Margaret Atwood's *Surfacing,*" *The Centennial Review* 25:2 (1981): 285–202.

Fee, Margery. *The Fat Lady Dances: Margaret Atwood's* Lady Oracle, Toronto: ECW Press, 1993.

Felski, Rita. *Beyond Feminist Aesthetics: Feminist Literature and Social Change.* Cambridge, MA: Harvard University Press, 1989.

Finnell, Susanna. "Unwriting the Quest: Margaret Atwood's Fiction and *The Handmaid's Tale,*" *Women and the Journey: The Female Travel Experience.* Ed., Frederick Bonnie and Susan H. McLeod. Pullman, WA: Washington State University Press, 1993.

Foley, Michael. "Satiric Intent in Margaret Atwood's *The Handmaid's Tale,*" *Commonwealth Essays and Studies* 11:2 (Spring 1989): 44–52.

Fullbrook, Kate. "Margaret Atwood: Colonisation and Responsibility," *Free Women: Ethics and Aesthetics in Twentieth-Century Women's Fiction.* Philadelphia: Temple University Press, 1990. 171–93.

Givner, Jessie. "Names, Faces and Signatures in Margaret Atwood's *Cat's Eye* and *The Handmaid's Tale,*" *Canadian Literature* 133 (Summer 1992): 56–75.

Goldsmith, Elizabeth, ed. *Writing the Female Voice: Essays on Epistolary Literature.* Boston: Northeastern University Press, 1989.

Grace, Sherrill E. *Violent Duality: A Study of Margaret Atwood.* Montreal: Vehicule Press, 1980.

————, and Lorraine Weir, eds. *Margaret Atwood: Language, Text and System*. Vancouver: UBC, 1983.

Hammer, Stephanie Barbe. "The World as it Will Be? Female Satire and the Technology of Power in *The Handmaid's Tale*," *Modern Language Studies* 20:2 (Spring 1990): 39–49.

Hengen Shannon. *Margaret Atwood's Power: Mirrors, Reflections and Images in Select Fiction and Poetry*. Toronto: Second Story Press, 1993. 110–16.

Howells, Coral Ann, and Lynette Hunter, eds. *Narrative Strategies in Canadian Literature*. Buckingham: Open University Press, 1991.

Keith, W. J. *Introducing Margaret Atwood's* The Edible Woman: *A Reader's Guide*. Toronto: ECW Press, 1989.

Lacombe, Michele. "The Writing on the Wall: Amputated Speech in Margaret Atwood's *The Handmaid's Tale*," *Wascana Review* 21:2 (Fall 1986): 3–20.

Lecker, Robert, Jack David and Ellen Quigley, eds. *Canadian Writers and Their Works: Essays on Form, Context, and Development*. Fiction Series 9. Toronto: ECW Press, 1987.

Leclaire, Jacques. "Margaret Atwood's *Cat's Eye* as a Portrait of the Artist," *Commonwealth Essays and Studies* 13:1 (Autumn 1990): 73–80.

Mackenzie, Manfred. " 'I am a Place:' *Surfacing* and Spirit of Place," *A Sense of Place in the New Literatures in English*. Ed., Peggy Nightingale. St. Lucia: University of Queensland Press 1986. 32–36.

McCombs, Judith, ed. *Critical Essays on Margaret Atwood*. Ed., Judith McCombs. Boston: G.K. Hall, 1988. 179–97.

————. *Margaret Atwood: A Reference Guide*. Boston: G. K. Hall, 1991.

McKinstry, Susan Jaret. "Living Literally by the Pen: The Self Conceived and Self-Deceiving Heroine-Author in Margaret Atwood's *Lady Oracle*," *Margaret Atwood: Reflection and Reality*. Living Author Series 6. Edinburg, TX: Pan American University, 1987.

Mendez-Egle, Beatrice, ed. *Margaret Atwood: Reflection and Reality*. Edinburg, TX: Pan American University, 1988.

Murray, Heather. " 'Its Image in the Mirror': Canada, Canonicity, the Uncanny," *Essays in Canadian Writing* 42 (Winter 1990): 102–30.

Mycak, Sonia. "Divided and Dismembered: the Decentred Subject in M. Atwood's *Bodily Harm*," *Canadian Review of Comparative Literature* 20:3–4 (1993): 469–78.

Nicholson, Colin, ed. *Margaret Atwood: Writing and Subjectivity*. London: Macmillan, 1994.

Pearlman, Mickey, ed. *Canadian Women Writing Fiction*. Jackson: University Press of Mississippi, 1993.

Perrakis, Phyllis Sternberg. "The Female Gothic and the (M)other in Atwood and Lessing," *Doris Lessing Newsletter* 17:1 (1995): 1, 11–15.

Rao, Eleonora. *Strategies for Identity: The Fiction of Margaret Atwood. Writing About Women: Feminist Literary Studies* 9. New York: Peter Lang, 1993.

Rubenstein, Roberta. "Escape Artist and Split Personalities: Margaret Atwood," *Boundaries of the Self: Gender, Culture, Fiction*. Urbana: University of Illinois Press, 1987. 63–122.

Van Spanckeren, Kathryn, Jan Garden Castro, and Sandra M. Gilbert, eds. *Margaret Atwood: Vision and Forms*. Carbondale: Southern Illinois University Press, 1988.

Sparrow, Fiona. " 'This Place is Some Kind of a Garden': Clearings in the Bush in the Works of Susanna Moodie, Catharine Parr Traill, Margaret Atwood and Margaret Laurence," *The Journal of Commonwealth Literature* 25:1 (1990): 24–41.

Suarez, Isabel Carrera. " 'Yet I speak, Yet I Exist': Affirmation of the Subject in Atwood's Short Stories," *Margaret Atwood: Writing and Subjectivity*. Ed., Colin Nicholson. London: Macmillan Press and New York, St. Martin's Press, 1994. 230–47.

Thomas, Sue. "Mythic Reconceptions and the Mother-Daughter Relationship in Margaret Atwood's *Surfacing*," *Ariel* 19:2 (1988): 73–85.

Tomc, Sandra. " 'The Missionary Position': Feminism and Nationalism in Margaret Atwood's *The Handmaid's Tale*," *Canadian Literature* 138/39 (Fall/Winter 1993): 73–87.

Wagner-Martin, Linda. "Epigraphs to Atwood's *The Handmaid's Tale*," *Notes on Contemporary Literature* 17:2 (1987): 4.

Wall, Kathleen. *The Callisto Myth from Ovid to Atwood: Initiation and Rape in Literature*. Montreal: McGill-Queen's University Press, 1988.

White, Roberta. "Margaret Atwood: Reflections in a Convex Mirror," *Canadian Women Writing Fiction*. Ed., Mickey Pearlman. Jackson: University Press of Mississippi, 1993. 53–70.

Woodcock, George. *Introducing Margaret Atwood's* Surfacing: *A Reader's Guide*. Toronto: ECW Press, 1990.

Workman, Nancy V. "Sufi Mysticism in Margaret Atwood's *The Handmaid's Tale*," *Studies in Canadian Literature* 14:2 (1989): 10–26.

York, Lorraine M., ed. *Various Atwoods: Essays on the Later Poems, Short Fiction, and Novels*. Concord, Ontario: Anansi, 1995.

Acknowledgments

"Atwood's Haunted Sequences: *The Circle Game, The Journals of Susanna Moodie*, and *Power Politics*" by Judith McCombs from *The Art of Margaret Atwood* by Judith McCombs. © 1981 by House of Anansi Press Limited.

"Future Tense: Making History in *The Handmaid's Tale*" by Arnold E. Davidson from *Margaret Atwood: Vision and Forms*, edited by Kathryn VanSpanckeren and Jan Garden Castro. © 1988 by Board of Trustees, Southern Illinois University.

"Margaret Atwood and the Politics of Narrative" by Annette Kolodny reprinted by permission of the Modern Language Association of America, from *Studies on Canadian Literature: Introductory and Critical Essays*, edited by Arnold E. Davidson. © 1990 by The Modern Language Association.

"The Artist's Marriage to Death in *Bodily Harm*" by Sharon Rose Wilson from *Margaret Atwood's Fairy-Tale Sexual Politics*, by Sharon Rose Wilson. © 1993 by the University Press of Mississippi.

"*The Edible Woman*'s Refusal to Consent to Feminity" from J. Brooks Bouson's *Brutal Choreographies: Oppositional Strategies and Narrative Design in the Novels of Margaret Atwood* (Amherst University of Massachusetts Press, 1993) © 1993 by The University of Massachusetts Press.

"*The Handmaid's Tale*: Dystopia and the Paradoxes of Power" by Glenn Deer from *Postmodern Canadian Fiction and the Rhetoric of Authority*, by Glenn Deer. © 1994 by McGill-Queen's University Press.

"You Are What You Eat: The Politics of Eating in the Novels of Margaret Atwood" by Emma Parker from *Twentieth Century Literature* 41:3 (Fall 1995): 349–367. © 1995 by Hofstra University.

"Optics and Autobiography in Margaret Atwood's *Cat's Eye*" by Molly Hite from *Twentieth Century Literature* 41:2 (Summer 1995): 135–155. © 1995 by Hofstra University.

"Atwoodian Gothic: From *Lady Oracle* to *The Robber Bride*" by Hilde Staels from *Margaret Atwood's Novels: A Study of Narrative Discourse*, by Hilde Staels. © 1995 by A. Francke Verlag Tübingen und Basel.

"*Cat's Eye*: Creating a Symbolic Space out of Lost Time" by Coral Ann Howells from *Modern Novelists: Margaret Atwood*. © 1996 by Coral Ann Howells. Reprinted with the permission of St. Martin's Press, Inc.

"Margaret Atwood's Modest Proposal: *The Handmaid's Tale*" by Karen Stein from *Canadian Literature* 148 (Spring 1996): 57–71. © 1996 by The University of British Columbia, Vancouver.

"Atwood's *The Robber Bride*: The Vampire as Intersubjective Catalyst" by Phyllis Sternberg Perrakis from *Mosaic* 30:3 (September 1997): 151–168. © 1997 by The University of Manitoba.

"Science for Feminists: Margaret Atwood's Body of Knowledge" by June Deery from *Twentieth Century Literature* 43:4 (Winter 1997): 470–483. © 1997 by Hofstra University.

Index